PRAISE FOR *EFFECTIVE BRAND*

'Very rarely do you find a book that tells you *everything* you need to know about its subject matter. This is such a book. And we will make it mandatory reading for every single marketer we teach. Because it's *that* good.'
Sherilyn Shackell, Founder and Global CEO, The Marketing Academy

'A beacon of clarity in a muddled marketing era. There is truth, provocation and practical help dripping from every page. Andrew Geoghegan has written the brand-building/effectiveness textbook for our times.'
Laurence Green, Director of Effectiveness, The Institute of Practitioners in Advertising (IPA)

'Helps you take control and focus on what truly matters for growth. Andrew Geoghegan has always been a far-sighted visionary who could see as marketers are increasingly overwhelmed by data, they needed a resource that could strip things back to what truly makes a difference. This is that book – essential reading for all marketers who want to drive sustainable growth.'
Syl Saller, CBE

'Practical and thoughtful and wise. Andrew Geoghegan's book sets out a positive and achievable route to successful brand building. It's especially strong on how to cajole the organization and the commentary on how to use data is spot on. Highly recommended.'
Dr Grace Kite, Founder, Magic Numbers

'Andrew Geoghegan is such a gifted human - incredibly smart, curious, thoughtful – always willing to share his knowledge and wisdom. This book now allows for that pragmatic, practical wisdom to be shared far and wide, helping marketers work out what to do to make their organizations grow.'
Ellie Norman, Chief Marketing Officer, Formula E

'Andrew Geoghegan is one of the most insightful marketers of his time. I urge you to rely on him to guide you with this book, enabling you to have a successful marketing career.'
Rosie Phipps, Founder, Oxford College of Marketing and Oxford Professional Education

'Andrew Geoghegan has written the perfect practical users' guide for anyone responsible for brand growth. He combines learning from academia with his own experience of commercial application to cover every aspect of brand strategy and execution.

'This is no "one view of the world" dogma, it simply puts down what works in a way that anyone could apply.'
Helen Edwards, Director, Passionbrand, and Adjunct Associate Professor of Marketing at London Business School

'Will help equip marketing leaders and their teams with cross-industry knowledge and approaches for effective brand building. With this book in hand marketers will be better armed to tackle the internal and external barriers to growth.'
Sophie Devonshire, CEO, The Marketing Society

'The more things change the more they stay the same. As the world evolves ever more rapidly this book is a brilliant distillation and reminder of how to build brands amidst the chaos and hype.'
Mark Evans, Honorary Fellow, The Marketing Society

'There are many books that focus on the theory of building brands. Not enough about the practice. Andrew Geoghegan's years of experience means he not only knows what to do, but how to do it. This is a practical book that is applicable across categories.'
Russell Parsons, Editor-in-chief, *Marketing Week*, and the Festival of Marketing at Centaur Media Plc

Effective Brand Building

*Unlock growth with strategy,
insights, and measurement*

Andrew Geoghegan

KoganPage

First published in Great Britain and the United States in 2025 by Kogan Page Limited

2nd Floor, 45 Gee Street
London
EC1V 3RS
United Kingdom

8 W 38th Street, Suite 902
New York, NY 10018
USA

www.koganpage.com

Kogan Page books are printed on paper from sustainable forests.

ISBNs
Hardback   978 1 3986 1859 6
Paperback   978 1 3986 1857 2
Ebook   978 1 3986 1858 9

British Library Cataloguing-in-Publication Data
A CIP record for this book is available from the British Library.

Library of Congress Cataloging-in-Publication Data
Names: Geoghegan, Andrew, author.
Title: Effective brand building : unlock growth with strategy, insights,
    and measurement / Andrew Geoghegan.
Description: London ; New York, NY : Kogan Page, 2025. | Includes
    bibliographical references and index.
Identifiers: LCCN 2024046257 (print) | LCCN 2024046258 (ebook) | ISBN
    9781398618572 (paperback) | ISBN 9781398618596 (hardback) | ISBN
    9781398618589 (ebook)
Subjects: LCSH: Branding (Marketing) | Brand name products–Management.
Classification: LCC HF5415.1255 .G46 2025 (print) | LCC HF5415.1255
    (ebook) | DDC 658.8/27–dc23/eng/20241018
LC record available at https://lccn.loc.gov/2024046257
LC ebook record available at https://lccn.loc.gov/2024046258

Typeset by Integra Software Services, Pondicherry
Print production managed by Jellyfish
Printed and bound by CPI Group (UK) Ltd, Croydon, CR0 4YY

For Emma

CONTENTS

ABOUT THE AUTHOR

Andrew Geoghegan is an experienced chief marketing officer, brand strategist, and innovator who has held senior roles at businesses including Diageo, PepsiCo, William Grant & Sons, and global beauty and personal care business PZ Cussons. He has set up a business, Future Conditional Limited, helping businesses to more effectively grow their brands.

He has worked on brands such as Guinness, Johnnie Walker, Tropicana, Walkers/Lay's, and St. Tropez. Andrew has been responsible for the design and implementation of world-class brand-building programmes from strategy right through to execution and measurement.

He is passionate about marketing effectiveness and creativity and his paper on how to create a culture of marketing effectiveness was awarded Gold, Best New Learning, and Best Use of Data by the IPA in 2020.

He was recognized as one of the top 100 marketers by *Marketing Week* in 2022 and 2023, and by *Management Today* in 2019 as a Male Agent of Change for his work on gender representation.

He has written a column for *Marketing Week* since 2018 focussed on providing practical guidance for marketers with the issues they face, and regularly contributes to industry events on marketing effectiveness.

FOREWORD

by Syl Saller, CBE

The magic of brands

Brands possess a unique magic. One of the greatest joys in marketing is working with brands, creating those intangible elements and emotional connections that resonate deeply with their audiences. Great brands make a difference – they help solve problems, enhance our lives, enrich experiences, and shape culture.

Many brands begin in the minds of founders, reflecting their personalities and the spark that inspired them to solve a problem more effectively than existing solutions. The best brands outlive their founders, staying true to their origins while evolving with culture through the collaboration and hard work of countless individuals over years, even centuries. Effectively growing brands is part art, part science – it demands the very best of us – our analytical rigour, curiosity, creativity, collaboration, and stellar leadership.

The changing landscape of marketing

Yet, it might seem that the golden era of brands is behind us, consigned to the late twentieth century of big brands, blockbuster advertisements, and iconic cultural moments around movies, sports, and music. For most of the twenty-first century, we've been navigating a second era of marketing. Data and technology have profoundly changed how brands connect with their audiences. The best brands do this in a way that feels intimate and personal, but many brands feel distant reflecting the paradox of social media that brings us together and isolates us at the same time.

This second era of marketing has responded to the age we live in, termed the "third information crisis" – a disruption as significant as the invention of writing and the printing press (Alderman, 2024). As in previous times of epic change, there are benefits to society but also profound disruption. This information crisis is altering humanity – how we communicate, see the world and each other, how we shop, and experience life. The overwhelming amount of information and shifting dynamics have democratized individual voices while creating new, unelected power centres. Today's most valuable companies are involved in data, tech, and online retail. They have highly concentrated market power, and this presents profound challenges for all of us.

The role of data and technology

Data has brought more certainty to brand marketing, making it something that can be managed with a high degree of control, but often at the cost of deep consumer insight and breakthrough creativity. Media is digital, targeted, and omnipresent. Data is a new currency, often more valuable than the profit from the associated tangible products, as seen in the smart TV market.

Marketers have had to continuously upskill in digital marketing, AI, social media, search, performance marketing, and a host of new capabilities to reach consumers. Most businesses weren't designed to keep pace with this level of change, putting enormous pressure on modern marketers. Outdated business systems, a drop in training and capability, and a drift in understanding marketing's role heighten the challenge. While some brands have shown incredible resilience, many have faltered.

Embracing the future

The information crisis is not going away anytime soon. But if we learn quickly, act bravely, and lead well, we will usher in a third era of marketing – one where brand magic integrates seamlessly with data and technology. At its best, this era will see brands and technology working harmoniously to serve consumers and help organizations achieve their goals in ways that benefit people and the world. At its worst, we'll have untrained brand teams mindlessly feeding unfiltered data into AI programs that spit out generic brand plans.

Don't get me wrong – I'm all for smart AI-assisted insight work and programs that reduce costs and the grunt work of marketing. However, as marketing leaders, we must control this change to ensure a future where tech, creativity, and humanity come together to drive growth.

The marketers who succeed in both business and their careers will be those who embrace change and upskill to meet new challenges. They will understand their role in leading a bold transformation to a bright future.

The purpose of this book

This excellent book is here to help. No matter what new marketing tech tools emerge, you must understand the fundamentals underlying the inputs you feed into a brand plan and analyse outputs for validity and their ability to be executed in a real market setting. The time saved in data processing should be invested in deeper insights, more creative work, and greater innovation. As marketers, navigating change is at our core. We must lead our organizations and put brands and consumers back at the heart of everything we do. We must tackle what we can control and focus ruthlessly on what matters.

Andrew's book helps you take control and focus on what truly matters for growth. He has always been a far-sighted visionary and could see that as marketers are increasingly overwhelmed by data, they needed a resource that could strip things back to what truly makes a difference. His deep experience, pragmatism, and compassion for the challenge facing modern marketing are a huge help in a world of biased data, hysteria over the dangers of AI, and a decrease in the ability to generate real consumer insight, as only humans can.

This book clarifies the fundamentals of consumer behaviour, demand, and insights. It helps you understand your organization's nature and its impact on your role as a marketing leader. It guides you in setting bold brand ambitions, making growth choices, creating holistic plans, and measuring and improving your efforts year after year. In short, it makes you a better marketer.

I wholeheartedly agree with Andrew's provocation – that dedicating even a small amount of time to quality thinking on brand strategy, consumer insights, and measurement will help focus your time and energy on the most impactful areas. This will undoubtably bring more certainty, joy, and success to you, your team, and your brands.

Reference

Alderman, N (2024) The third information crisis, BBC Radio 4, 9 July, www.bbc. co.uk/programmes/m0020xrs/episodes/player (archived at https://perma.cc/ 59G6-3GB8)

ACKNOWLEDGEMENTS

Thank you for taking the time to read this book. My aim was to offer practical help to people wanting to grow their brands in a confusing world where there seems to be more criticism than encouragement for marketers. There is a lot written for agency folk and by consultants, especially on creative effectiveness, but not enough for marketing practitioners trying to deliver end-to-end effectiveness while dealing with day-to-day organizational challenges. I hope I've succeeded in making things simpler and in provoking you to think about how to create a more effective system in which your brand can thrive, and that you will apply some of these approaches with your own team and brand.

Special thanks to Emma who supported and encouraged me during the process of developing and writing the book. Emma is an exceptional human who has my back no matter what life may throw at me. Her wit, compassion, and integrity have been a source of inspiration since we met in 1996. In supporting this book, she will be relieved to know she has more than paid off the debt of endless cups of tea I provided while she completed her doctoral thesis. Special thanks also to Stella, my constant companion throughout the writing period, selflessly volunteering to take me for extra walks to help me work out what I needed to write next. Thank you to friends and family, especially Jo and Vic; I wonder what Patrick would have made of this?

The following were kind in helping me with the book – Jason and Christene volunteered as readers, Laurence and Alexandra at the IPA gave me access to their vault of incredible case studies, Syl wrote a thoughtful foreword, and Alison and Isabelle checked in on me during the writing process. Thanks to Donna and Jeylan, and all the team at Kogan Page, for their guidance and making the whole process pleasurable.

This book is the product of almost three decades of working in marketing, innovation, and strategic planning roles. There are far too many people to name individually who've had an impact on me and therefore directly or indirectly shaped this work, but here are a few, not repeating those named elsewhere – Alex, Alicia, Alison F, Amrit, Catherine, Colette, Colin, Dawn, David B, David G, Deb, Doulla, Gareth, Grainne, Grania, Helen, James, John, Julie, Justin,

Karen, Liz, Malcolm, Marie, Mark H, Mark M, Mark S, Michael, Nick, Nik, Paul, Pete, Rick, Megan, Michelle, Russell, Sarah, Steph, Sherilyn, Simon, and Will. I am so grateful for the people I met on the journey who had the courage to lead with fearless authenticity, especially those who became friends.

A final mention to two groups who were part of overlapping life changing experiences: the Covid-19 cohort of the Marketing Academy Fellowship, and the 2023 Pearls of Wisdom – the latter emboldened me in summer 2023 to take the path which led to this book and new beginnings in the garden of forking paths.

CONTRIBUTORS

I interviewed almost two dozen people while writing this book to capture a range of geographic and industry perspectives. Most were chief marketing officers or the equivalent, but I also spoke to marketers specializing in measurement, insights, revenue growth management, and select external partners. Many are listed below, and I thank them for their generosity.

Becky Brock
Ben Curtis
Bridget Angear
Craig Mawdsley
Ellie Norman
Grace Kite
Gurpreet Bhinder
Helen Bass
Jane Ostler
Jerry Daykin
Katie McAlister
Kerry Chilvers
Kiel Petersen
Nick Graham
Paul Cowper
Ross Farquhar

Introduction to effective brand building

1

What is effective brand building and why is it important?

Introduction

First and foremost, welcome. It makes sense to start by explaining a bit about this book and how to use it. The purpose is to be useful – to be useful to marketing leaders and their teams in increasing the impact they have in their business, and in creating predictable and effective growth on their brands. It's written to be practical, easy to understand, and something you and your teams can refer to at the points in your business cycle where different elements of it are relevant. It's something to have in your kit bag to save you time in working out how to approach an element of brand strategy, planning, insights, and measurement and agreeing collectively on the best approach.

It's not an academic book, or a training course. I don't claim to have ground-breaking new theory or evidence. I would encourage you as a marketing leader to invest time in understanding the theory of marketing, how the principles are evolving over time, and what the current conversations are in the industry and the implications for you. My aim here is to make it easy to implement effective brand building within an organization. This book is less of an observation on 'how brands grow' and more of a guide to what you need to do to make it happen on the ground. While you are being pulled in all directions, this book covers the things for which you should make time.

That said, I do have a point of view based on my experiences and talking to people across different industries, from those who are frustrated, to those striving to improve their impact, right through to those who are knocking it out the ballpark delivering their numbers. I believe most of us get stuck in the weeds, fighting the day-to-day battles, and reacting to all the volatility and uncertainty being thrown at us. If we could find just 10 per cent of our time to plan the future based on deep understanding of consumer opportunities for growth, and another 10 per cent of our time to understand the impact of our actions on our brands and their performance, we'd be more effective, and able to demonstrate it.

In this book I want to make this easier to do, so when you put aside that time for strategy, planning, and measurement you have the prompts and questions to help you be more strategic, have better insight, and understand more about what works to spend your money wisely. The vast majority, or 80 odd per cent, of your time should be spent on execution, but more deliberately, consciously, and therefore more effectively.

Building capability

A lot of capability building happens through training courses – there are many excellent commercial courses available for marketers, and some businesses invest in creating bespoke training for how they want their marketers to work together. I am a fan of training, especially when it is a collective experience and focuses on how to apply learning to real brand issues. However, the learning from a training session decays quickly. My aim in providing this book is that you will be able to use it individually and collectively, when you really need it. For example, when you come to do an annual audit of the situation you face, you'll be able to refresh your memory about the key questions you should be asking.

There are many ways to skin a cat. A common issue this book seeks to resolve is that in teams, people will have slightly different tools and languages to approach common elements of brand building. I am not here to argue for the merits of one tool or another, but to recognize that not having agreed a way to do things wastes time and confuses your stakeholders. In this book, I will offer up what I have found to be the most useful and straightforward. I aim for the least amount of the most powerful tools and approaches. I'll give you suggestions on language, and tips for running sessions together.

I lean towards asking questions rather than providing templates. This is because in my experience, the templates used in many organizations create something of an industry – people fill them in, rather than spending time thinking about what to do.

Often these complex approaches are there to prevent mistakes rather than inspire brilliance. If you have found an approach which works for you for brand positioning, defining a creative idea, or whatever, my advice is to use it and embed it consistently in your team and organization. Have one common approach for each key thing, and ensure they link together to form a way of working. Where I have provided templates, adapt them to suit your own circumstances if they are useful.

Industry applicability

Another consideration is how transferable these approaches are across different industries. My belief is that they are – these are the fundamentals. It's easy to fall into the trap of saying tourism, finance, insurance, sports, tech, and consumer goods businesses, and even business to business, are so different there is no common ground, but when I talk to peers it becomes clear that we have common challenges within our organizations – in defining the role of marketing, in ensuring we lead a growth agenda, and in designing and executing programmes which will recruit buyers faster than our competition. It's important for you as a reader to think about what's similar and what's unique about your industry – whether it's mass or niche, who your customers are, what their decision-making processes are, what the frequency of purchase is, whether you interact directly with customers and so forth.

To do this I spoke to senior marketing leaders across different industries and brands covering diverse markets and geographies, all leaders or chief marketing officers. They were predominantly in business to consumer environments, but I also spoke to marketers working business to business – where there is surprising commonality albeit radically different audiences and channels. I spoke to marketers in businesses which are brand-led and where marketing is central, but also in those not led by marketing, which probably represent the majority and where marketers work hard to cut through. In listening to them, their experiences, and how they think and act, I have been able to appreciate similarities and differences. My aim is to combine simple, repeatable approaches with inspiration from people who've been successful in effective brand building.

They also gave me examples. Where possible I have made explicit which brand or segment these are from, but often anonymized or embedded their experiences into the text. This has enabled me to focus in on the challenges we face without making anyone feel uncomfortable – some of the experiences they related to me were from peers in other organizations.

In addition, I spoke to some of the brightest brains from organizations who partner great marketers in delivering effective brand building. Marketers don't work alone, and it made sense to combine internal views with some critical external perspectives – concerning data, consumer behaviour, research, creativity, and measurement.

I got a sense from these conversations that there is frustration about some of the narratives in the marketing and brand building industry. I heard from marketing leaders that they felt judged or ridiculed – as though they must be lacking somewhat in their capability when work was called out, as it so often is, for being substandard or not reflecting what was obvious to some commentators; *'did "brand x" really just change its 100-year-old logo?'*. Instead of criticizing, could we show empathy for the challenges marketers face to create great work, celebrate successes, and generously share knowledge?

Beyond the specific anecdotes, you will see occasional references to recent IPA effectiveness award winners. These awards are important in bringing to life what effective brand building looks like – understanding the situation the brand faces, cracking a great strategy, consumer insight, developing and deploying a creative idea to address challenges across different touchpoints, integrated with other brand activity, and quantifying beyond reasonable doubt the impact and value of that work, along with fresh learning for other brands.

How might this help you?

I've written this book to help marketing leaders and their teams be influential – to do the right thing, be able to explain what you are doing and why, and to create short- and long-term value. Marketing leaders face real challenges in the boardroom. The availability of data means more and more other functional leaders have a point of view. Data and tech have shifted marketing activities disproportionately toward the tactical – if once marketers 'did the pictures' perhaps now we spend too much time optimizing the impact of individual social posts rather than curating and executing a holistic brand experience? The role of marketing feels as though it is blurring – we are being asked to spend more time evaluating the impact of things like the metaverse and AI than we are in setting the strategy for growth and operationalizing it.

Marketers receive less formal training at work, and this means less emphasis on building core marketing capabilities – despite the short-term gain in productivity from the savings made, this is having a long-term negative effect on the impact marketers have.

In my conversations, it became clear that although there are many differences there are overwhelming similarities. I learned that we are all consumed by time spent on execution, and delivering the non-negotiable revenue or whatever targets we have, while trying our best to add more value for the long term, and better understanding and serving our consumers. The practical approaches I want to share are relevant if you are the chief marketing officer of a consumer goods business, a luxury business, a world leading football team, a travel company, quick service restaurant with a franchise model, a big brand, or a small brand. None of us have enough time or resources to do what we think is possible, and we imagine everyone else has better data and martech (marketing technology tools) to manage a seamless consumer experience when ours doesn't really work that well.

This book seeks to meet its audience of marketing leaders where they are – putting their heart and souls into building their brands, their teams, navigating complex external landscapes, and challenging the inner work-ings of their businesses. *Marketing Week's* Career and Salary survey (2024) was illustrative not only of the skills gap marketers perceive, but also how core marketing is undervalued by their businesses – over 50 per cent citing that marketing strategy was not valued and almost half that brand manage-ment was not. We should be celebrating the best work, encouraging marketers to help cross-functional colleagues better understand the commercial value of brand-building approaches, and continuously improve and learn.

I know there are still a handful of organizations with comprehensive and well enshrined brand-building practices. I believe this book can be useful to marketers in those organizations but have a significant impact on small and medium-sized businesses, domestic and international, start-ups and scale-ups. I am writing this book to help you succeed. There is no right or wrong way per se, but it is important you have a consistent and joined up way of working.

I believe that you have all the answers. My job here is to provoke you with the right questions at the time when you need them, to coach you to unlock the potential for you, your teams, and your brands.

A word on language

Depending on the industry, the words consumer and customer may be used. For the sake of consistency, I will use 'consumer' to talk about end users, even though in industries such as hospitality, travel, and insurance, 'customer' is more prevalent. In consumer goods businesses customers are typically retailers or resellers who sell on the goods. In truth, I would rather we talked about people or humans, but this is jarring in some contexts. 'Consumer' reduces people down to the relationship they have with your product or service when we should consider them holistically.

At the end of each section, I'll ask you some questions to reflect on what the content means for you, and what action you should take.

Reflections

What are the biggest challenges you and your team face?

How well does your organization understand brands and brand building?

How strong and consistent is your brand-building capability?

How is this book organized?

Part One – Introduction to effective brand building

How on earth do we go about creating a model which stacks the cards in our favour, helps us win over the competition, and enables us to demonstrate positive commercial impact, getting the organization comfortable with brand building investment?

I suspect you are keen to jump into the brand strategy and planning sections, but before we get to that we need to zoom out. Effective brand building thrives when the total system accepts and is aligned to the benefits it provides for long- and short-term performance.

Part One of the book is concerned with establishing some of these foundations. For example, in **Chapter 2**, we will consider the significance of the most recent thinking on consumer behaviour.

Chapter 3 examines whether your organization has the right conditions for brand building. The nature of an organization, its goals, culture, and how it creates value shape the role marketing and brands play. We will reflect on the elements which can enable or inhibit brand building, from tangible things such as business strategy, how leaders are rewarded, and what processes and capabilities are established. In addition, we will contemplate the less tangible elements of culture – values and beliefs around brands and the stories your organization tells. The chapter outlines an approach to conducting an audit to enable you diagnose how ready you are, and what interventions you might need to consider. You may be able to make interventions to better enable brand building. At least it will allow you to see where to focus your attention and recognize where system bias may work for you and against you.

Unlike many other functions whose activities have been more closely codified, marketing has not. Though marketing theory abounds, translating this theory into everyday competencies is still not present in many organizations. It does reflect the fact that many organizations do not have a common view on what marketing should do, and often marketers allow their role to be defined by someone else. This is an issue when working cross functionally with general management, finance, and sales, but also human resources. For example, if your human resource partners don't understand the work involved in building brands, then they will not be able to adequately support you in creating the right marketing organization and wiring it into the total business.

In **Chapter 4** I will propose a framework of core marketing capabilities against which you can evaluate your team. We will examine whether and how to embed this into an annual cycle. It's important to have a capability framework which combines skills and behaviours alongside a brand-building model as it elevates your marketers from everyday executional tasks and considers their skills and the skills you may require in a broader framework. It will enable you to identify gaps which you can fill with new hires, training, and coaching.

The final section of Chapter 4 will address leadership. There is no single answer to this, but I want to share perspectives as to what makes for successful marketing leaders from the people I consulted preparing this book.

Chapters 5 and 6 are about the foundations of effective brands – their characteristics, the importance of understanding brand and category stage of development, the drivers of strong brands, and the importance of understanding the drivers of consumer demand.

The final chapter of Part One, **Chapter 7**, is on consumer insight – a critical discipline which enables brands to apply consumer understanding to their toughest problems, and inspire effective solutions.

Part Two – Creating an effective brand strategy – where to win

Part Two provides guidance on how to create an effective brand strategy, synthesizing approaches from different industries into one coherent approach which you should be able to adapt to your brand and category.

Chapter 8 addresses what strategy is, and how to align brand strategy to your business planning processes. **Chapter 9** outlines tools you can use with your team to understand the environment in which your brand operates, its growth potential, and introduces an effective brand model to enable you to understand how strong your brand is today.

In **Chapter 10** we will reflect on the role brands play in a portfolio to deliver an organization's goals, how to think about investment across the portfolio, and how to develop a long-term brand ambition.

An effective brand strategy has a red thread running through it from powerful analysis of the external environment and organizational capabilities to the development, deployment, and measurement of consumer-facing activities. In **Chapter 11** we will address how to use the marketing audit to make choices about what you will prioritize to grow.

In **Chapter 12** we will devote attention to two fundamental elements of brand building: brand positioning and visual identity.

Part Three – How to win and how to keep winning

In the third part, we will focus on how to turn what you have done into a repeatable brand building model, which you can optimize with each new wave of learning.

In **Chapter 13** we examine how to connect with your target audience, the kind of creative your brand may aspire to, and how to brief and work with agency partners.

In **Chapter 14** we will translate the building blocks you have established into a 12-month plan. We will define some important terminology to help you organize consumer-facing work against strategic priorities, and choose the right mix of activities, thinking about whether you are spending enough on the most effective and efficient things. To ensure you develop a holistic plan we will consider how to integrate things such as pricing, promotion, range optimization, and innovation alongside media and communications.

In **Chapter 15** we will look at how you can turn this into a growth plan – bringing to life the growth your plan will deliver, and the investment required to support it. We will discuss setting key performance indicators and developing a learning plan.

Chapter 16 will cover measurement and invite you to develop a measurement framework and toolkit to ensure you are set up to understand the impact of your work, be able to adapt, and make better future decisions about how best to deploy your marketing investment.

An effective brand-building model is a wheel – measurement creates new perspectives which influence future decisions. It is a wonderful balance of art and science, magic and measurement – a skilled craft combining experience, judgement, and evidence. Brands run in cycles, which is one of the issues marketers face in their organizations. It is rarely the case that you will fully establish and codify a growth model on your brand and portfolio in year one. Occasionally a brand will hit it out of the park, but patience in embedding over two or three years is what will pay significant dividends for the long and short term.

Though the scope of the book is ambitious, it's worth acknowledging some things which are out of scope, or which may be better served with a dedicated text. These include innovation, category management, as well as going into detail into aspects of physical availability, shopper, and customer marketing. The book does not go into everyday execution as these differ by brand due to channels, audiences, and route to market and are shifting dynamically due to technology.

Topics such as ESG (environmental, social, and governance) and DEI (diversity, equity, inclusion) are among other pressing subjects for brand marketers considering effective brand building for which space does not allow coverage.

What is effective brand building and why does it matter?

Marketing suffers from poorly defined terms. 'Insight' is one of them, which we will cover in Chapter 7, and indeed the role of 'marketing' itself is perceived inconsistently across organizations and industries. The classic definition is that marketing is about satisfying consumer needs (Kotler *et al*, 1996). In thinking about brand building, we are more concerned with what marketers do and how they add value to an organization, its customers, and consumers.

If you asked senior leaders and other stakeholders in your organization what they would say about the role marketing plays and the value it adds? I hope they would describe you and your team as business leaders whose deep understanding of the consumer and market opportunity defines where growth will come from, and translates that into programmes in partnership with other functions and agencies to create sustainable incremental revenue and profit. I hope they would be able to cite examples of brand work, innovation, and other actions which have made a difference to business performance, and in delivering its long-term vision.

What do we mean by effective brand building?

We could describe brand building as the core competencies needed to create sustainable top- and bottom-line growth; brand building puts consumer insights at the heart of the business and applies those insights to unlock growth. A business concerned with brand building understands both the power of brands as shortcuts to consumers in the moment of choice, and that strong brands are its most valuable asset, correlating with the perceived value of the business as a whole. A brand-building model balances building positive associations in the mind of its target audience, with harvesting those strong perceptions to generate sales in the short and medium term.

By bringing 'effective' into the equation we are explicitly signalling how central 'marketing effectiveness' needs to be in brand building. Often the phrase marketing effectiveness conjures up measurement tools. These can be a silo alongside core marketing processes, and backward-looking in nature. Effectiveness should be central to brand building – focused on ensuring businesses meet their revenue and profit goals by recruiting customers in the most cost-efficient way, enabling ever better future decisions about brand investment. By putting 'effectiveness' at the heart of brand building we are choosing to focus on a more transparent, commercial, forward-facing, and repeatable model. We need not complain any more that half of the money spent on advertising is wasted, as Lord Leverhulme or John Wanamaker are reported to have said.

Brand building is an important term as it makes the distinction that it is not just the concern of the marketing team; the whole business must be 100 per cent consumer-focused – at all levels, in all functions, and across the total business system including agencies, partners, and suppliers. This must be underpinned with the right ways of working – a combination of brand building expertise, leadership behaviours, and the systems and processes which create competitive advantage. In the same breath, marketing champions brand-building – consumer-centred growth, strategy, and activation.

BRAND BUILDING CREATES COMMERCIAL VALUE

- Between 1982 and 2019 Audi estimates that for every £1 it invested in communications it returned £2.33 through work built around the idea of 'Vorsprung durch Technik' ('progress through technology') (Lion and Gwin, 2020).

- Guinness quantified the value of its creative platform to be £1bn in the UK and Ireland between 2012 and 2019 (Stoney and Mawdsley, 2020).

- Between 2015 and 2019 Tesco estimated the incremental revenue contribution from marketing to be £4.3bn (Gregory and Parnum, 2020).

- Cadbury believes its marketing between 2017 and 2021 not only helped rehabilitate positive perceptions of the brand in the UK but delivered £261m additional revenue per year (King *et al*, 2022).

The challenges marketers face building brands effectively

In trying to create a culture of effective brand building marketers face many challenges, both internal and external. Here are some of them which provide context for what this book seeks to help marketers achieve:

- Volatility – impacting consumer behaviour, supply chains, and costs. This makes forecasting tricky and can constrain consistent marketing investment which is a characteristic of effective brand building.

- Changing media environment, with global advertising revenues focused on big platforms in search, social, and retail media making connection planning difficult and reducing buying power.

- Despite financial analysts acknowledging the importance of brand strength (IPA, 2023), brand and consumer measures are not typically part of business reporting, and do not reflect the three- to five-year cycle brand and innovation programmes take to mature.

- Organizations designed to deliver short-term goals of public and private investors rather than a long-term consumer opportunity.

- Lack of clarity on the impact of marketing activities on business outcomes.

- Lack of brand-building capability with few organizations having common brand-building language, framework, and tools.

- Data overload, often focused on evaluating the performance of short-term tactics at the expense of brand strategy and long-term outcomes.
- Complex internal stakeholder management and approval processes for marketing programmes.

Reflections

What does effective brand building mean to you?

What is the commercial value brand building adds to your business?

What are the internal challenges and pressures you face to deliver effective brand building?

References

Gregory, S and Parnum, J (2020) From running shops to serving customers: The Tesco turnaround story, in *Advertising Works 25, Proving the payback on marketing investment*, ed. S Unerman, pp 47–86, IPA Effectiveness Awards 2020, Ascential Events (Europe), London

Institute of Practitioners of Advertising (2023), Brand finance investment analyst survey, https://ipa.co.uk/news/investment-analyst-survey/ (archived at https://perma.cc/24T6-NNQH)

King, A *et al* (2022) Cadbury 'There's a glass & a half in everyone': How intrinsic purpose can transform a brand's fortunes, in *Advertising Works 26, Proving the payback on marketing investment*, ed. H Singh, pp 41–75, IPA Effectiveness Awards 2022, IPA, London

Kotler, P *et al* (1996) *Principles of Marketing*, 7th edn, Prentice Hall, Upper Saddle River, NJ

Lion, W and Gwin, T (2020) Audi, the value of 'Vorsprung durch Technik' over four decades, in *Advertising Works 25, Proving the payback on marketing investment*, ed. S Unerman, pp 87–117, IPA Effectiveness Awards 2020, Ascential Events (Europe), London

Marketing Week (2024), Career and salary survey 2024, www.marketingweek.com/2024-career-salary-survey/ (archived at https://perma.cc/K2T6-EKSW)

Stoney, L and Mawdsley, C (2020) Guinness 'Made of more' 2012–2019: consistency x creativity, in *Advertising Works 25, Proving the payback on marketing investment*, ed. S Unerman, pp 147–95, IPA Effectiveness Awards 2020, Ascential Events (Europe), London

2

What are the fundamentals of consumer behaviour?

- What are the key principles concerning buyer behaviour which underpin effective brand building? p. 15

What are the key principles concerning buyer behaviour which underpin effective brand building?

Though this book is not intended to be an academic textbook or contribution to marketing theory, I think it's critical to start by laying out the principles which underpin how we think about building brands today. The point of doing this is twofold – firstly, these principles inform assumptions on how to build brands in the rest of the book, and secondly, I think it is important for any organization to have a philosophy of brand building, understood cross functionally.

Marketing teams and their cross-functional peers need to be on the same page. Changes in how we think about growing brands has largely come from two angles – firstly, the digital era has created new datasets which enable us to observe how audiences behave like never before, and secondly, practitioners of behavioural economics have reframed how we think about consumer behaviour and how to influence it.

Though the last 15 years have been dominated by the embedding of these ideas, I anticipate that our learning will continue to grow, especially with new thinking from psychologists and neuroscientists, while technology continues to evolve the media landscape.

There is a short reading list at the end of this chapter, including a handful of texts which have changed our views on marketing in profound ways since *Principles of Marketing* (Kotler *et al*, 1996) was developed.

Here are four things to consider:

1 Consumers don't care about your brand.

2 Consumers buy from a repertoire of brands within a given category.

3 You need to get each consumer to choose your brand over the competition every time they shop the category.

4 Consumers will only buy your brand if it comes to mind and the right offer is available and easy to find.

Consumers don't care about your brand

Some of the most exciting developments in the last 15 years have been in behavioural economics – the application of psychological insight into how people make economic decisions. One of the texts which has most influenced marketers is *Thinking, Fast and Slow* (Kahneman, 2011). I also recommend reading some of Dan Ariely's work – it is illuminating about the *Predictably Irrational* (Ariely, 2009) drivers of consumer choice.

This work has sharpened marketers' focus on changing consumer behaviour, perhaps more than on changing attitudes. It has helped illuminate the importance of the emotional and instinctive drivers of choice in a world where many brands are still in an arms race to present ever more extreme product features – for example, do deodorant manufacturers really believe that the average man does not shower for 4 days or 96 hours?

System 1 and system 2 thinking

System 1 thinking is the fast, instinctive, and emotional way we respond to everyday situations and stimulus. Ever experienced arriving somewhere in your car and not been sure how you got there? That automatic pilot is the system 1 brain in action. It is also how we make most of our choices as consumers and how we consume marketing communications – seemingly passive, but in fact undertaken by a brain built on years of experience of making the complex simple, knowing what to ignore and what to tune into.

In contrast, system 2 thinking is more analytical, deliberate, and rational. We use that to make sense of unfamiliar situations. Most of us have a bias that we use this mode of thinking more than we do. We like to think of ourselves as more conscious and in control of our decisions than we are. If we had to use system 2 thinking from the moment we got up, we might never get out of the house in the morning. Do you remember the exercise where people are asked to explain how to make a cup of tea? It turns out to be extremely complicated – our morning routine is full of things like brushing our teeth, buttoning a blouse or shirt, tying our shoelaces, which would be exasperating if we were not able to do them automatically.

In the past marketers referred to the decisions consumers made as based on 'limited problem solving' or 'extended problem solving'. It turns out that we have all over-emphasized 'extended problem solving'. That is not to say we should put it aside entirely. New category entrants can be a great source of business, and if that is important to your brand you will need to understand how new consumers make sense of your category as they approach it for the first time.

In the past we typically prescribed 'extended problem solving' to higher value categories, and 'limited problem solving' to lower value categories. It turns out we approach most of our category choices in an instinctive and emotional way once we have understood how it all works – we are creatures of habit. The implications of this for brands is that they must ensure consumers can instantaneously decode them and understand what they are all about without having to expend too much cognitive effort.

It also gives us some clues as to why challenger brands can be so effective in upsetting the apple cart. A great recent example is Mockingbird smoothies in the UK. This brand is disrupting the mainstream juice and smoothie category. It observed how juice consumption was changing among leading-edge consumers and how this in turn was showing up on the high street with chains such as Joe and the Juice. Consumer requirements were changing in a way that the main established competitors available in grocery retailers had not understood. Of course, this is ironic when you consider that the main brand, Innocent, had disrupted the category 20 years earlier, and before that Tropicana had done the same in shifting the default from ambient UHT juice from concentrate to pasteurized chilled juice not from concentrate.

Recognizing the importance of system 1 thinking in decision making is not only about making it easy for consumers to buy your brand, in understanding the drivers of choice and the shortcuts consumers make, but also in recognizing how evolving culture can tip consumer behaviour in favour of one brand over another.

Do consumers love brands? Well, you know what, some of them might do, especially if they share values and beliefs (Collins, 2023). There are certain categories where I am interested in brands, want to know what they are doing, and am keen to see what their new range of products might be. I love what they do! They play an important role in my life, who I am, how I see the world, and how I want to spend my time. Music, sport, and entertainment brands are categories which may have characteristics like this. But for the most part, I'm trusting my gut reactions and my system 1 reptile brain, and that means I may well buy a competitor product instead if it suits my needs just as well as or better than the one I think I prefer. That is what most of your consumers do too. It can be a trap to think too much about those highly engaged consumers who would recommend your brand as they still probably fulfil a proportion of their needs from your competition. They may love you but want an open relationship.

Consumers buy from a repertoire of brands within a given category

Putting into perspective the role categories and brands play in your consumers' lives is both liberating and slightly daunting. Instead of seeing them as friendly, well-disposed people who generously want to give you the time of day, we can see them as they really are – busy people juggling multiple priorities in their lives. Our job as marketers is to make their lives easier, not harder, and to have primed their system 1 brains with the shortcuts which will get them to choose us over the competition in that moment of choice – a nano second which goes under the radar for them, but in aggregate for us means the difference between winning or losing market share.

Alongside the work of Kahneman *et al*, the work of the Ehrenberg Bass Institute has had a significant impact on how marketers think about brands, especially since the publication of *How Brands Grow* (Sharp, 2010) and its sequel *How Brands Grow Part 2* (Romaniuk and Sharp, 2016).

One of the main contributions to marketing practice of *How Brands Grow* was to shine a light for the broader industry on understanding consumer-packaged goods businesses had from the shopper behaviour datasets they bought from businesses such as Kantar and Nielsen IQ. These datasets are based on continuous panels of shoppers recording their purchasing data across categories. Core analyses focus on understanding the drivers of purchasing behaviour – the relative importance of heavy, medium, and light buyers, the number of brands in shopper repertoires over a period of time, how shoppers fulfil their needs by shopping across brands, how a buyer base is composed of new, lost, and retained buyers, and where incremental volume gains come from – typically more from switching from other brands in line with their relative size versus being incremental to the category.

If you had been working in a packaged goods category with the benefit of these datasets, you may have found the implications self-evident, but the Ehrenberg Bass Institute smartly zoomed out and were able to see that the same patterns appeared across multiple categories, including luxury categories at higher price points. A rigorous evidence base brought these ideas into plain sight and challenged many marketing theories accepted at the time.

Understanding how consumers make decisions, and the rigorous evidence of actual shopper dynamics, challenged long-held notions that marketers need to focus on recruiting new consumers, and then develop their loyalty – increasing both the brand's share of their category requirements and the depth of connection they feel. Fuelled by the prevalence of the Pareto principle that claimed that roughly 80 per cent of sales come from 20 per cent of buyers, marketing has focused on creating and retaining heavy buyers. Supposedly, these buyers become loyal, ultimately dropping other brands from their repertoires.

However, the data does not support these long-held assumptions. In fact, over the course of a year or longer all brands lose a significant proportion of their buyer base to competitors. To maintain or build a buyer base means recruiting new buyers at a faster rate than you lose them, and retaining existing buyers as best you can. Your brand is like a leaky bucket.

These datasets also make clear that most shoppers buy from a repertoire of acceptable brands within a category. If you think of your own behaviour, this is self-evident. If, as a staunch drinker of Guinness, arguably one of the most remarkable brands in its category, you walked into a pub to meet your friends and it was not available, it is unlikely you would leave but instead you would choose a different beer or something else entirely.

In fact, a Guinness drinker is likely to drink a range of different brands and drinks based on the occasion, who they are with, and whether food is present, amongst other factors. Think of your own behaviour – you might choose still wine or lager to unwind in the evening, pair red wine with certain types of food, champagne or cocktails for a celebration or special occasion. Trying to get that same consumer to choose the same thing when their motivations and occasions can be so different seems insane when you think about it. The same is evident in other industries – the different types of financial products you might need, the different leisure and tourism activities you might undertake, the types of transport you might choose for different types of journeys.

The data around the contribution most brands get from their heavy buyers supports this. In fact, the contribution from light buyers is much more significant. Growth is more likely to come from influencing their behaviour than it is heavy buyers. This has profound implications for you as a marketer – it means your success is more likely to come from influencing the most fickle buyers, and those who may know the least about your brand and proposition. Not only are we trying to influence people on autopilot, but we are also trying to influence the least interested consumers.

You need to get each consumer to choose your brand over the competition every time they shop the category

Another important cross category learning is the importance of penetration to brand growth. Sales are a function of how many consumers you have, how much they buy, and how much they pay for those goods and services. In theory this means you can grow by increasing your buyer base, increasing the average amount each buyer buys over a given time frame, or increasing the value of those transactions.

The evidence shows across different categories that those brands which experience most dynamic growth do so as they increase the number of consumers they have; this is expressed as percentage penetration – the percentage of category buyers who buy your brand over a specified time frame – or as an absolute number of buyers in a time frame.

The evidence also shows that brands with higher penetration tend to have a higher buying rate or average frequency of purchase – the average number of times each buyer buys. This means that if you were to focus on getting your existing buyers to buy more often you are less likely to grow than if you focus on penetration alone.

Think of your own buying behaviour across a range of categories and this will start to make sense. There are a finite number of potential needs or purchase occasions for most categories. Take mobile phones – you may own one, or maybe two if you have a personal and a business phone. Even if I tried, I would be unlikely to succeed in persuading you to buy a third phone. It would be just as hard for me to get you to go on an extra holiday each year – you probably don't have the money or additional days leave. Do you think you can persuade your brand's buyers to wash their hair more often, to drink more cups of tea, to have multiple bank accounts? Though not everyone is the same, categories have natural ceilings for demand.

A primary focus on penetration, however, does not mean you should ignore the buying rate. A great source of growth for a strong brand can be to get people to buy it in adjacent categories. Most importantly, you should never ignore the value of every transaction. In addition to ensuring you recruit new buyers faster than you lose them, you should focus on ensuring the price your brand commands can at a minimum keep pace with the category, ideally growing ahead of it. Brand building is about profitable growth, and as well as recruiting new buyers, the other main impact of investing in brands is to create pricing power. Alongside penetration, premiumization is the second main strategy for growth.

Given the importance of penetration for brand growth it is something you should measure alongside that of your competitors. We will talk more about this when we discuss measurement, but it is often a missing piece in marketers' toolkits, and overlooked with brands which have primary data on their own consumers, but not necessarily a view on their competitors. Thinking about the typical purchasing cycle will be important in working out how you do it, and how frequently you do it – it might be that you need a weekly or monthly read for the fastest moving categories, whereas in automotive or insurance a longer time frame will suffice, given the much lower frequency with which people buy those categories.

Consumers will only buy your brand if it comes to mind and the right offer is available and easy to find

This new thinking has helped crystallize what lies at the core of the marketing task and provides a framework to think about achieving growth by expanding your buyer base.

There have been many models historically which have tried to do this – one of the oldest is 'AIDA', standing for 'awareness, interest, desire, action' which captures in a linear way how consumers go from never having heard of a brand to buying it. Marketing funnels have become common currency in the last few years, especially given the growth of retailer advertising platforms, the most significant of which is Amazon Marketing Services (AMS), albeit they are prevalent with online and offline retailers including giants such as Walmart and Tesco, and in specialist sectors such as Boots in the UK, and Ulta Beauty in the US.

Retail media has become one of the most significant channels for advertising spend in the world (Statista, 2022). It demonstrates how this mindset of 'upper funnel' in which brands build positive associations, and 'lower funnel' in which they seek to convert those to sales, may no longer be entirely practical. Certainly, there are traps for the marketer with lots of evidence of sales going through these channels being validated by attribution analytics which only account for the advertising effects on their own platform and not those created elsewhere.

It helps marketers to consider that they have two jobs to do – create consideration for their brands and convert that consideration into sales – even if these two things have more synchronicity than perhaps we thought they had (Roach, 2021). The terms 'mental availability' and 'physical availability' became embedded in the language of marketing long before the blurring of advertising channels and retail channels.

Mental availability is often defined as the likelihood of a brand to come to mind in a buying situation. It stresses how building brand associations only matter if they are effective at the moment of choice. Physical availability is often defined as whether the brand is available in a buying situation – be that in a store or online, it means that it is visible, shoppable, and available to purchase in that moment.

The 'availability' model is useful as it sharpens our attention to creating the conditions for winning over the competition right there in that moment. Even brands which own their own physical and digital stores have reliance on other retailers. Brands for travel such as booking.com or expedia.com are faced with the same challenge. They still need to consider how they ensure those disengaged repertoire shoppers think about them when they are considering booking a hotel, that they are visible, have the right offer at the right price, and that it's easy to book. There's so much that can go wrong, and effective brand building is simply a set of principles and approaches to follow which can give you the edge and advantage in that precarious buying situation.

Though we recognize mental and physical availability are mutually reliant like yin and yang, having them as distinct concepts is important in a world where performance marketing and retailers are encouraging us to spend more on conversion at the expense of consideration.

The implication of this is that brand owners must understand the path to purchase – their consumer journey and brand experience, built on insight into the most fertile moments in which to influence behaviour.

What are the implications for brand building?

I promised this book was not going to be a heavy theoretical tome, but it is important to establish a common framework of understanding. This is for your team, but also for your broader business who care about different things.

So, we've established that effective brand building is hard – consumers don't really care about your brand, and that once they are used to buying a category, brand choice almost happens automatically from a repertoire. But we also know we need to focus on ensuring that, when they do make a purchase, your brand stands out from the crowd, is relevant and memorable, present and visible.

This is where measurement and learning come into the picture. Ensuring you invest in an appropriate framework of key measures is the only way to understand the impact of your marketing endeavours holistically – to do more of the things which work, to evolve or stop those which don't, and to continuously shape the mix of activities so you engage your distracted consumer. This must be a measurement framework which goes beyond measuring the immediate things typically covered by performance marketing metrics – concerned as they are typically with the effects of individual digital assets in driving traffic or converting sales, versus their role in in an overall brand-building system. You need to be able to see the wood and the trees.

Reflections

What beliefs exist in your business about brands and consumer behaviour?

How embedded are these?

Are they reflected in how you operate as a brand or business?

What actions should you take to establish and embed a philosophy of brand building?

References

Ariely, D (2009) *Predictably Irrational: The hidden forces that shape our decisions*, Harper, New York

Collins, M (2023) *For the Culture*, Macmillan Business, London

Kahneman, D (2011) *Thinking, Fast and Slow*, Farrar, Straus and Giroux, New York

Kotler, P *et al* (1996) *Principles of Marketing*, 7th edn, Prentice Hall, Upper Saddle River, NJ

Roach, T (2021) The sales funnel is wrong but it's here to stay, so let's fix it, www.thetomroach.com/2021/09/01/the-sales-funnel-is-wrong-but-its-here-to-stay-lets-fix-it/ (archived at https://perma.cc/7UUV-C3W9)

Romaniuk, J and Sharp, B (2016) *How Brands Grow. Part 2*, Oxford University Press, South Melbourne

Sharp, B (2010) *How Brands Grow*, Oxford University Press, South Melbourne

Statista (2022) Leading media companies worldwide, ranked by advertising revenue, www.statista.com/statistics/261827/leading-media-companies-worldwide/ (archived at https://perma.cc/4WTU-PPQ5)

3

What are the conditions required for brands to thrive in my organization?

Why does understanding my organization matter?

In general, when marketers embark on a journey to improve their impact on brand building, they get stuck straight into reviewing things such as brand positioning, creative work, and investment levels. In my experience, and in my conversation with marketing leaders, attempts to embed brand building rarely fail because of the brand positioning, the insight, and the marketing, and more likely due to organizational culture, structure, and design.

Brands thrive in organizations where everyone is on the same page in understanding what they are there to do combined with consistent values and behaviours. In effective single brand organizations and service businesses, how the brand is seen internally is typically in synch with what the consumer or customer sees, albeit the language and concepts used might differ to reflect the needs of those internal and external audiences.

Creating the right conditions in your organization is critical to increase brand building effectiveness. Do not pass go until you are confident these are in place, or you are aware of potential traps and how to resolve them. So much of what you need to be successful in building brands is contingent on recognizing the needs of the organization, what it is motivated by, and what it celebrates. The importance of understanding your organization as much as your consumer is often overlooked by marketers, especially those who have spent most time in the same or similar organizations.

Let me give you a cautionary tale shared with me by the marketing leader in a well-known branded consumer business where brand building was core to the business strategy and the CEO was a strong advocate. The organization had identified which of the brands in its portfolio were the most important for the future, and the marketing leader in question set about doing the work on a market-leading brand which had lost its way. As well as the CEO they had the support of the managing director of their business unit and the chief marketing officer.

Working with their brand team and a strong advertising agency, they identified the biggest challenge the brand faced and uncovered a consumer insight which would help reframe the brand from being in an unremarkable functional space into an emotionally potent one relevant to the lives of their target audience. A strong brand campaign was aired across channels and touchpoints and the marketing director could see in the retail sales and performance data that something appeared to be happening in the short term – which is unusual even though in this case media was well coordinated with instore activity and promotions.

The scale of investment was enough that marketing mix modelling was commissioned to evaluate the impact of the work with a view to making improvements and proving the case for future investment. The results were stunning. I reiterate at several points in this book that effective brand building requires patience – unlike in this example, rarely do you get things right first time, and most often it takes humility and courage to learn, improve, and resist the temptation to throw out a strategy and start again.

The marketing mix modelling demonstrated that the campaign was highly effective – enabling the marketing director to optimize aspects of the campaign, including the mix of channels, the media plan, and focusing on the campaign assets and formats which had worked the best. In fact, the work smashed industry norms by more than three times, was profitable in the short term, and the econometricians recommended that up to four times the amount could be spent on media without seeing diminishing returns.

These moments don't happen often in your career, and given the organization was under significant cost pressures elsewhere, the marketing director was not seeking to max out investment on this brand alone but start a journey year by year to increase investment profitably and make the brand vibrant again. There were exciting plans for innovating into adjacent spaces, and things looked positive.

Fast forward a year, the campaign had not been re-run, and the innovation had stalled. In fact, the brand had rolled back on some associated price increases enabled by its renewed strength and reverted to the same short-term sales tactics and promotions it had sought to avoid. So, what happened? At the end of the financial year in which the campaign ran, there was a change in managing director. The new managing director was still tasked with overcoming the many performance difficulties of the business, but their experience had been shaped in an era when the business was not focused on brands.

The replacement managing director had no experience or understanding of the effects of media and was more focused on the percentage gross margin and short-term sales, using limited editions and other tactics to hit numbers, negotiating cautious targets they could be certain of delivering. With a productivity mindset focused on removing all costs they perceived to be unnecessary, investment in marketing represented risk to the delivery of the numbers which delivered their bonus. In the system they were in, this productivity-led approach was not entirely 'off strategy', and it incentivized them to 'sandbag' to achieve their personal goals.

Despite the rigour of the analytics supporting the investment case, the managing director was happy to discount them and not engage. Despite having a suite of powerful and proven activities, the business did not invest. The brand continued to track against the market, gently losing equity and share, and pricing power. It would be easy to point fingers – perhaps the marketing director was not influential enough, did not allay the concerns of the managing director with their fixed mindset and low appetite for risk. This, however, is to miss the real drivers – reward, decision-making and process, skills and capabilities. The system the managing director had been trained in was one where hitting short-term numbers triggered financial bonus payments and missing them was likely to result in poor career progression or being fired. The time horizon in which people held roles was insufficient for them to have to address the most significant challenges.

In this hierarchical business, the managing director was solely responsible for decision-making, and neither they nor their finance partner had experience with a broad set of commercial drivers. In short, any investment in brand created perceived risk to short-term delivery and would not be countenanced until everything was going well – in essence, brand investment would be permissible at low levels only when sales levels were secure versus being understood as a driver of those sales and an ability to manage pricing.

Does this cautionary tale resonate with you?

What can we learn?

- Despite the company articulating 'brand building' as core to its strategy, this was not consistently understood by senior leaders in the business.
- Reward, both in terms of overall objectives and bonus, were linked to short-term sales and did not include any brand measures – be they brand strength, market share, market pricing, or promotion levels.
- A broad commercial skill set was not developed, reducing the understanding of the perceived levers for growth. Alongside this issue on capability, information flows were poor, meaning that the scope of inputs into key decisions was limited.
- Finally, decision-making sat with the managing director solely in a hierarchical culture.

As leadership changed in the course of this work, we can wonder how the marketing director might have responded differently, but it's hard to see how things would have turned out differently given the experience and perspectives of the managing director and what was really going on in the organization.

Reflections

What are seen as the most important things in your organizations?

How does the organization see the role of brand in creating value?

Have you experienced situations at work where people may have behaved in a way which seems counter to the overall mission? Why might this have been?

Have you experienced situations at work where people have championed brands despite potential risks to short-term delivery? Why might this have been?

How might I think about the organization as a system?

When you are in a system, it can be difficult to diagnose what's going on. There are, however, lots of organizational design models that you can use to help understand and tackle the factors likely to drive or inhibit brand building in your organization. All of them have pros and cons, and although it goes beyond the scope of this book, it is worth knowing there are more recent transformation models which more explicitly seek to guide organizational change.

For our purpose, the most common design models are sufficient – these include Galbraith's Star Model (Galbraith, 1973), Weisbord's six box model (Weisbord, 1978), and McKinsey's 7S design framework (Waterman *et al*, 1980). These models help us understand the organization as a system and diagnose how it might shift to a desired future state. For example, the McKinsey model combines hard elements such as strategy, structure, and systems, with softer elements such as skills, staff, style, and shared values. The Galbraith Star Model is simpler, although it does not include the critical lens of culture – the often-unspoken values and behaviours which characterize how a business works, nor does it include an external point of view. Focus on the impact of external change is present in Weisbord, which is why I suggest considering using a slightly hybrid approach. Use one of them, but ensure you capture the missing element of either culture or external environment.

At the heart of a brand-building model is maintaining a consistent brand core while continuously aligning and realigning your brand to the ever-changing landscape of culture and your consumers so this external lens is critical. As you consider how well your organization is set up to build brands, external understanding will help you understand how your organization needs to adapt to thrive in the next three to five years. Remember, brand building is a cycle and in Part Two we will discuss developing a robust lens on how the market is evolving. Once you are clear on your brand's ambition and source of future growth you should iterate this work.

You can use this organizational change framework to identify the barriers and enablers to brand building in your business, either from the perspective of marketing, or holistically – though marketing may champion brands, brand building thrives when everyone in the organization sees themselves as brand builders. If you use an external party to conduct this analysis, it will give it more clout and objectivity, increasing the likelihood of making a case for change, getting the commitment and resources you may need to tackle barriers. Regardless of how you do this work, speaking to a broad range of influential stakeholders will flush out not only the issues, but also check for congruency. If you think of the example above where the cards were stacked against brand investment from the start, one of the core issues was the lack of congruency between the stated brand-building strategy, and the way senior leaders were rewarded, talent, and capability, and culturally there was no consensus around the definition of brand building.

Remember that changes in the external environment affect your total business, and that all external and internal elements interrelate with each other to create the system in which you and your team find yourself.

The criteria you should consider as you think about your organizational readiness for brand building are:

- external environment – the forces shaping your category and consumers;
- culture – the values and behaviours prevalent in your organization;
- strategy – the choices your organization has made to achieve its ambition;
- structure – how teams and tasks are organized, decision-making, power;
- processes – repeatable ways of working, information flows;
- reward – what motivates people, how compensation is decided, what is incentivized and celebrated;
- people – talent, skills and capabilities, mindset.

Reflections

How would you describe your organization?

How would other people describe your organization?

How does the organization talk about itself?

How might I audit my organization to identify opportunities?

As mentioned above, you can conduct this analysis yourself to understand the nature of your organization and its readiness for brand building. Ideally you would present findings to your broader business leadership team to develop the thinking, identify critical areas, and create an action plan. If you are going down the path of doing a more rigorous audit, include senior leaders of key functional areas, and some of their direct reports. This ensures you gather a broad range of functional perspectives, including from those with the greatest influence, and those closer to day-to-day operations. In this instance the purpose of this audit is to diagnose readiness for brand building, to establish strengths and where there may be gaps, and to understand areas of consistency and incongruency. Table 3.1 covers some of the questions you might ask against each of the most important criteria.

TABLE 3.1 Prompts for understanding organizational readiness for brand building

Area	Prompts
External environment	What are the key forces shaping the landscape in which you operate? Consider the context, category, competition, consumer, customer/channel, and company.
Strategy	How does your business create value? What are the business's vision, mission, and core values – what is it here to do? What are the two to three priorities for the organization to achieve its vision? How intrinsic is brand in achieving it?
Structure	How is the business structured (roles, functions, organizational design such as business units, legal entities)? What is the operating model (traditional functional model, tribes, partnership model etc.)? Is it flat or layered? How does this serve the strategy? Where do power and influence sit? How are decisions made considering levels of seniority, rigour, pace etc.?
Process	What are the core processes in the business and how do they enable the structure and support the strategy? Remember to consider vertical processes such as target setting and budgeting, as well as horizontal processes which enable frictionless delivery of the work between functions day to day. How does information flow around the organization?
Reward	How does the business manage performance and determine how people are rewarded? Is it congruent with the long-term strategy and its delivery in the short and medium term? How does the business enable or constrain growth, innovation, investment, experimentation? What motivates people?
People	People are a critical element to strategy delivery; this is about understanding the strength of the critical capabilities required to deliver the strategy, as well as training, and how HR policies ensure you are evolving to have the right people for the present and future work. What is people's mindset?
Culture	Culture is 'how people do things around here' – what are the stories people tell about the kind of business it is, its shared values, style, the preferences of teams and individuals in terms of motivations, behaviours? These less tangible human elements create a sense of identity for a business. In a single brand business these are often symbiotic with those of the brand itself.

The importance of culture

Culture is nuanced and can be opaque to people, especially those who may have worked in a business for a long time, or who have limited experiences of working in different environments. It is worth underscoring here, as it is material to how you approach this book. The book is not intended to be deployed wholesale, but for you to think about what elements of effective brand-building culture may already be present and strengthened, which elements are absent and should be addressed, and ask what would and wouldn't work in your organization. My encouragement is to adapt and amend the frameworks and tips you find in this book in a way which works for you and in your industry. For example, you may not spend sufficiently to warrant marketing mix modelling, but you still need to identify an affordable way to determine the longer-term effects of brand campaigns versus KPIs.

The importance of culture came through in the interviews I conducted across marketing leaders from different industries. For the interviews, I had outlined the content and flow of the book so they could contribute more meaningfully. Some were at pains to point out that their business was more like the 'wild west' than having a conscious and deliberate way of behaving which we may think of ideal. In truth, most brand businesses are more like the wild west – becoming more effective is about learning to manage the tension between chaos and consistency!

Another critical point made was how the role of marketing differs in different companies and therefore the importance of brand. In some businesses marketing is central, and leads the growth agenda, defining where to win and how to play. This is typical in some, but not all, consumer-packaged goods businesses. It is important to use 'central' rather than 'lead', so as not to denigrate other functions.

In contrast, in other industries – such as sport, automotive, and entertainment – marketing may not be central, and marketers need to keep things simple and tap into the language and rhythm of what is core to the business – the team, races, the entertainment properties. It does not mean brands owned by such businesses cannot be highly effective but that marketers need to work and influence in a more nuanced way. The same is often said for founder-led brands and scale-ups. Remember, in all business and industry types, brand building should be seen as a team sport in which everyone plays a role, even if marketing champions brands.

To build on this, a couple of my interviewees framed a critical question marketers need to ask a priori to understand their role in the organization: how does your business create value? Understanding this clarifies the role marketing will play, its scope, how it interacts with other departments, and cultural biases. Think about how an insurance business is likely to be similar to and different from a football team franchise in the role marketing plays.

The key point on culture is to think about the nuances of your business as you consider how to approach brand building. Listen to what people say about how they perceive the business, how decisions are made, and what is valued. Businesses describe themselves as 'entrepreneurial', 'anti-establishment', 'data-driven', 'process-oriented', 'relationship based', 'biased to action', and so on. These are all important clues as to how to approach things. For example, in a complex multi-brand, multi-category multinational it's highly likely you will codify terminology and core processes for brand building to save time, build brands consistently, and have a common language. In that environment you may need a common philosophy of marketing, a 'laws of growth' programme, a non-negotiable set of 'brand pillars', 'must win battles', a 'way of brand building', a 'brand growth wheel', or whatever bespoke model the company uses to express the common approaches in this book.

You may also need to tackle some deep-seated beliefs – one of the marketers I spoke to was clear that the biggest hurdle to overcome was a decades-old belief that brands needed to demonstrate functional differences. In a single brand start-up or scale-up business you may not need this level of codification at all – it may be sufficient for you to align your leadership team to a common view on brands, to role model a culture of effective brand building through your behaviour – the questions you ask, how you coach and develop your team, and how you define the work to be done may be the only change required.

What have you learned? What are the areas which support brand building? How does your organization make decisions? What changes would have the biggest impact – people or evolving capability, more effective cross-functional ways of working?

This type of analysis has been used to inspire different change agendas, including some of the things below:

- intervention in marketing talent and capability;
- change in reward to include market and consumer measures which indicate progress towards longer-term vision;
- revisiting business and brand strategy – to get clarity on key choices, and where growth will come from;
- culture programme to build new leadership values and behaviours.

When you reflect on power and decision-making in your business it will give you clues as to how to seek alignment to the change required. If there are things to do within marketing this is more straightforward, but by its nature a view of your organization as a system is likely to reveal opportunities with cross-functional interdependencies.

In these instances, think about how you work with others to build consensus around the benefits of change, and define shared actions. It may be useful to share the analysis with your business's leadership team, with individual functional leaders, or with your CEO. The analysis may be useful to provide an evidence base to support the change, but in most instances focus on the benefits of what you are proposing for the things your CEO and business care about and make the actions you recommend tangible and specific.

Reflections

What elements of your organization's system promote brand building?

What elements of your organization's system inhibit brand building?

What is the culture of your organization?

What are the congruencies and incongruencies between marketing and the business?

What internal changes would most significantly enable brand building?

References

Galbraith, J R (1973) *Designing Complex Organizations*, Addison-Wesley Longman Publishing Co.

Waterman, R H (1980) Structure is not organization, https://tompeters.com/docs/Structure_Is_Not_Organization.pdf (archived at https://perma.cc/YN65-NGLF)

Weisbord, M R (1978) *Organizational Diagnosis: A workbook of theory and practice*, Addison-Wesley, Reading, MA

4

How do I ensure I have the right marketing capability?

- Why do marketing capability frameworks matter? p. 35
- What leadership behaviours foster effective brand building? p. 43

Why do marketing capability frameworks matter?

Having the right marketing capability to deliver the work you need is critical for brands to thrive in your organization. It is worth digging deeper into this aspect of 'people' which we addressed in Chapter 3.

I believe there is a crisis in brand-building capability, exacerbated by some of the forces shaping our industry in the last decade: the shift from consumer goods as the centre of gravity in brand building to tech; the plethora of new things brand owners have had to make sense of, from digital media, big data, blockchain, the seemingly short-lived metaverse, and now generative AI; and a skills crisis in marketing as training has been de-emphasized, due to cost pressures and remote working but also the inevitable intensity of working through wave after wave of crisis. Research from Jon Lombardo quoted in *Marketing Week* (2023) showed in markets such as the UK, Ireland, Canada, Australia, and New Zealand most marketers were untrained, with the percentage trained as low as 23.9 per cent in the UK and 27.5 per cent in the US.

A marketing capability framework can help develop the individuals in your team and shape your team to ensure they have the right mix of skills and experience to do the work you need to grow your brand.

How do you develop a marketing capability framework?

Herein lies a recommended framework you can adapt to match your needs. In line with the book's structure, this could be organized around 'where to win', 'how to win', and 'how to keep winning'. There are other ways you can do this – strategy, planning, and execution, or diagnose, plan, create, execute.

Organize it in whichever way makes sense for you, align it to the language of your brand or employer brand, or indeed take it wholesale. A capability framework is not a job description. You don't need everyone in your team to be rockstars at all of it – the larger the brand, the more likely you are to increase the focus and specialism of roles.

Below is a summary of the key areas.

WHERE TO WIN:

- understanding the environment;

- brand and category understanding;

- consumer insights;

- defining opportunities for growth.

HOW TO WIN:

- annual planning and project management;

- developing a creative platform, activities, and assets;

- connection moments and media;

- maximizing presence and revenue;

- innovation.

HOW TO KEEP WINNING:

- data analysis;

- understanding performance;

- measurement and learning.

The following tables, 4.1–4.3, summarize the competencies you should expect to see in each of these areas:

TABLE 4.1 Where to win

Understanding the environment	Brand and category understanding	Defining opportunities for growth	Consumer insights
Analysing and understanding the changing external environment	Identifying and quantifying attractive and accessible motivation-based segments	Identifying, quantifying, and selecting growth opportunities	Being curious and constantly learning about culture, consumer attitudes, and behaviours
Understanding the drivers of consumer choice	Deciding which brands can best compete and meet consumer motivations in priority consumer segments	Determining strategic brand actions to address growth opportunities	Having deep understanding of consumers and their changing motivations and behaviours
Understanding future trends shaping consumers' attitudes and behaviours	Articulating a three- to five-year brand ambition	Identifying growth opportunities beyond the core, and developing an innovation pipeline	Creating powerful insights into consumers which can be applied to opportunities for growth and inspire breakthrough ideas and actions
	Setting long-term category and brand objectives		

TABLE 4.2 How to win

Annual planning and project management	Developing a creative platform, activities, and assets	Connection moments and media	Maximizing presence and revenue	Innovation
Setting long- and short-term objectives and expressing the actions to deliver them	Defining a relevant and credible brand positioning	Understanding and managing an effective consumer experience across touchpoints	Identifying revenue opportunities through understanding of distribution channels	Developing propositions against identified innovation territories
Developing a 12–18 month plan across all relevant consumer touchpoints	Developing a creative platform to support strategic brand actions suitable for content across all channels	Understanding consumer connections across the media landscape	Developing brand range, pack and price architecture to best meet consumer demand	Understanding new technology to reach and meet consumer motivations effectively
Prioritizing marketing activities most likely to deliver objectives effectively	Defining distinctive brand assets	Developing an effective integrated media plan	Setting profitable and competitive pricing and promotion principles	Designing packaging that is distinctive online, in store, and in use
Developing a project plan with an integrated set of objectives, strategies, activities, timing, and allocated resources	Writing single-minded and inspiring briefs	Applying an audience-led approach to media planning to maximize reach	Collaborating with sales and customers, to develop trade plans that maximize sales, providing customer materials on time	
Developing new product launch plans	Working with agencies to develop consumer-facing activities aligned to growth priorities			
Gaining commitment to the plan from internal stakeholders, including roles, responsibilities, resources, and timings	Working with agencies on the production of activities across channels in line with brand guidelines and growth priorities			
Monitoring project delivery versus KPIs and course correcting as necessary				

TABLE 4.3 How to keep winning

Data analysis	Managing performance	Measurement and learning
Writing succinct research briefs	Cross-functional understanding (sales, research & development, supply, operations, finance etc.)	Creating and managing a learning plan to consistently understand and improve your brand's performance
Keeping up to date with latest research, analysis, and data acquisition techniques		
Analysing information, identifying critical learnings and actions	Managing brand P&L, integrating predictable short-term delivery with long-term brand-building investment	Conducting post-campaign and post-innovation launch reviews to understand the effectiveness of different elements of the marketing mix and to optimize future investment and incremental profit from marketing
	Setting and measuring brand, campaign, and activity KPIs against objectives and versus competition	Defining opportunities to drive more effective future decisions

The tool above is comprehensive, and some elements relate more to product brands than to service brands. There may be things which need more emphasis for your brand – all media channels including TV have been digital for some time and enable selective buying of audiences, but your business may need to underline digital. Conversely, for brands reaching broad audiences you may need to stress the capabilities required to do that well with a generation of marketers more familiar with social media channels, influencer marketing, and user-generated content.

Do all capabilities have equal importance?

Some of these capabilities are used more frequently than others, and it's worth paying attention to those which are critical but used infrequently. For example, the capabilities in 'where to win' are only likely to be properly revisited every three to five years, given the typical growth cycle of a brand. It's important to revisit key strategic assumptions annually and identify changes based on new competitive activity and developments affecting your consumers. These capabilities are, however, the foundation of effective brand building – identifying the right opportunities for growth from robust analysis of the external environment and translating them into specific actions the brand needs to do creates the red thread of effective brand building.

Doing this well, but infrequently, enables you and your team to focus most of your effort on 'how to win' – this is about breaking down your long-term ambition into plans for the next 12–18 months, ensuring you have the right plans and activities to execute. This should be where around 80 per cent of your effort goes – focused on winning in the short term, but in a way which supports the growth priorities you have defined versus being reactive.

Executional elements are those which differ most across industries and types of brands. Elements to consider are how long the gap is between purchases in your category, seasonality, the value of transactions, whether it is a product or service, planned or unplanned, bought in the moment or in advance, sold directly by you or indirectly. The nature of content is important – for some brands, such as in sport or entertainment, content is part of the brand offer – it drives fan engagement and provides value way beyond what happens on the pitch or racetrack. This can even be true in consumer-packaged goods – think about Red Bull – beyond the drink, do the extreme sports constitute advertising content or a core part of the offering?

If 'where to win' is one end of the red thread of effective brand building, 'how to keep winning' is the other. Often, given the pressure of delivery and budgets, this is where marketers scrimp on dedicating time and focus. However, in taking the time to look objectively at your work you will start to quantify the effects of brand-building activity and create a virtuous circle which enables improvements and better future outcomes from your investment.

How to get value out of the marketing capability framework

Firstly, adapt or amend it to best meet the needs of your brand or team. You can take a modular approach focusing on where to win, how to win, or how to keep winning, or you can cover off all of them.

A lo-fi version is to get members of your team to conduct a self-assessment where they rate themselves versus a scale and capture evidence – projects or work they have done which demonstrate their experience.

A formal manager assessment can be conducted for comparison, or the self-assessment used to understand the strengths and development areas of each person in your team, and for them to create a development plan. For each core area members of your team wish to focus on they can decide whether they plan to do this through on the job experience, training, mentoring, or other avenues. It will enable them, and the marketing leader, both to play to the latent strengths of the team as well as coordinate developing the team based on the brand work to be done.

Typically, an assessment such as this would be completed annually to enable the team member and leader to understand what progress was being made against the development objectives. Team members changing roles should create a fresh development plan given the new challenges ahead and possibly revisit this sooner given the tenure of roles – often disappointingly short for marketers.

A more comprehensive and valuable approach to this is to use one of the many free online survey platforms to collect this data, or to use an internal HR or external partner to manage this for you if you have the budget. Including identification data such as job level, gender, number of years' experience can enable you as a marketing leader to get an aggregated view of the strengths and development needs of your team more comprehensively. The data can then drive a robust plan to build the key areas of capability you require for the future. Using the same framework consistently allows you to repeat the exercise every one to two years to see progress, the impact of turnover in your team, and ensure you are maintaining and building the team you need to grow the brand and business.

It will also allow you to deploy individuals in the team against their key strengths, to be deliberate in developing them, understand gaps you may need to fill with external hires, and to direct learning resources towards the areas which will most benefit your team and the work required on your brands.

Though the marketing team leader will want to take ownership of the strategic dimensions of this exercise – shaping the team for the future and defining a learning curriculum with support from HR, it's important each member of your team owns their own development.

Table 4.4 gives an example of what this might look like for the 'Where to Win' capabilities, but could be applied to all three sections.

TABLE 4.4 Measuring capability

Where to win					
Understanding the external environment					
	Baseline	Experienced	Mastery	Evidence	Action
Analysing and understanding the changing external environment					
Understanding the drivers of consumer choice					
Understanding future trends shaping consumers' attitudes and behaviours					

(continued)

TABLE 4.4 (Continued)

Brand and category understanding					
	Baseline	Experienced	Mastery	Evidence	Action
Identifying and quantifying attractive and accessible motivation-based segments					
Deciding which brands can best compete and meet consumer motivations in priority consumer segments					
Articulating a three- to five-year brand ambition					
Setting long-term category and brand objectives					
Defining opportunities for growth					
	Baseline	Experienced	Mastery	Evidence	Action
Identifying, quantifying, and selecting growth opportunities					
Determining strategic brand actions to address growth opportunities					
Identifying growth opportunities beyond the core, and developing an innovation pipeline					
Consumer insights					
	Baseline	Experienced	Mastery	Evidence	Action
Being curious and constantly learning about culture, consumer attitudes, and behaviours					
Having deep understanding of consumers and their changing motivations and behaviours					
Creating powerful insights into consumers which can be applied to opportunities for growth and inspire breakthrough ideas and actions					

Reflections

Are you clear on the capabilities you need in your organization to build brands?

What are the strengths of your team?

What are the priority capabilities you need to develop in your team?

How will you go about developing those priority capabilities?

What leadership behaviours foster effective brand building?

It seems important to conclude this chapter with some discussion on leadership. In my conversations with CMOs across industries there were two common ways of framing this:

- marketing leadership behaviours which support core marketing tasks;
- more nuanced views on what great leadership is depending on the type of business, industry, and local cultural norms.

The former is easier to define as the 'how' of effective brand building, whereas the second is a combination of situational criteria and emergent beliefs around leadership for which there are many academic studies and theories. Below are some of the common elements people reported.

What are some of the leadership behaviours which support effective brand building?

- Be a business leader first and foremost – as committed to delivering the overall business vision and objectives as anyone.
- Champion the consumer and customer, and bring the outside world into the organization.
- Be curious – about the consumer and the market, and about what's going on in the organization.
- Create a shared vision of success, keep people focused on stepping towards it every day.
- Set direction – be clear on what that vision means for your priorities and those of your team.

- Understand broad internal audiences and inspire the business with story-telling.
- Collaborate effectively by building powerful cross-functional internal and external agency and supplier partnerships with common focus and ambition.
- Develop brand marketing capabilities, building confidence in the effect of every dollar, rupee, or pound spent on building the brand and business with consumers.
- Have a learning mindset – ask what's working, strive to make things better.

Everyone I spoke to was passionate about leadership qualities. I was struck at how much emphasis leaders placed on doing work on themselves – making the connection between more effective leadership and more effective brand building. There was a real awareness that personal growth had come from understanding internal and external barriers to their own growth as well as that of their brands.

Based on my conversations, an effective marketing leader is aware of their motivations, their values, what they want, and where they want to be. These leaders were clear on what they were like to work with – understanding their own strengths and limitations, and the positive and negative impact their working style and preferences might have on others.

Finally, I heard things which speak to a more emergent style of leadership – a desire to shift from a more authoritarian, tell-do leadership to one more characterized by spending time with and listening to different people, to being comfortable with ambiguity, building cultural intelligence, and being more vulnerable and being prepared to learn, unlearn, and relearn.

There was also a big theme around humility – being prepared to own your development, your mistakes, being curious about yourself, and striving to be better.

I was struck by these themes – there was no less drive to win, but it was tempered by the recognition that effective brand building, characterized as it is by transforming deep consumer insight into work which wins with consumers, was more about deep empathy than the rigour of measurement which perhaps gains more of our attention when we think about effectiveness.

Reflections

What kind of leader are you?

What are your motivations, values, and what are you like to be around?

What kind of leadership is valued in your organization?

How might you have to challenge your own leadership and self-insight to become a more effective brand builder?

Reference

Ritson, M (2023) Effectiveness ignorance has left American marketing lagging behind the rest of the world, *Marketing Week*, 13 November, www.marketingweek.com/effectiveness-ignorance-american-marketing/ (archived at https://perma.cc/6J4P-ANDH)

5

What are the characteristics of effective brands?

- What are the characteristics of effective brands? p. 46
- Why does understanding brand and category stage of development matter? p. 53

What are the characteristics of effective brands?

Great brands live in the minds of consumers – people who may never have bought your brand before, who have bought it in the past, and who may buy it again in the future. We know from Chapter 2 that consumers are busy people, acting on autopilot, and our job as marketers is to stack the cards in our favour so that it's our retail brand that gets visited, or our brand that gets clicked into the basket.

However, so often in our busy working lives we get bogged down in execution – the creation and implementation of what the consumer sees, without being as conscious as we might be about what we are trying to achieve. It helps to devote time to strategy, insights, and measurement so the bulk of our effort on execution is more deliberate.

As a practitioner it can also help to look at other brands, not to copy or emulate them, but to envisage the kind of brand you want to nurture. This section covers some of the characteristics of effective brands, distilled from my own observations and talking to people from different industries and markets. Many of these characteristics are not visible to consumers, but they contribute in significant ways to what the consumer sees and experiences.

What are effective brands made of?

Effective brands:

1 know what they are about – have a clear mission;
2 know who they are for – focus on a credible market;
3 are relevant – leverage strong consumer insight;
4 have a remarkable product or service;
5 stand for something remarkable in the mind of consumers;
6 stand out from the crowd;
7 are creatively interesting – in how they behave and where they show up;
8 are present;
9 innovate imaginatively to grow the core and beyond;
10 display sound judgement – rigour, instinct, creativity.

Not all brands have all these qualities, but effective brands will over-index on most or many.

EFFECTIVE BRANDS:
KNOW WHAT THEY ARE ABOUT – HAVE A CLEAR MISSION
Effective brands know what they are about and where they are going. This might build on the positive role they want to play in the world like the much-lauded Patagonia, and Tony Chocolonely's aim to make all chocolate *100% slave free*. A vision or mission might not be so high-minded, for example Red Bull's mission to 'give wiiings to people and ideas', but like this example it should reflect the core human motivation the brand seeks to satisfy and be grounded in the product or service.

The industry debate on 'brand purpose' is worth mentioning here. I am not sure it is as polarizing as it is presented – for some brands, environmental or societal impact might be inherent in their mission, intrinsic to their product or service and the human motivation they seek to satisfy. For many brands it might not be, and their mission, or why they exist, might be just as valuable to their consumers without purporting to do something noble. Oreo's purpose is about playful connection – isn't that valuable to people and grounded in its product?

Nike's often quoted mission exemplifies this as it aims 'to bring inspiration and innovation to every athlete in the world', noting that if you have a body, you are an athlete. At the core of its business is the human motivation to be the best you can be in sport or physical activity, regardless of level, and therefore reap the benefits of that in your life. Nike's role is to facilitate that in everything it does. This drives all aspects of its products and services – committing it to serving the best athletes in the world and everyday people.

The fact that many of these missions are familiar demonstrates how effective they are when congruent with our needs and experiences – like Google's mission to organize the world's information and make it universally accessible and useful, or Airbnb enabling guests to connect with communities in a more authentic way.

The British handmade cosmetics company Lush is a lovely example of how a clear mission has directed the business for over 25 years. This is 'We Believe' and it's worth quoting it here as it is a more comprehensive manifesto:

Lush: We believe

We believe in making effective products from fresh, organic* fruit and vegetables, the finest essential oils, and safe synthetics.

We invent our own products and fragrances. We make them fresh by hand using little or no preservative or packaging, using only vegetarian ingredients, and tell you when they were made.

We believe in buying ingredients only from companies that do not commission tests on animals and in testing our products on humans.

We believe in happy people making happy soap, putting our faces on our products and making our mums proud.

We believe in long candlelit baths, sharing showers, massage, filling the world with perfume and in the right to make mistakes, lose everything and start again.

We believe that all people should enjoy freedom of movement across the world.

We believe our products are good value, that we should make a profit, and that the customer is always right.

* We also believe words like fresh and organic have honest meaning beyond marketing.

A mission should be more than a bland strapline on a corporate website – the best ones will materially shape what a brand or business will or will not do, how it will achieve its financial aims as well as the contribution it may make to consumers or culture. The worst are vague or bland – more intended to sound good on a corporate website than to drive action.

KNOW WHO THEY ARE FOR – FOCUS ON A CREDIBLE MARKET

We'll cover this in more detail in Chapter 6, but effective brands are crystal clear on what they do and for whom. This means they have a relentless focus on the most attractive segments they serve and what the drivers of demand are in their category – be they consumer motivation or needs, occasions, or something else.

We often hear the mistaken conclusion that marketing segmentation is no longer relevant to marketers as our job is to drive penetration amongst all category users. First you need to understand meaningfully what category or segment you are playing in or trying to disrupt. This drives targeting and messaging amongst other strategic decisions. Secondly, if you are a practitioner with finite resources, segmentation will be critical for allocating marketing spend. Most brands simply can't afford to talk to everyone, and it's critical to work out how to find balance.

The same is true regarding who your target audience is. We may be trying to attract these seemingly amorphous 'light buyers' but it is valuable to understand them so we know what drives them and what we may need to overcome to recruit them. Deep consumer understanding matters even more to win over the disengaged.

Think Under Armour, Glossier, Headspace, Hello Fresh.

ARE RELEVANT – LEVERAGE STRONG CONSUMER INSIGHT

It's that feeling in your gut when you've cracked something powerful about your consumers that you can use to unlock a barrier to growing brand penetration. Consumer insight fuels brands challenging the status quo, enables established brands to remain relevant sometimes over centuries, can reframe tired ones or entire categories. It inspires communications, innovation, shopper activity, and all aspects of your brand mix in a way which will resonate more with your audience.

Insight is magic dust though the term has been much overused and become interchangeable with information and data. It's so important that Chapter 7 is devoted to it.

Think McDonald's, Aldi, Tesco, Cadbury.

HAVE A REMARKABLE PRODUCT OR SERVICE

Being remarkable matters and it is a characteristic of the next few elements in this list – from what the brand offers, to what it stands for, and how those things show up in the world to consumers.

I am deliberate in using the word 'remarkable' here. In *Purple Cow* (Godin, 2003), Seth Godin tells us you can either stand out or be invisible. For me the word 'remarkable' captures a key characteristic of effective brands – remarkable in a holistic sense, and relative to other available choices.

'Remarkable' also helps us avoid the debate about differentiation versus distinctiveness. Though in academic literature they mean different things, many often use them interchangeably, and we no longer believe having a differentiated functional benefit or USP (unique selling point) is the be all and end all of successful marketing.

Historically, many brands identified the most differentiated feature of their brand and anchored their marketing communications around it. If you reflect on what we know about consumer behaviour today this may or may not be useful, and certainly the Ehrenberg Bass Institute have evidence to dismiss it (Sharp, 2010, pp 112–33). The point is that if most decisions come from the gut, and that consumers are buying from a repertoire of brands at a similar price point which meet their needs, then focus on a perceived difference, and typically a perceived functional difference, is unlikely to be effective, especially if your brand's difference isn't a leading motivator in the category.

It doesn't mean, however, you should not strive for your brand to deliver a superior or distinctive product or service. Being clear on the brand and product attributes you want your consumer to perceive and remember is likely to play a role in your marketing – in alcohol marketing, for example, where all alcohol products deliver the same functional effect, albeit at different strengths and with different taste and sensory experiences, this is often called 'the bar defence' – a couple of reassuring facts a bar tender might give to recommend a brand. Over time, however, competitors catch up and new entrants can change what consumers value. Ultimately, once all the diaper brands available are effective in keeping your baby dry, and you have enough razor blades to shave without irritation, you're not going to get far demonstrating your brand does it better.

A differentiated product or experience might be one way to stand out, but it it's not the only way – you can do it through packaging – structure, substrate, and semiotics, by having a distinctive style of advertising, colours, logos, endlines, celebrity endorsements, cultural relevance etc. Ideally, you want a combination of these things.

There is compelling evidence which links being remarkable to superior brand performance which is something we will consider later.

Think WeChat, Sephora, Airbnb, Little Moons, Oreo, Nespresso.

STAND FOR SOMETHING REMARKABLE IN THE MIND OF CONSUMERS

Closely linked to having a remarkable product or service is standing for something remarkable in the minds of your consumers. Though I believe this should be grounded in what you do for them, finding something relevant to consumers which is credible coming from your brand enables you to elevate your brand in the mind of existing and prospective consumers, build belief about your brand and confidence in its choice. Standing for something remarkable creates an emotional connection, cultural traction, and social currency. If your brand has something worth talking about this can create the ripples which may help it win, especially in mature categories in developed markets where shoppers have come to expect a baseline of quality and performance in most brands they could buy in the category.

The tool which helps us define this consistently is brand positioning. Positioning matters not only to drive relevance and consistency, but to inspire creative people.

Think Lifebuoy, Patagonia, Red Bull, Dove, Jack Daniels, Patek Philippe.

STAND OUT FROM THE CROWD

Just as great brands will stand for something remarkable, they will be visually remarkable. In a world where shoppers are on autopilot, this means your brand stands out, and the combination of colours, logos, fonts, and other elements you choose can be the signifier for the meaning you encode in your brand.

There are so many examples of brands instantly recognizable not from their wordmark, but from their logos through years and years of investment. For new brands or insurgent brands, a key element of how you design your pack and brand needs to consider this – how you reflect some category codes, but also have the courage to stand out and disrupt.

This means going beyond just a logo – a visual design system will inform your packaging, communications, and other elements of your mix.

Think Magnum, Google, Coke, Starbucks, Kit Kat, Disney, KFC, Apple, Guinness, Chanel, Louis Vuitton.

ARE CREATIVELY INTERESTING – IN HOW THEY BEHAVE AND WHERE THEY SHOW UP

Effective brands not only stand for something relevant and have remarkable products or services and are visually remarkable, but they understand the power of great creativity and media to cut through with their consumers with imagination in the moments they are most receptive to their message. In a world where we are bombarded with largely irrelevant communications, being able to connect is critical.

Think Nike, Guinness, Netflix, Snickers, McDonald's.

ARE PRESENT

This means being available where consumers want to buy them with the right format and pricing for the channel and occasion.

Think Apple, Coke, Budweiser, Louis Vuitton.

INNOVATE SELECTIVELY TO GROW THE CORE AND BEYOND

There is a real art in getting this balance right. Effective brands are constantly refining their core offering to keep ahead of or challenge the category – reflecting changing tastes and behaviours, technological advancements, and so forth. They understand the right amount of innovation to create excitement such as formats, fragrance, and flavours, and how selective innovation relevant to different channels, consumer types, or occasions can help recruit new buyers and increase profit margins.

Think Tiffany & Co, Amazon, Canva, Eventbright, Disney, Wagamama.

DISPLAY SOUND JUDGEMENT – RIGOUR, INSTINCT, CREATIVITY

Effective brands find the sweet spot of rigorous evidence-based understanding, instinct which is inspired by learning and observation, and creativity that enables novel approaches to the problems and opportunities brands identify to grow.

Think Cadbury, Walmart, Ulta Beauty, Johnnie Walker.

Reflections

Which of these criteria are the most and least important to your brand and
  category?

Which of these criteria does your brand excel at?

Which criteria are opportunities for improvement?

How do your closest competitors perform against these criteria?

Why does understanding brand and category stage of development matter?

The final foundational concept to introduce in this chapter is that of brand and category stage of development.

It is worth calling out as inevitably it is big established brands which get cited in books such as this and academic papers. This is for various reasons – simply to aid comprehension as it would be confusing for a reader only to have examples of single market brands which not everyone has heard of, but also because bigger brands tend to have the data and resources to make their cases or end up as case studies in academic papers.

There are three stages of brand development – we can call them seeding, scaling, and maturing. There's possibly a fourth one – declining.

Along with industry type, development stage is one of the biggest drivers of the kind of work you need to do as a marketing leader, the type of environment you are in, and the resources you may have available. If you refer back to Chapter 3, it is another lens to think about the kind of organization you may find yourself in – perhaps founder led if you are in seed or scale phase, and perhaps a multi-brand publicly listed multinational if you are a mature brand, or a brand in different stages of development in different markets.

What characterizes these stages?

SEEDING

Brands in the first stage of development focus on becoming available and establishing what makes them remarkable. Distribution focus may be in more niche or premium outlets, or direct to consumer to build premium perceptions or drive advocacy. Joanna Jensen who founded Childs Farm, the B Corp kids personal care brand, focussed on country shows and schools fayres where she knew prospective consumers with an affinity for her brand would be. Seedlip, the 'world's first distilled non-alcoholic spirit', founded by Ben Branson, focussed on being available in Michelin-starred restaurants, and Little Moons was also available in high-end restaurants signalling the product quality – if it was good enough to be available there, it would speak volumes later to retailers. Though clearly in this phase driving consumer engagement and excitement is important, this is about building a narrative to gain broader distribution later – to demonstrate how other retailers may be missing out on the opportunity.

Whilst marketing budgets in this phase are typically small, the speed with which portfolio brand businesses can seed is much faster given the customer relationships they already have. Paradoxically, they often lack the skills to create disruptive and authentic new to world brands – often buying in seeding brands from outside when they reach a point of scale.

As well as building distribution, new brands focus on succinctly telling prospective consumers what they offer and when or how to use the product, ideally in a way which gives a compelling reason to buy it over what they already buy and use.

It's difficult to put a time frame on this phase of development, but it often lasts a couple of years. Start-up brands in this phase do not typically have traditional data to understand how their penetration may be building, but those built on a tech platform will benefit from what they can learn from their first party data.

For those brands which do have an established route to the consumer already and are using innovation to build out their portfolio into other spaces, you might argue they quickly or automatically jump to the next phase because of their ability to quickly penetrate the market.

For the pure start-up brand, the shift into the next phase may simply be characterized by achieving that first main listing. Though it is hard to be definitive, brands in this stage will typically have about 0–20% penetration relative to the category leader.

SCALING

Scaling is characterized by building out distribution and it is in this phase that marketing budgets may scale in line with brand availability. With the brand still nascent, most will continue to focus on building the right experiences and associations for the brand, rather than achieving scale. Alongside the type of work described above, many brands seek fame in this phase – with limited budgets how can they create desire, drive advocacy, be interesting enough to earn media, and deploy user-generated content to get their message across?

Successful brands in this phase often grow ahead of their innate capability, though this is the phase in which marketers will seek to build a clear understanding of how to grow, start to get data on performance, and seek more input from consumers – in a founder-led business marketing often acts in a mediating role between the founder's intent for the brand and how it is received and consumed.

With tight resources, focus during this phase may be on more affordable media channels, especially social, PR, and experiences. It's difficult to put a time frame or key measures on this, but even the most successful brands may spend 5–10 years in scaling, be it in one market or in multiple ones simultaneously.

In this phase brands typically have reached 80% of the available distribution and need to focus on activities which ensure they are getting consumers to repurchase while recruiting new ones.

Brands in this stage may have 30–60% penetration relative to the category leader.

MATURING

The market for maturing brands is typically when scale distribution has been reached and further growth will come mainly from building rate of sale and increasing penetration, with innovation increasingly important. In this phase marketing matures too – understanding triggers and barriers to penetration informs growth strategies, data is abundant, and so are budgets. If the first stages focus on enabling prospective consumers to understand how the new brand might be relevant to their needs, and to be distinctive, this third phase focusses increasingly on salience – how easily your brand comes to mind.

For those fortunate – and determined – brands which do reach this stage, the biggest risk is that their salience in the marketplace starts to over-index against their relevance. We will see in Chapter 7 how McDonald's, a brand with exceptional awareness, effectively met some of those challenges.

Category stage of development   Category stage of development is another important lens to consider. In markets where a category is underdeveloped it is common that a single strong brand emerges, almost as an icon and signifier of that category. This is especially the case in emerging markets where there is often a formal and an informal category. An example of this might be in household hygiene where consumers will use simple soaps, as well as homemade or unbranded cleaning products as formal brand products may be aspirational but unaffordable. In an instance such as this the category will develop as more affordable brands launch and consumer wealth increases.

This phenomenon may be easily explained through developing market examples, but we also see it happen in developed markets especially in tech enabled categories – consider how quickly alternatives to Uber appeared on the market offering a similar service but at a more affordable price. In the food delivery market, Waiter may have been first, now trading as waiter.com, but now consumers can choose between Ubereats, JustEat, Deliveroo, Skip the dishes, Doordash, Grubhub, Wolt, and so on. The same is now true of subscription entertainment brands.

Brands such as McDonald's, Airbnb, Netflix, Uber, and Atom Bank are examples of those which created new categories, or regenerated mature ones. New brands entering developed categories must find distinctive ways to compete or disrupt.

In the UK, Magnum ice cream is over 30 years old – a mature brand in a mature category. Magnum's focus is on recruiting and re-recruiting people into core Magnum over time, continuously renovating and ensuring product delivery is ahead of the category, meeting consumer expectations. In essence, Magnum meets the need for pleasure but cuts through by acting more like a glitzy high-end fashion brand than it does an ice cream, as exemplified by its affiliation with Cannes Film Festival.

In many of Magnum's other markets, however, the brand is less well known, and the category underdeveloped. In China, for example, the brand is known and respected as an international or imported brand, and Magnum invests time in driving more local connection and relevance – some minimal product adaptation to cater to local tastes, and more culturally relevant communications.

In the US, in contrast, it tackles a competitive issue. There the brand shares its name with a leading condom brand. One could argue they both play in a similar consumer territory of pleasure, and flirt with language around size, but there is a big task to do to ensure Unilever's Magnum brand comes to mind with US consumers with the right associations.

The point of this is that a single brand which operates in multiple markets might be at different stages of development in different markets and the category may be nascent or developed. Such a brand needs to develop a model which balances the efficiency which comes from consistency with recognizing that brand will have different tasks to accomplish and need different types of work in different markets to succeed. It must protect against proliferating local work when brand campaigns can be reapplied. It must understand what is similar and different in how local consumers meet the core need it offers and the context around that – be it the consumption moments, brand and category perceptions, or the competitive context.

> **Reflections**
>
> What is the stage of development of your brand?
>
> What is the stage of development of your category?
>
> What does this mean for the organizational context in which you operate?
>
> What are the most important drivers for growth at the different stages, and where does marketing or brand building fit into this?

References

BBC Radio Four (2022) You and yours, Gapfinders: Joanna Jensen, founder of Childs Farm, 1 December, www.bbc.co.uk/sounds/play/m001fmr6 (archived at https://perma.cc/FJ4G-298M)

Godin, S (2003) *Purple Cow, Transform Your Business by Being Remarkable*, Portfolio, New York

Google: www.google.com/intl/en_uk/search/howsearchworks/our-approach/ (archived at https://perma.cc/7X2Q-W2TV)

Lush: weare.lush.com/lush-life/our-company/what-we-believe/ (archived at https://perma.cc/KRT3-RGRM)

Nike: www.nike.com/help/a/nikeinc-mission (archived at https://perma.cc/EW6B-7SH7)

Redbull: www.redbull.com/gb-en/energydrink/company-profile (archived at https://perma.cc/65G4-RHT6)

Sharp, B (2010) *How Brands Grow*, Oxford University Press, South Melbourne

Tony's Chocolonely: tonyschocolonely.com/uk/en/our-mission (archived at https://perma.cc/MR94-YU62)

6

How can understanding brand strength and the drivers of consumer demand help effective brand building?

- What can brand strength tell me about how brands create value? p. 58
- How do effective brands use understanding of consumer demand? p. 65

What can brand strength tell me about how brands create value?

The double-edged sword of data

One of the major shifts in the last decade has been marketers' ability to understand the drivers of growth using empirical data. Using data smartly is one of the characteristics that sets effective brands apart.

Data is, however, something of a double-edged sword. At the same time as data has helped us make sense of the drivers of brand growth, it is also being used aggressively with marketers to promote specific channels and platforms.

In the boardroom, the proliferation of data can mean everybody has a view on how effective the marketing is, but as we saw in the cautionary tale in Chapter 3, members of your leadership team may not always look at the data through a lens of understanding the critical levers of growth from consumption back to purchase, and sales out. This can be particularly true when considering some of the long-term aims of brand-building work.

With so much data at a micro level, so much bias, and capability levels lagging our ability to understand what's going on, using data effectively can be challenging for marketers. As brands scale up there is an initial buzz that comes from being able to afford data, but this can turn into paralysis, causing stake-holders to second guess, and introducing uncertainty where there was confidence.

There is hope, however, as organizations independent from those selling us their media or distribution are making exciting breakthroughs – pulling together datasets which go beyond what happens on the digital or physical shelf into understanding the interplay of motivations, attitudes towards brands, and behaviour. These datasets are compelling in their ability to make the link to sales and commercial outcomes and look beyond consumer-packaged goods into other categories including things such as entertainment streaming platforms.

For many marketers brand guidance systems, often called brand equity or brand strength measurement, have fallen out of fashion. These systems are lagging, slow-moving indicators in a world where fast-moving and seem-ingly more actionable datasets have grabbed our attention. This has led to the commoditization of brand equity measurement – marketers looking for the most cost-effective option rather than the system which will add most value to their decision-making. We have also seen a plethora of new entrants in brand measurement with affordable offerings based on technology and AI but often without the social science understanding to back them up.

Just as we see increasing evidence that correlates certain dimensions of creative pre-testing with market performance, we are in an era where marketers need to reconsider the role data and brand guidance can play in understanding the latent growth potential of their brand relative to their competition, and what they need to do to go after it.

An overarching brand guidance system can be useful as 'air traffic control' at the heart of a measurement system as it has the power to diagnose, drive action, and contextualize the micro-level data we have, especially from social media and retail platforms.

What can we learn about brands from brand guidance systems?

Kantar has unique access to datasets from different categories and industries which enable it to cross-pollinate how consumers think about brands, how they use them, how they shop and buy brands, and how those brands perform. Kantar's understanding of how these things connect has been developing in the last few years culminating in the publication of its study 'Blueprint for Brand Growth' (Kantar, 2024).

Kantar has discovered that brands which outperform the market have certain common characteristics, and that those which are 'meaningfully different' outperform the stock market by up to five times, are more resilient and recover more quickly from adverse conditions like a recession. 'Meaningful difference' also correlates strongly with pricing power, accounting for about 94% of it (Kantar, 2024) – pricing being a critical lever to develop margin and outperform competition in revenue terms. This data provides evidence that success goes beyond the product and service a brand offers, and that people's perceptions and attitudes to a brand affect not only how they think about it and buy it today but also affect and predict the brand's future performance as well.

Marketing thinking and action has been built on the notion that attitudes and behaviours are linked, but now data is showing us much more specifically how they are linked and the actions brands can take to leverage those links.

BEING MEANINGFULLY DIFFERENT TO MORE PEOPLE

Let's unpack what Kantar understands by these terms; meaningful, different, and salient. These are qualities brands must have, and to succeed they must be stronger relative to their competition.

Being 'meaningful' is about meeting consumers' needs or motivations – this comes down to both the functional needs a consumer has from a product or service, and their emotional needs – things such as how they want to feel, how they want to be perceived, or the experience they want to have.

There are simple and cost-effective ways you can measure these dimensions over time, asking consumers to rate your brand and those of your competitors on the efficacy and suitability of your brand for their needs. Having a meaningful brand – one that performs well against my expectations – is critical, and it gets you into a consumer's consideration set which means repurchasing is more likely.

Being 'different' is more complex. 'Different' is the language Kantar use, and as you know from Chapter 5, I prefer the term 'remarkable' as it avoids the false opposition we often see in debates in marketing where 'differentiation' is used to reference functional differences and 'distinctive' is used to refer more holistically to the attributes which will make a brand stand out, including things such as the values and beliefs a brand may share with prospective consumers. In this section I will stick to Kantar's terminology, but to be clear it is also talking holistically in the same sense as I mean remarkable. Being different is about relative difference, not about being unique.

Kantar can demonstrate that being different matters as the greater the relative difference to competition the less willing consumers will be to substitute a brand for another in that category. Again, this relative difference is easy to measure in a research context – it is about understanding within your competitive set which brands stand out and are seen to be leading the way.

The third element in this model is 'salience' – this is more than just whether people have heard of or are aware of your brand but how easily it comes to mind when a consumer encounters the category. As with the other dimensions, salience is simple to measure, and with mobile-enabled measurement is normally cost-effective, quick, and accurate.

The combination of these three factors – meaning, difference, and salience – is predictive of future penetration growth. Core brand equity measures are no longer rear-view mirror but reveal 'Future Power', as Kantar calls it, and therefore a vital diagnostic for understanding brand strengths and opportunities relative to your competitive set.

Kantar observes three growth accelerators depending on your brand's maturity, and its category.

PREDISPOSE MORE PEOPLE

Predisposition is about increasing consumers' sense that your brand is the right one to buy. The first growth accelerator is about loading the dice in your brand's favour and is just as important for frequently bought categories as it is for infrequently bought ones such as cars.

Successful brands predispose more people by investing in the right activities and experiences – high quality, relevant, and engaging messages delivered through advertising, media, influencers, brand- or user-generated content, events, usage, and so on. When these touchpoints build meaning and difference, they increase predisposition and up to nine times more volume share growth and improved margin.

Brands with strong predisposition tend to have better pricing power, up to twice that of other brands, and this increases the likelihood of driving value share by four times. Kantar's evidence shows benefits for brand penetration now and two years into the future.

This notion of 'predisposition' can be quantified through understanding the relative meaning and difference of your brand among other attitudinal and predictive measures.

The notion of 'predisposition' is similar, but not identical, to the idea of 'mental availability' or the propensity of a brand to come to mind in a buying situation which has been a common concept in marketing in the past decade.

BE MORE PRESENT

The second growth accelerator is 'Being More Present'. This is about being present along the consumer's path to purchase and includes media connections, range, distribution, pricing, promotion, and any activity which converts predisposition into purchase. Being in the right places matters and explains why digitally born brands such as Harry's and Glossier sought to shift into physical retail, ensuring they were more available to more people.

Robert Woodruff, President of Coca-Cola, stated Coke's aim to be 'within arm's reach of desire' – a paradigm of being present everywhere people are. Coca-Cola today boasts the world's second highest household penetration of any brand at 49% (Kantar, 2024).

Occasionally mainstream brands talk passionately about the importance they place on selective distribution as though this somehow makes them more precious. In truth, they are typically missing out on sales or may not have as strong a brand and proposition as they believe. Brands that are present on all relevant buying occasions attract seven times more buyers than those present on one half of buying occasions – deliberately limiting distribution is not a growth strategy other than for the strongest luxury brands.

Even luxury brands understand the importance of being present and they ensure the shopping experience in different locations is appropriate for their brands – think about beauty brands, Apple's bold decision to invest in its own network of stores, and the private sales of watch and whisky brands.

The rise of retail media is enabling brands to focus on targeting people at the moment of choice with the right trigger, advancing the precision with which effective brands convert sales amongst predisposed consumers.

This notion of 'being present' is similar, but not identical, to the idea of 'physical availability' – being available and easy to shop in a buying situation, as Kantar stresses the importance of the quality of a brand's presence, as well as the scale.

FIND NEW SPACE

The third growth accelerator Kantar observes is about how brands sustain growth into the future. The strategies will differ depending on brand size, lifestage, and category. This is about finding new space in which a brand can credibly and incrementally grow – be they motivations, occasions, categories or services. An example of this is Heinz's co-branded entry into pasta sauces with Absolut Vodka – combining the 'meaning' or relevance for that category which comes from how consumers perceive Heinz with the difference 'Absolut' can bring from the spirits category. As such this makes the proposition more than just another jarred sauce.

Finding new uses for your brand doubles your chances for growth. For example, Kantar found increasing use cases for a brand by 10% results in growth of 17% (Kantar, 2024). This means that beyond ensuring prospective buyers understand what you are about as a brand at scale, and being present, you should focus on how to credibly expand that offering into new, relevant spaces in their lives.

DIAGNOSING ACTION

This framework enables brands to audit where they are, using data for their brand and category, and define critical actions.

Many brands may be 'meaningful' – meeting the requirements of their audience, but unremarkable. Insurgent brands may be distinctive in spades but not actually as good at delivering their product and service as established brands, and of course are less likely to be known by as many prospective buyers. In contrast, some of the world's best-known brands run the risk of lagging on meaning, as high-growth brands create new expectations for what a great product or service experience might be.

A brand lacking in difference may investigate what its innately differentiating features are and double down on these in communications, packing, presentation etc. Or it may seek through innovation to make its offering less substitutable. Being more predictive of future outcomes means brand guidance systems powered by core research data, AI, and predictive models are coming back into their own for a new generation of marketing leaders.

THREE BRAND BEHAVIOURS

From this work Kantar have observed three behaviours successful brands display.

Being consistent – instead of burning calories always doing something different, deliver consistency in communications, channels, and other activities underpinned by an enduring view of what your brand wants to stand for in the consumer's mind.

Being connected – leverage distinctive assets, tonality, language, and other devices across the different channels and activities you use to ensure your consumer experiences your brand in a connected manner in all touchpoints.

Being optimized – adopt a culture of curiosity, testing, and learning. Experimentation creates new data which can test hypotheses and embolden action.

An example of this model in practice would be in the US streaming market. Analysis combining data into consumer attitudes to different streaming brands with behavioural data was able to explain why Amazon Prime had much higher churn rates than Netflix. Though both brands are well known, Netflix is seen as offering better content. As such Amazon was reliant on promotions including free trials and other discounts to drive subscription numbers, but those new users fell away at a higher rate. The implication for Amazon is to improve its content offering versus Netflix.

HOW IS THIS DIFFERENT?

This work builds on the work of the Ehrenberg Bass Institute as it is based on analysis of ten years of data. It provides evidence about a brand's potential future performance, related more holistically to the broader drivers of consumer behaviour, and its relative strength to competitors.

Brands are substitutable, and there is a basic threshold of utility every product and service must meet if people are going to purchase or repurchase it. There is, however, a broad range of tactics which can be deployed to increase brand value, from developing product and service intrinsics, to activity and media channel selection, and beyond.

It provokes us to think about how brands are increasingly presented to us – served up by algorithms on TikTok or through content generated by an influencer rather than through a media schedule brought by a marketer against an audience and time of day.

The ever-changing nature of these algorithms is a challenge to marketers who are used to the control which comes from developing and signing off professionally made, well-branded content for use in channels where you can be more certain of reaching the audience you have paid for with an appropriate number of impressions.

These worlds co-exist, despite what we might hear, as consumers still seek communal experiences around live TV broadcasts, go to the movies, sit on public transport being exposed to so-called 'traditional' media as well as or even at the same time as scrolling through reels. Separating these worlds in how we operate as marketers is artificial – it only happens because we might buy exposure on Youtube.com direct from Google, and not as part of an integrated media buy from an agency.

Rather than becoming engulfed in tactics, a framework such as this challenges us to step back to see the bigger picture of what we are trying to achieve.

Data organized against a growth framework is a massive advantage, increasingly enabled with predictive models. Especially in a world where technology will continue to evolve how consumers discover and interact with brands, and volatility and uncertainty are norms, it helps to understand how data intersects with human emotion, and the seeming irrationality of behaviour.

This surely must help marketers in a boardroom setting where numbers drive decisions and people still struggle to draw the line connecting emotions and growth.

Reflections

Do you have an established approach to understanding the strength of your brand versus the competition?

What are the criteria which mostly strongly correlate with growth?

How strong is your brand versus its closest competitor?

What are the areas which you should address to ensure your brand is fit for future growth?

How do your brand strategy and your consumer experience support strengthening your brand?

How do effective brands use understanding of consumer demand?

What are the drivers of choice? How do you break down consumer behaviour into something you can influence and be able to fund? How do you define your category?

You will hear that you should simply reach everyone in your category, but in truth no one can afford to do that! And what exactly is your category? What if you have a portfolio of brands?

Being consumer-centric means stepping back from a trade view of the category

There is a lot of rhetoric from brands and businesses about being consumer-centric, human-centred, or people-focussed. It's true we should strive for that because ultimately it is those people who are good enough to part with their time, cash, or attention that make our brands thrive.

However, an awful lot of businesses are intermediated by trade or retail partners. As a result, the lingua franca of businesses is often more about how we talk to the trade than it is about how we think about consumers. We are concerned with how we describe our category and how we describe the competitive set to trade, or sometimes even more internally focussed about how or where our products are manufactured.

Effective brands hold this obsession with the trade and a simultaneous obsession with consumers. If people don't buy your product or service, it won't continue to be available in shops, online or the high street. Obviously if it's not in the shops, people won't buy it. Both trade and consumer demand are essential and need to be in balance, but we do need to recognize most businesses venerate the trade slightly more than they venerate the people who buy their brand. Effective brand builders get this balance right, and in doing so, are better at shaping their own future and the success of the category than those that think mainly in terms of the retail category status quo.

We've mentioned a couple of times the issues with the word consumer – it is a symptom of neglecting the end buyer, as for many businesses it does not go further than thinking that the person's role in life is to buy my soup, t-shirt, or soap. They might need these things over the course of a typical day, but they are incidental. People are more focussed on being as happy as they can be, looking after their families, spending time with their friends, pursuing work and their passions. Along the way they might need soup or deodorant or on demand streaming video services.

This means that it is fulfilling a need that gets a brand purchased or repurchased. The better you are at fulfilling people's needs, the more likely it is that you will be a successful brand. Thinking about what we learned about the drivers of strong brands, fulfilling that need or being useful is a minimum threshold.

You need to go beyond understanding motivations or needs

When businesses think about motivations they often do so in a myopic way. They may say the need is hunger, feeding my family, impressing my friends, and only consider how to do this in a cheaper, more convenient, healthier, or more culturally relevant way. However, the danger here is assuming people fulfil all their needs through buying things. We get lulled into the false belief that motivations are adequately fulfilled in a given category, but something newer eventually will come along and change the category rules.

Evidence shows that motivations are universal – they cross geographic boundaries, age cohorts, and so forth. They may be disrupted by life stage changes, but thirst, the need for emotional fulfilment, to belong, to stand out, evolve at best at a glacial pace. People don't suddenly need to drink more, so growth through increasing the amount of volume bought, rather than through penetration, has always been a bit of a myth. How many cars, mobile phones, or TV subscription services do people need? How much time do we have to go on extra holidays, go out to eat more, or go to the movies?

So, if needs are largely stable, then how come behaviours and categories change so much over time? The answer is that culture is unstable. Marketing has often been defined as primarily concerned with needs, but I want you to pay more attention to the interplay of needs with culture. The context around consumer motivations is where the focus should be – effective brands focus on consumption moments as these are where motivations and needs manifest in our target audience's lives. Sometimes these are called category entry points, but that terminology seems dehumanizing.

Let's take status as an example. It's an enduring human need, and prevalent in so many categories. In cars, BMW did an amazing job at fulfilling this need for decades. In the UK, Audi took a share of this market through its 'Vorsprung durch Technik' positioning. Arguably the cars are comparable in terms of performance and range, and one did not evolve to outperform the other. If the cars did not change, then culture and notions of taste must have. Though in sales terms BMW may still be the world's no. 1 luxury car brand, Audi has been able to develop its brand and sales over the long term impressively.

Needs endure but how they are expressed in culture evolves

This happens as culture evolves, or when someone does something new in the category. Often it is a combination of the two, as the new thing which catches people's attention is likely to be more on the front foot of culture than the dominant brands. When this happens, it challenges and changes the norms. Take banking, for example; arguably our basic need to manage our money day to day has not changed, but how we fulfil it has. Innovation has taken us from branches and cheque books to telephone banking, and now to online and mobile banking. In brand terms, this means traditional UK banks like Lloyds and Barclays have gradually become displaced initially by First Direct in the 1990s, and ultimately Starling and Monzo, albeit over a 30–40 year period.

All these banks meet core needs – to have control over my finances, to manage my spending, to be trustworthy – but each does it with a different set of norms. Change is not overnight – there is still vocal backlash from many consumer segments about the closure of branches, or when physical bank account books are discontinued, but equally many consumers have never been into a bank branch in their lives.

If you simply assume consumers have a repertoire and all brands are interchangeable you are missing the point that the make-up of those repertoires and how consumers fulfil their needs are constantly evolving. It looks static when you look at the data because you are looking at a point in time, and the change is obvious when you look backwards, but it is happening right now in your category and with your brand.

If you think of a brand as a product wrapped up in a myth, a marketer's job is to ensure that myth remains true to the brand's core while keeping it fresh as taste, ideas, science, tech, and other things shape culture around it.

At a product or service level, it's easy to think that brands are interchangeable when in fact they are doing something quite different. Think of Tony's Chocolonely, Candy Kittens, or BrewDog. BrewDog beers challenged the dominant idea that beer had to have provenance. Over a period of half a century beer went from being hyper local, to regional, national, and then international with a plethora of exported brands playing on the imagery associated with their provenance. In fact, consumers and BrewDog realized that big beer companies were no longer always brewing these brands where they had originally come from, and there was therefore inauthenticity. BrewDog challenged this not with a different take on provenance but with a punk ideology which challenged the rules major manufacturers used to present their brands. It changed the rules – especially around naming. At the same time, there was little real innovation on the beer – perhaps the biggest change was the shift from either being cold with not much taste or having a more characterful taste but not served chilled. Now you could have chilled, flavourful beer with anti-corporate attitude.

In the ice cream category Little Moons has done something similar. For decades the dominant formats of ice cream have been tubs and handheld. These are great and will continue to be sold and meet the needs of most consumers. If you take tubs, however, there are some issues with the format. Thirty years ago, we were used to seeing them presented in popular culture, especially in American TV shows, with people eating straight from the tub on fun nights in sharing with friends or alone. As attitudes to health and well-being have changed so have some consumers' attitudes to this format – they are concerned with the risk of overeating, and the imagery around this format we see in culture has shifted from one associated with release and decadence to gluttony and loneliness. In contrast, Little Moons – bitesize balls of Italian gelato surrounded with mochi dough – offers the consumer indulgence with portion control in that dessert or snacking occasion, wrapped in a different set of myths and cultural associations than the Americanized category norms for ice cream tubs. Little Moons is exotic – 'ice cream from another world'. The brand has expertly understood the overall consumer need for pleasure, and that we still want that sweet sign off to a meal, but that it can be fulfilled in a different and surprising way from what we are used to. In so doing, it recruited consumers from the core ice cream category and engaged consumers who may have rejected the category.

This all seems simple with hindsight, but it does not happen by accident. Effective brands go beyond needs and have a relentless focus on the context around those needs. This is not just the cultural context, it's about understanding where to find them – what occasions do they show up in, with what type of person?

Needs alone do not drive choice

Consumers will use your product however they want – they may eat potato chips for breakfast or breakfast cereal as a quick snack while binge watching something on Netflix. They don't always have agency over their choices, either – the context can dictate to them how to behave. For example, I may have an incredibly wide range of alcoholic drinks or brands in my repertoire, but the moment I walk into a pub on a Friday night with a couple of close friends, my choice narrows right down to the same shared choice of beer, and nothing but beer. I may prefer the taste of a gin and tonic, but my choice has been dictated to me by the need to connect, being in a group of close friends, and in a pub, reflected in the ritual of shared choice.

People's needs show up in different ways at different times of day, in different places with different social groups. As much as our needs fluctuate throughout the day, the week, the year, maybe even a lifetime, there are predictable patterns to those fluctuations of needs. It is nuanced, but essential to understand the forces at play around your brand, competitors, and the other things people may do to satisfy that motivation which do not involve buying a product or service at all. You need to aggregate and map these drivers to really understand your market and where your brand plays.

Effective brands recognize the value in being able to understand motivations and the contextual drivers of how those needs are met in a way that makes them locatable for developing your core proposition, identifying opportunities for innovation, marketing, and communications. How the need is satisfied is largely driven by those contextual factors – beyond the specific alcohol example above, it is the case that choice in that category will be dictated by whether the occasion is in or out of the home, whether food is present or not, and whether it is an intimate or larger group occasion. What does this look like in your category? In leisure travel it might be whether it's a day trip, weekend break, or main holiday. Domestic or foreign? Am I going with my family, a partner, or friends?

With different means, different people will have the ability to spend at different levels and this tends to create price tiers within each of these occasions or 'demand spaces' as they are often called: family holiday, couples city break, perhaps with value, mainstream, and premium or luxury offerings for each type of excursion.

Think about the drivers as who, what, when, where, and why. All of these 'w's are involved in choice, but depending on the category some are more important than others. In the alcohol example it's a combination of why + occasion (where, when, and who), whereas in personal care it might start with 'what': 'I want a shampoo' and then 'who' and 'why'. In snacks and beverages 'who' plays a big role, for example, with potato chips or snacks for kids which will also differ from a sensory standpoint from crisps for adults – often crunchier with more sophisticated gourmet flavour descriptors. 'Who' is also important in high-cost, low-frequency categories like cars and holidays, and in sports where following your team can be an important marker of your identity.

How to balance trade and consumer language

Let's come back to the point around the difference between language for trade, and language for understanding people. To go to the trade, you must talk about your competitive set as the things that are on the shelves or on the web page beside you – so that it's easy for people to find you when they go searching for painkillers or shampoo on Walmart.com. In real life, what people use to fulfil their needs is broader – and may not be a product or service at all. If you take a category like analgesia, for example, we know that there's any number of other things that people do, from simply resting, to having a massage, using heat treatment, perhaps a tens machine, and therefore an oral analgesic brand alone only has access to a small proportion of the total market. If you think purely through a manufacturing and category lens, you risk missing opportunities. What is my role as a brand – to meet people's needs in the moment, or to sell them the product or service I manufacture?

A great example of an insurgent brand that really gets this is Vivobarefoot. Yes, it is a barefoot shoe company, but it understands its target market wants to reconnect more deeply to the earth. This means not only does it offer a range of shoes for different activities, but also online courses, recycling, and upcycling of products. It is more than just a minimal shoe designed as an alternative to the overblown norms of the sneaker industry. In the same industry Veja, who offer more fashion-conscious sneakers, has opened stores dedicated to recycling, not selling shoes – it understands its consumers' need to feel more responsible while being able to enjoy the fashion side of modern footwear. It is trying to enable its consumer more holistically which would be missed if we looked purely at a trade segmentation.

Similarly, North Face and Patagonia might have products on the same racks in a shop, but as consumers we are presented with different mythologies wrapped around the products. One appeals to our need for exploration or to see ourselves as adventurous, while the other appeals to our desire to enjoy the outdoors without doing harm.

Volvic and Evian are two bottled water brands sold by the same business. Evian is about innocence – water as pure as melted snow, whereas you had better believe Volvic surges from the earth itself. Yes, these things are interchangeable on one level, but effective brands invite us to participate in something deeper which can be about who we are, or how we want to live our lives. All things being equal, when I choose Volvic over Evian it is because there is something deeper at play, not entirely rational. And it is something which consumers would add more value to over say Dasani which is in effect bottled tap water – but just as clean and effective in meeting the basic need for hydration.

All of this is going on subconsciously. There's more to this than being a big brand with a distinctive logo, with unavoidable visibility in a buying situation. Fans don't just swap their Manchester United season ticket to another top tier English Premiership club at the end of the season because it's more visible and front of mind. To drive effective growth, you will need to deeply understand your consumer's motivation, the contextual factors which enable you to influence choice, and how to wrap your product or service in a relevant mythology which will appeal to these consumers living their lives and acting on autopilot.

What do you do about this?

Focus holistically on your consumers – this is about seeing your brand in the full context of everything else going on in their lives and how changing culture is invisibly influencing them. When you identify the moments in which they use your brand, put them under a microscope. You need to figure out what's going on – what are the characteristics of those moments and how does your brand stack up against them.

Ask yourself what value your brand is bringing to their lives. This is the heart of the matter and helps to make effective brands remarkable. Look at what your brand competes with, by which I mean including the other things consumers may choose to do beyond buying a close alternative to the product or service your brand offers. Look at these other things that deliver not dissimilar value to their lives, whether they pay for them or not, whether they're packaged or not. This is your real competitive set. Your mission is not only to understand what's going on but how you could add even more value.

That's something you can do in a relatively qualitative way at quite a small scale with a little bit of intelligence and intuition. Or you can do it at a very big national or international scale using quantitative techniques. The degree to which you want to bring sophistication to your understanding of it depends on the size and type of business that you are. Have you got one brand? Have you got many brands? If you've got one brand, your chance of competing with yourself is zero, so you don't need a massive quant study, which is appropriate for multi-brand businesses covering multiple motivations and wanting to ensure they do not inadvertently compete with themselves.

In this instance, you are playing in a repertoire category where people want to be able to make a choice between different variants or products. In these types of categories, like cereal or cookies that will just get eaten once they are in the home, your job really is to get them bought and into the home. Most of us eat a broad repertoire of products like this – we'll eat whatever cookies are in the jar. But if the driver of cookie consumption in the home is largely around distraction, then that might be the business you are in. What are the other ways people distract themselves in the home, seeking a pause in what they are doing, and can you learn about the characteristics of the other things which they find just as effective as dipping their hand in the cookie jar? What is the headroom for your existing business? How might you convert people from those other distractions into your core offering, or innovate to better satisfy how those motivations manifest in that distraction moment?

We've mentioned the kind of 'demand space' projects which multi-market branded businesses may use. A demand space is just a located bundle of needs. Those big businesses manage complex portfolios to try to ensure they have discrete pockets of growth. With scale they do need to understand their market and its drivers with this level of granularity. If you work in that type of business, the economics will probably allow you to conduct this work or have access to it. It will enable you to understand the landscape and competitive environment through that human lens. It will explain the different dimensions which deliver value to consumers and enable you to understand how effective your brand is at meeting them versus the real competitive set.

This kind of approach allows you to understand your presence in the space versus your fit – how effective you are at satisfying the key dimensions. For many big brands their presence is ahead of their fit and this leaves them vulnerable, especially to those insurgent brands which may not yet have the same presence or level of awareness, but which may be better suited to meet the different dimensions of consumer needs.

For smaller brands where growth is about share steal, not necessarily category growth, you can create an appropriate and cost-effective understanding of demand spaces using intelligence, intuition, and a little bit of qualitative research or even simple and affordable quantitative research. If you can work out how to outperform those strong brands, you can blindside them over time and take their business away from them. Small brands create meaningful new businesses often without the scale brands noticing that some of their business has been nibbled away.

A lot of this comes back to the impact of changing culture, harnessed by brands which challenge and disrupt. Those brands are either meeting these category triggers differently or better, or they're subtly changing the dimensions which drive satisfaction in the moment. The banking example is a good one. Our choice of bank might be based on which has the nearest and best branches. Now, having to go to a branch to do something might be seen as inconvenient, and you'd wonder which has got the most accessible and easy to use app and who gives the best interest rate on your savings.

Once we are crystal clear on these things it enables crisp measurement. You can measure your brand and competition over time in how each is performing against this mix of dimensions which are so important to consumer behaviour, and which for most consumers are automatic and even invisible to them.

If you are Starbucks, for example, you achieved scale by providing a better space in which to have coffee. But the music has changed over time. Now, many customers might not frequent Starbucks because the environment matters most to them, and they can find that better in Black Sheep or Blank Street. Starbucks are probably still front of mind to most consumers if asked to recall coffee brands, but there is more to effective brands than salience. McDonald's is another good example – a brand with mass awareness, but which, having learned the lesson, today has relentless focus on ensuring all aspects of its offering keep pace with changing consumer expectations, the competitive landscape, and culture.

Clothing retail is interesting as well. Though founded in 1975, it was in the early 2000s when Zara disrupted global fashion retail. Before Zara you could either have quality clothes sold in quality retail environments for high prices or cheaper, less style-conscious clothes, maybe even sold in a yard sale or thrift store. Zara thought about the drivers of choice like a graphic equalizer – it kept prices down, while creating a nice environment which felt more like an expensive boutique. It was able to give this value to consumers – the sense that the clothes had more value than they perhaps intrinsically did with a relentless focus on materials, labour, and manufacturing. It was staggeringly successful, hitting established clothing retailers with many other businesses emulating its fast fashion model such as Primark, Asos, and H&M, albeit at different price points and with different offerings. Now, of course, culture is changing again, and Zara will be thinking about how consumer attitudes to sustainability may challenge its 'fast fashion' model longer term.

All these businesses knew what they were doing – knowingly or intuitively. BrewDog, Zara, Monzo, Little Moons. None of them had accidental success – each understood how its brand could better or distinctively deliver against the moments in which people sought to satisfy their needs. If you think about those characteristics as elements of a value graphic equalizer, they changed the mix. Meanwhile, the competition continued to think about consumers and how the trade was organized, missing the opportunity to remain relevant. That orthodox view of the category you have when you talk to the trade has its place but limits your mindset in how you keep pace or exceed the value your consumers are seeking. You need both – and you also need to be able to translate what your brand does into language the trade will understand so they see the value to their business and get behind you.

Brands which innovate within the framework of how the trade see the category invariably add little value – new flavour or fragrance variants which provide some news but little incrementality or bigger plays which somehow miss the boat – Coke Life was a recent example in a long line of 'half sugar', 'half caffeine' type innovations. I would guess that it was not successful as although it offered a more natural sweetener, the absence of calories remained a critical characteristic for consumers on the target occasions, and for those who may have tolerated or ignored the calories, they would have continued to meet their needs from the plethora of other beverages inside and outside the carbonated soft drinks category – herbal teas, kombucha, water, etc.

Understanding the drivers of demand, your real competition, the characteristics of key consumption moments or category triggers, and how culture is shaping them is critical. Effective brands don't leave these things to the next people, and this is why some brands like Johnnie Walker can last for centuries, not years – surviving things as profound as the industrial revolution, world wars, major technological change wrought by electricity or telecommunications. Effective brands bake this understanding into their mission and values, and it becomes something the whole organization is passionate about. These things may seem conceptual or hidden away from the day to day of sales targets and KPIs but without them you become complacent, short term, and ultimately set up your brand and business for obsolescence.

Reflections

What is the core consumer motivation that your brand satisfies?

What other ways do people have of meeting that motivation?

What are the key moments in people's lives when this motivation is relevant?

What are the characteristics required to effectively satisfy this motivation in those moments?

How are these changing over time? Which characteristics are becoming less important, and which are becoming more important?

What does this mean for your brand, your broader business today and for the future?

Reference

Kantar (2024), Blueprint for Brand Growth, www.kantar.com/campaigns/ blueprint-for-brand-growth (archived at https://perma.cc/3P8U-49K9)

7

Consumer insights

Introduction to consumer insights

Eureka! It's that moment you uncover a consumer insight and experience that feeling in the solar plexus as you make a powerful connection between one of the opportunities or threats your brand faces and what you've learned about what motivates your consumers and shoppers. It's one of the best parts of building brands – a rush, a moment of clarity, the distillation of something powerful which will inspire creative people to develop work which will engage consumers.

Work powered by insight is distinctive, is more likely to be remarkable, and have the power to change behaviour and create emotion, enabling your brand to increase penetration by overcoming a barrier or leveraging a trigger. Having insight as this pivot between an opportunity for growth and an idea which can unlock it is powerful in other ways; for example it enables you to understand why something works to influence consumer choice, be that on your brand or one of your competitors'. Unpicking the insight behind brand campaigns is a great everyday habit to develop, and it will tune you into what's going on in culture, how other brands are thinking about presenting themselves to the world, and give you mastery in dissecting brands and their plans – spotting great ones, and those going through the motions.

As mentioned in Chapter 5, 'insights' is an overused term. It's used interchangeably to mean things such as data, trends, and information. Perhaps most worryingly it is used on many marketing dashboards – presenting information about exposures to advertising, the proportion of people who may have clicked through a piece of content, and other in-platform metrics. These are not insights but good performance data or input into understanding whether something is working or not.

Intelligence, or consumer intelligence, might be a contender for alternative terminology. Intelligence is used in various contexts including the military, and in organizations to describe the collection and analysis of information to give guidance and direction in decision-making. It's not quite right – when data helps inform a decision it is undoubtably useful but not exactly what we mean by insight. Intelligence gives us understanding and confidence to act, but it doesn't have that feeling of a powerful breakthrough.

We need to reclaim consumer insight as a term and be specific in how and when we use it versus 'intelligence' or 'information'. It makes sense to have a definition, think about how to generate and apply insights, and consider the behaviours your team should adopt to increase the chances of uncovering a powerful one. We'll focus more on the definition in the second section of this chapter, but think of an insight as a profound evidence-based discovery about human motivations, behaviours, or attitudes which a brand can apply to the opportunities it faces to unlock growth.

Insights in action

Before discussing how to create insights, it's worth bringing to life why insights matter. Insights are the lifeblood of brands. We talked in Chapter 6 about how consumer motivations are static overtime and across geographies, but that culture is not. Culture is in constant motion and differs across geographies and communities. Thanks increasingly to technology, culture has a global dimension to it as well – how we live our lives can feel both similar and different as they are shaped by local, national, and international forces. Needs may be static, but culture affects how those needs are expressed – the context around them which shows up in people's values and beliefs, their different eating habits, working patterns, how family and relationships are constructed, how leisure time is spent, the kind of homes people aspire to, and so on. Understanding how culture constrains and enables people's needs is at the heart of insights.

To bring this to life, let's look at an example of a brand which has excelled in using consumer insight to drive growth over a long period of time. It's a brand which comes to mind easily with strong associations. It's a mature brand which everyone knows and has probably used at some point, albeit relevance may be an issue. This brand would see me at best as a light category user, but in the right moment, I might choose it over alternatives. Even for someone like me who is not often in the target market, and has few available occasions, this brand stands out strongly and I could talk about what it stands for, its products, consumer experience, and so on. I know lots of people who would advocate and speak up for this brand, perhaps in a way which might be surprising given some of the cultural and perceptual challenges surrounding it and which shape its category.

The brand is McDonald's, and this case is detailed in the gold-winning IPA Effectiveness awards paper (Sussman, 2022). The paper covers a 15-year period and tells the story of how McDonald's in the UK impressively turned around a negative trend in customer visit numbers, the brand's measure of penetration. McDonald's had been in consistent growth since its arrival in the UK in 1974, never knowing a period of decline. Growing for 30 years consistently does not happen without challenge, but I imagine the business did not have the muscle memory to be able to make sense of and respond to finding itself suddenly losing consumers.

In 2006 the brand was in the midst of a PR storm with a backlash against fast food, and research revealed that 44% of its customers were openly critical of the brand. More broadly, attitudes to food and health were changing in the UK, and there was a government select committee reviewing food labelling and advertising in response to obesity. McDonald's was no longer expanding its estate of restaurants, so the turnaround needed to come from directly addressing its role within UK life.

It's a classic example of what we've been talking about – there was probably no material change in the occasions and needs McDonald's satisfied – convenience food on the go, fun and sociable treat, etc. but the changing cultural landscape meant that just redesigning the nutritional profile of the menu would not cut it. McDonald's understood the issue it had to address was trust and love, *and that in this complex food environment, with the food they loved under regular attack from worthy-sounding critics, consumers wanted reassurance about the choices they were making.*

This insight enabled McDonald's to create work which reminded its audience of the positive role McDonald's played in British life, dramatizing that 'we all have McDonald's in common', while also running work which reassured on the integrity of its ingredients, reflected in the idea of 'simply doing nothing', all about the fun and play inherent in kids and the McDonald's experience. Consumer insight enabled McDonald's to frame itself as permissible – a fun part of UK life for everyone. Without insight it may well have tried simply to defend the nutritional elements, and I suspect would have achieved far less.

This work was successful, but more challenge lay ahead. By 2012 McDonald's was under siege from shifts in its competitive set – challenged by speciality coffee chains, home delivery, value brands such as Greggs, and premium burgers in casual dine-in chains. Growth in visits slowed. McDonald's used insight again to its advantage. As with the previous example, evolving the core product offering was an element, but not the real story. Understanding that *people didn't just want a better coffee, but a nicer environment in which to hang out*, McDonald's redesigned its restaurants to be places people would be more comfortable hanging out in, which was a big driver for the coffee chains. It understood what consumers enjoyed about the coffee occasion but that some cafés could be expensive and pretentious, enabling it to bring to life the great value and hipster-free no nonsense of McCafé while upgrading its drinks offering. The work leveraged the same confidently humble brand tone, UK slice of life casting, and instantly recognizable brand assets – combining what it knew people love about McDonald's.

Just as things were going well again, Covid hit, closing its restaurants. McDonald's understood that lockdown, with the government's ever-changing rules, could feel more like a war than a recession. Its insight was that *without a solution in sight, people were looking for reassurance from leadership, wherever they could find it, even from brands*. To address this, McDonald's brought qualities of wartime leadership to its work – demonstrating confidence and compassion to its audience, especially those acutely affected, such as NHS workers. This work was also underpinned by consistent value messaging and that so familiar tone of voice.

McDonald's business results over this entire 15-year period were strong – a turnaround and long-term increase in customer visits, and an increase of between 30% and 46% revenue per restaurant during the different phases of this work.

Just as we learn from other brands such as Cadbury, Audi, and Tesco which have stayed the course, the core motivation you serve may not change, but changing culture and therefore the context in which that motivation is satisfied can be quietly killing your brand. Tuning in to the interplay of culture and consumer needs and applying what you learn to your biggest problems in a way which is credible from your brand is how to remain relevant. This is what insight is all about.

Insight solves problems

What's great about the McDonald's case study is that it demonstrates how insight can solve different types of problems – in helping the brand navigate culture, in refining and innovating core product and service offerings, in helping the brand understand and respond to a changing competitive environment. New entrants are often more agile in identifying how to challenge the dominant category characteristics which consumers are looking for to meet their motivations. Successful new entrants will shift the expectations people have and if your brand does not keep pace with these evolving category triggers over time it will become irrelevant.

This can be especially true with mega-brands with near universal awareness and scale. At Meta HQ, the dramatic slowdown in the growth of active Facebook users in the last few years was one of these moments – against which they have been acquiring brands which better meet the characteristics consumers are seeking from social media, and updating their own brands, as you can see in the evolution of Instagram to keep pace with TikTok.

Reflections

What does 'insight' mean in your organization?

How is consumer insight used to solve the problems and opportunities your
   brand faces?

What is a consumer insight and when do I use it?

If an insight is not information, data, intelligence, or observation – even though all these are routinely presented to marketers as such – what is it?

Dictionary and other definitions bring out common elements – seeing the inner nature of things, having deep understanding of a complex situation or problem, perceiving the world in a way which challenges conventional perspectives, discerning relationships differently, uncovering the true nature of things, and so forth.

Other definitions of insight stress rigour, logic, data, or a revelation. The quest for an insight fuses analytical rigour with moments of revelation and clarity.

In defining insight as far as it applies to effective brand building, I think there are three ingredients:

- a profound evidence-based discovery about human motivations, behaviours, or attitudes;
- the potential to unlock the opportunity or threat the brand faces;
- the ability to inspire credible action leading to category or brand growth.

All three elements are critical. The need to ground insight in needs or motivations, behaviours, or attitudes is generally understood but it should be backed up by evidence. It is the next two elements which enable insight to be effective. To be useful, an insight needs to solve the problem in hand. This means first having a well-defined issue, and then that whatever you uncover about the consumer is relevant to that issue.

Finally, an insight is not valuable unless it provokes clear actions and can inspire creativity grounded in something credible coming from the brand.

If you think about the insights McDonald's developed to address the three threats it faced, they all met these criteria. Firstly, the brand had a strong understanding of the problem it faced: that its customers were becoming overtly critical of the brand as part of a backlash against fast food, that it was becoming less relevant a place to visit than competitors, or that consumers were hesitant to return after the trauma of Covid lockdowns. It can help to reframe the opportunity or threat as a question:

- How do we overcome scepticism about McDonald's food and get people to return to the restaurants?
- How do we get people to choose McDonald's on casual coffee occasions?
- How do we get people to come back to McDonald's after Covid?

The insights it uncovered had the power to reframe the problems. For example, in the first instance the brand focussed on reminding people that McDonald's was about fun times together and was something we 'all had in common'. Addressing nutritional concerns alone may not have been sufficient, and this insight helped it remind people why they enjoyed going to McDonald's.

In the instance of McCafé, the brand was able to build awareness for its new offering in a way which was credible. We know McDonald's is known for its value and would be able to compete better on those terms than it could on competing on drink quality. Had McCafé tried to copy Café Nero or one of the other chains which was affecting McDonald's footfall it would have lacked the credibility for translating the insight into action.

To validate the insight you have developed it's useful to ask:

- Is the insight relevant to the opportunity or threat?
- Will it inspire action which is credible coming from the brand?

If not, then it's likely you have something which may be a useful observation about your consumers, or a piece of information rather than a powerful vehicle to drive change.

When to apply insights

Insights play a role at various points in effective brand building and can be used both in strategy and in execution.

In strategy the most common use of insights is in brand positioning, but as we saw in the McDonald's example, insights can be applied to the opportunities and threats a brand faces to inspire integrated brand campaigns, including individual assets or activities. The McDonald's IPA case study, for example, references how insight informed particular creative executions. Insights are used not only in communications development across all channels, but also in media understanding, in developing shopper marketing work, brand experiences, innovation, and so on. In almost any situation where you want to translate your business objective into something consumer-facing, an insight can play a role.

Reflections

How does consumer insight inform your brand positioning?

What consumer insights have been used to develop your current work?

Reviewing your competitors' activities, what consumer insights are they using?

How do brands uncover consumer insights?

There are two key dimensions to this – one concerns the latent behaviours within an organization and the other is about having discipline in ensuring consumer insights are created at those points when they matter. Let's start with how you focus your team on being curious.

Insightful behaviours

Having an enquiring mind is probably the most important characteristic for you and your team to excel at in order to develop powerful insights. Brands and businesses tend to be overwhelmingly internally focussed. When businesses talk about being consumer-centric it is often within a narrow trade or category perspective, and they struggle to see the big picture of how brands and categories fit into our lives and in turn how culture shapes behaviour over time.

As mentioned previously, the word 'consumer' itself is problematic as it focusses on the individual at the point at which they interact with the product or service, and often this is seen as the buying, not usage, occasion. It's important to consider the people who use your brand holistically. When we focus on the product or service interaction we may conclude that consumers don't care much about brands. People may not care about a lot of the brands they buy, but the need those brands are trying to satisfy is important to them.

Take a bar of soap or shower gel, for example – it's a low interest category where many brands have become commoditized. Consumers do care, however, about their hygiene – it's important to how I feel about myself, and how I fit into society. Deny someone the ability to wash and bathe and the psychological impact is significant. Brands which are curious about their consumers create much more value in the category, for example recognizing that what's on display in the home communicates something about the household's values and taste, right up to recognizing hand washing and bathing rituals can be elevated to experiences worth paying ×30 the price of staple brands, as brands like Molton Brown and Aesop demonstrate. Missing the broader context can cost your brand a place in the category; it compromises your relevance as a brand, and your business will suffer.

Marketing must be externally attentive and challenge the whole organization to be so too. It is critical for effective brand building. You must constantly scan what's going on in the world outside your business to uncover new things about consumers, customers, competitors, and the cultural landscape that will help you unlock new opportunities for growth.

Here are some mindsets and behaviours which help develop an external radar:

MAKE IT A DAILY HABIT

Take time to look at a broad range of media. Be deliberate in continually breaking out of your own filter bubble and look at different sources. Get in the habit of considering source credibility and biases – who owns the media and what is their agenda? Be sure to look at sources covering politics, economics, social, and cultural topics. This should include traditional and contemporary sources, opinion leaders, and trend setters. Think about your audiences and what they are consuming. By reading and observing what's going on you will develop more intuition about the world in which activities from your brand appear.

HUMAN-CENTRIC, NOT BRAND-CENTRIC

Even the best brands fall into the trap of thinking 'brand out' – we ask ourselves how our brands can take advantage of what we are seeing, not about how our brands can add value to people. To be human-centric marketers we need to put people first. It's critical to understand the shifting context around our target audiences, and the forces shaping their lives and choices which may be invisible even to them. By immersing ourselves, it enables us to reveal more around their lives and understand how a brand can add value to them.

BE MORE SHERLOCK HOLMES

Having the mindset of a detective will help you spot patterns, make deductions, and find connections between different pieces of information. It may not be so apparent to us day to day, but we live in an interconnected local and global system. Our recent experience with Covid-19 was a great reminder of this – a new virus brought up questions of personal freedoms, affected how we work, connect, and brought aftershocks in so many areas – political, economic, technological. What interconnecting system do your consumers live in and how does that relate to your brand, and the experience it offers?

MAKE IT A SHARED EXPERIENCE

Many leaders encourage their teams to go on inspiration days and conduct cultural immersions. This means going to events, museums, exhibitions, new retail formats, and so forth. It does not matter if these things do not feel 100% relevant to the day job – these behaviours enable you to tune in and you will be surprised how what you learn influences your decision-making, inspires creativity, and fosters closeness to your audience.

Spend time with your consumers and in trade. Be aware that as you get more senior, people may want to impress you more than illuminate you. Be wary of staged trade visits with remarkable execution, and consumer immersions to impressive but atypical households. Your behaviour as a leader will set the tone. How can you serve your consumer if you don't respect them or are prepared to walk in their shoes? It is a privilege to step into someone's world. Without empathy, you will not be able to build brands which cut through and meet your consumers where they are. Perhaps even immerse yourself anonymously to ensure you are experiencing something real.

Make time to do this with your team, and with your cross-functional leadership team. Create space to have conversations which elevate consumers in your business. It's reportedly the case that in some businesses there is an empty chair in key meetings – one symbolizing the real boss – not investors or the chair of the board, but our consumers.

Here are some thoughts on where to focus your attention during these immersions:

OCCASIONS AND MOTIVATIONS

Though spending time in your consumer's world is not a luxury for marketers but an essential practice, it's still important to turn what you experience into action. Great marketers have strong gut instincts, but those instincts are not innate. We are not our consumers, and we typically have more privileged lives than they do. Think about these habits as probiotics – a healthy gut means healthier gut instincts.

Consumer immersions are a great vehicle for understanding motivations and occasions. For example, for sports teams such as Manchester United, identity and belonging are critical motivators ('who I am'), for Costa Coffee, KFC, and Magnum ice cream it is more about occasions (where + when), or experiences in the travel industry, and for luxury brands it may be about status or discernment – showing my place in the world or my taste.

By understanding the occasions on which your products are used you can better understand how those important characteristics or category triggers manifest, and really understand how you are tracking versus consumer expectation, how things may be evolving, and what other brands may be doing better than you. What's the tempo of the occasion? Where does it happen? What's the mood and environment like? What are the cues which drive choice – visible brands, a menu, a recommendation from a waiter? If, as is the case with Magnum, your brand is about pleasure, what can you learn from other occasions with the same motivation which may be outside your product category?

This is about bringing the time you spend immersing right into focus by being clear on the framework in which your brand exists – what problem you are solving for the consumer or what value they are seeking in that moment or in their lives.

BE A CULTURE VULTURE

Alongside occasions and motivations, focus attention on changing cultural forces – those things which affect our attitudes and behaviours, what's considered good taste, innovative, acceptable or not, and how we think about living a good life.

Effective brands understand the positive role they can play in consumers' lives. When McDonald's was under pressure, it did not shout about fat and salt reduction, but reminded us about its role in UK life – casual fun and inclusive moments.

Culture is a product of macro-environmental forces including social, technological, economic, environmental, political, and ethical. Many brands create a framework of the main forces shaping their world, monitor them, and consider how those forces intersect with occasions.

COMPETITORS

Understand your competitors in the context of the moments in which you and they compete. How do they meet the desired characteristics of a given situation, including functional, sensory, and emotional ones?

It is also important to look at your competitors from a lateral standpoint. Competition may not come from within – there may be many other ways your buyers satisfy needs like belonging and status, and there may be other ways they solve life's problems – like how to get rid of my headache, how do I get to a desired destination, how do I store my possessions? Solutions may come from adjacent or entirely different categories. Too often we are myopic and think the only way people can meet their needs is to buy something. This is a symptom of the trap of thinking about 'consumers' rather than people. If I can meet a need without spending money, I am likely to do so – perhaps I can cure that headache with rest, water, or exercise without reaching for painkillers.

Though we live in an age of consumption, many consumers actively seek to reduce consumption. Brands which have understood this have created entirely new offerings from re-use and repair services from Nudie Jeans to the Octopus Club for all things baby, kids, and maternity, to Vinted for clothes, and Vinterior for furniture. It would be easy for clothing, furniture, baby products, and retail brands to overlook these platforms as important competitors, reshaping how consumers fulfil their needs as a desire to live more sustainably becomes a more prevalent feature in society and culture.

What are the other ways in which your audience can meet the motivation at the heart of your offering beyond substitutable product and service offerings?

Human-centricity

Being human-centric is so much more than being consumer-centric. Effective brands know the whole person, not just through the lens of the other similar products they may buy. You and your colleagues are not your consumers. Walk in their shoes – think about their lives, how the culture they see through the media they consume influences them, when and how they shop, and how they use products or services – the experiences they seek and the problems they solve.

Spend time observing consumers – in situations related to buying or using yours and your competitors' products, but also beyond them to understand their lives in a broader context, and the other ways in which they meet relevant needs. This latter point is so useful to uncover characteristics in those moments which you might be able to bring into your brand's world and challenge the current dominant characteristics which drive satisfaction.

Finally, remember that so much of our own lives, motivations, and behaviours are invisible to us. Talk to experts from broad fields – especially cultural experts such as semioticians, economists, sociologists, behavioural scientists, culture makers – musicians, writers, travel experts, etc. Closer in, talk to your salespeople, customers, and your agencies who work across different brands. Use your first party data if you have it. Doing this in person is amazing, but technology and social media mean people are closer and more approachable than ever before. It's never been easier to see what people, albeit those either engaged or enraged, are seeing about brands, and to ask them provocative questions.

Reflections

What behaviours do you, your team, and colleagues from other functions do to
    stay close to consumers?

How do you share and derive value from what you see and learn?

How do I generate and apply consumer insights?

Being externally attentive improves your judgement, enables you to spot
opportunities and threats, and align with emergent culture better than the
competition. However, how do you turn this awareness into insights which
will improve your brand's performance?

Criteria for great insights

Gary Klein's work on insights across a whole range of industries is worth
investigating (Klein, 2014). He defines an insight as having caused an unexpected shift in understanding. Great insight reframes how you see things, so
ask yourself if your understanding has fundamentally changed, and whether
this inspires hitherto unseen possibilities.

   To apply this approach to your brand's performance, it may be that you
have observed a change in sales – be it a deviation from your run rate, or
more or less than you would have expected versus previous year's sales.
This is an observation, not an insight. If you find out that the reason for
the change in sales is merely down to an increase or decrease in promotional intensity or distribution, it is not an insight. If, however, you uncover
an unplanned driver of these sales – perhaps triggered by unexpected
coverage on TikTok with someone suggesting a surprising usage for your
brand – then you might have an insight. Insights have implications, which
can lead to actions you can take to get your audience's attention and
convert that to sales. The children's toiletries brand Childs Farm, for example, saw sales start to shift when users generated and shared images of the
remarkable impact the products appeared to have in clearing up long-
standing skin issues. It enabled the brand to double down on its sensitive
skincare messaging.

   Remember the importance of connecting what you have observed back
to a business or brand challenge. If you take the time to ask how it links

back, an insight can be more than a revelation; it can be a key to unlock brand growth.

Lots of organizations have screeners with mnemonics to help their markets check their insights. As well as considering whether a potential insight is actionable, whether it tackles the issue, they include things such as these 5Ts:

Tension – does the insight uncover a tension in people's lives, especially between the forces of culture outside our control, and our inherent desires and motivations? If so, it might be a tension your brand can help resolve.

Tacit – understood at a deep level without being explicitly spoken. Insights may come from seeing patterns, and observing things which people may not be able to explain or understand – much less articulate – directly themselves.

True – of the consumer and of the brand. To inspire well-branded work a great insight needs to be grounded in something true of the brand which may be aspects of its product or service, or things for which it is known. Being true from a consumer perspective is about being scalable – not necessarily universal but prevalent enough in your target market that work created from it will resonate widely.

Touching – will inspire work which provokes an emotional response. In a world where people are bombarded with messages, the evidence for the greater effectiveness of emotional work is compelling.

Timely – ensure insights lead to action and are applied with pace. As culture evolves as too do current affairs with even greater pace, you may need to revisit which insight will unlock the challenge your brand faces. For example, think about how different the consumer insight is which drives Noom versus the Slimming World and Weight Watchers brands which preceded it, albeit all ultimately tackle the same business opportunity and consumer need.

Generating insights

We know the criteria for an insight, but how do you generate them practically?

The classic approach to insight generation used is simply asking 'Why? Why? Why?' after each new answer until you get to an actionable place.

Here's a simple example:

> It's wintertime and you've noticed that body wash sales are increasing, and bubble bath sales are decreasing despite winter being a season during which more people enjoy a soak in the tub. As a leading manufacturer of bath products, you want to know what to do. This process provokes you to ask 'why?' or 'why is that important?' to get to the root of the driver.
>
> *Body wash sales are outstripping bubble bath sales*
>
> Why? People are showering more.
>
> Why? They are showering more in preference to having baths.
>
> Why? Showers use less hot water.
>
> Why? People are concerned with hot water usage.
>
> Why? Hot water costs more because of energy prices.
>
> Why? Energy prices have gone up due to inflation.

So what?

We must remind people of the experience they are missing out on when they take a shower over a bath, making the benefit of a bath feel worth more than the perceived extra energy cost.

Creatively, this is quite a rich territory – you might seek to bring to life the relaxation and indulgence that you get from having a bath, or that baths promote better sleep when taken before bed as they lower your core body temperature.

Imagine what your competitors in shower gels might do with this. They might be happy with the extra growth, or they might think about how they can encourage people to make this behaviour stick. They might try demonstrating that showers can be both indulgent and economical – helping people create the mood and experience of a bath as effectively without the expense.

There are other sequential approaches to generating insights which can help. The approach below lends itself to a workshop context – ideally preparing and aligning the problem to solve in advance and then working stages 2–4 sequentially over a couple of hours. This approach helps find new ways of unlocking an issue, in preparing an agency brief, or even working the process backwards to decode competitor activity and what insight it might have unlocked.

1   What is the opportunity or threat the brand faces?

2   What do we know that can help us address the opportunity or threat?

3   What have we learned about consumers that can be applied to solve the problem credibly from the brand?

4   What different consumer-facing activities might we do based on the insight?

WHAT IS THE OPPORTUNITY OR THREAT THE BRAND FACES?

We've all heard the quote about a well-defined problem being half-solved. This is true when trying to discover insights, especially when you think about opportunities or threats to penetration.

For brands, a well-articulated issue will express something around current consumer behaviour and your understanding of the triggers or barriers to penetration.

Often a well-articulated issue is a succinct description of the change in behaviour you are trying to achieve such as: How do I get [insert target consumer group] to choose [brand x] on their [z] occasions over [competitor brand] by overcoming [insert trigger or barrier]?

This approach encourages you to find the key to unlocking the trigger or barrier. It also centres in on the consumer – not on the brand or an observation about your market share position. Some brands like to express this issue using 'I' as though the consumer was expressing it.

WHAT DO WE KNOW THAT CAN HELP US ADDRESS THE OPPORTUNITY OR THREAT?

With a well-defined problem, examine the different information you already have to unlock it. To fuel a workshop this can be provided as a data pack in advance. If you have a lot of information, a good approach is to divide up data sources and ask people to come prepared with the 5–10 most significant things they have pulled out of the information which may be relevant to the problem. Getting people to undertake a fresh consumer immersion ahead of such a situation is ideal – it may provide more vivid stimulus than they may have read in your research materials.

Good sources for information include your own consumer research – qualitative and quantitative, syndicated and bespoke as well as other external sources – trend reports, contextual information, expert information, social media listening, reviews, and cultural insight studies. If you can, get information about extreme brand and category consumers, including both outright rejectors and superfans if possible – these often provide surprising clues. An insight generation session benefits from having a diverse cast, so include research and development colleagues, sales, operations, etc.

Collect people's observations in turn and post them up on the wall. A pre-task means you benefit from independent thinking without the bias of groupthink or hierarchy. As the information goes up on the wall it is important to create an environment where people listen without judgement – listening deeply without thinking about what you want to say has become a rare commodity.

At the end of this exercise, you can look at the information in different ways. First and perhaps most obviously, you can create themes. Secondly, you can seek connections between what you've learned and the problem in hand. Be curious and interrogate the information more by asking 'why?' to go deeper. As well as looking for convergence look for contradictions, tensions, and allow yourself to be drawn to things which perhaps don't appear logical at first.

As well as asking 'why?', some people use a Venn diagram to find patterns – with circles representing information about the consumer, the brand, and culture, or sometimes just the consumer and brand. Spot over-laps and commonalities between what the consumer seeks at a deep level and what the brand offers.

WHAT HAVE WE LEARNED ABOUT CONSUMERS THAT CAN BE APPLIED TO SOLVE THE PROBLEM CREDIBLY FROM THE BRAND?

This is where consumer insights take shape. Identify potential areas and mine each one to get to the heart of it.

Remember how we defined an insight earlier: 'A profound evidence-based discovery about human motivations, behaviours, or attitudes which a brand can apply to the opportunities it faces to unlock growth'. Remember also the characteristics of insights and the 5Ts screener.

Information is fact, observation, data, requiring little or no interpreta-tion, often directly from research. Insight typically contains something of the consumer's desire or motivation juxtaposed against a tension that comes from culture or some other constraint. Insight offers new perspective about how to approach your problem or opportunity.

There are different ways to express insights, and it's useful to decide how you will approach this.

Some people like to express an insight through the eyes of the consumer. A way to do this is to first describe the current situation and current behav-iour, then to express the limitation or frustration which the consumer experiences, followed by what the desired state might be (Dalton, 2017).

Imagine you were a cycle company trying to get people to switch to your puncture proof/run flat tyres.

I enjoy cross country cycling, but I am always worried about getting a puncture. It would be great if I could cycle worry free and without having to carry a bulky puncture kit.

An alternative approach is to capture a combination of cultural tension or context along with what the consumer desires.

Getting a puncture can ruin a cyclist's day, cyclists just want the freedom of cycling without worry.

In this instance the insight is relevant to the issue as it connects what the consumer really wants and what a puncture-free tyre offers – FREEDOM.

WHAT DIFFERENT CONSUMER-FACING ACTIVITIES MIGHT WE DO BASED ON THE INSIGHT?

The final stage in a working session is to brainstorm the actions you might take as a result of the insight.

Our cycle company would no doubt be thinking about how it can bring to life the freedom which comes from being able to cycle worry free – either literally or by finding powerful metaphors to use in communications, in events, and in other consumer-facing work. 'Freedom' as a platform has the potential to be powerful as it connects to what the cyclist really wants to experience.

It is important to be able to summarize succinctly the implication of the insight you have uncovered. In this instance it may be as straightforward as saying 'we need to bring to life the freedom which comes with using our puncture-free tyres'.

This stage is all about what we should or might do as a result, and that is different from the execution in market which the consumer sees.

Sometimes people are more comfortable describing a potential executional idea, or a specific product innovation. If so, you can ask them why or how it applies the insight to unlock the opportunity you have identified to grow penetration.

If you see some powerful competitor communications, you can ask similar questions:

- What was the barrier or trigger the brand was tackling?
- What did the brand learn about the consumer's desire?

You can get to this by first describing the execution you are seeing – tell the story, recount the details, and then work backwards to decode what the brand had learned about the consumer.

It remains the case that much consumer-facing material has no insight – it merely presents the product or service to the world without understanding its relevance or the audience's context.

Beyond your working session, it is important to present insights in the context of the problem you set out to overcome. This will enable you to use insights consistently in the moments which matter – such as briefing agencies, evaluating potential consumer-facing work, and setting context for stakeholders on the work you are deploying. Be clear on:

What is the problem or opportunity?

What is the insight?

How does the insight address the opportunity?

How does the brand support the insight?

Given the power of insights to enable more distinctive brand positioning, innovation, communications, media connections, shopper marketing, and suchlike, it is great to have a marketing team and broader organization familiar with insights development and the commercial value it can bring.

Reflections

Do you routinely spend time articulating a well-defined issue before starting development work?

Do you have a process for generating insights on your brand?

When and how is this process deployed as you develop work?

Do you have a common approach to writing insights?

Are you and your team able to recognize a powerful insight and explain why it is so?

Do you routinely examine what insight your and your competitors' consumer-facing activities are deploying and what problem they may be using them to solve?

References

Dalton, J (2017) How to write a powerful consumer insight statement, https://
thrivethinking.com/2017/10/09/write-a-powerful-consumer-insight/ (archived at
https://perma.cc/MMH6-Y6HV)

Klein, G (2014) *Seeing What Others Don't*, PublicAffairs, New York

Sussman, T, (2022) McDonald's. How we got customers lovin' it and kept them
lovin' it, no matter what', in *Advertising Works 26, Proving the payback on
marketing investment*, ed. H Singh, pp 193–245, IPA Effectiveness Awards 2022,
IPA, London

PART TWO

Creating an effective brand strategy – where to win

8

What is brand strategy?

What is strategy?

What do we mean by 'strategy'? A bit like 'insights', it's one of those words used in many contexts in a brand and business environment.

It can be a word loaded with bias – 'strategic' may be a judgement about something or someone. Sometimes it is positive, or perhaps used to denigrate something 'tactical', and it can be the reverse – meaning impractical, academic, overly complicated.

Looking online for definitions of business strategy can prove frustrating – lots of jargon, consultant speak, and proprietary models. Strategy is often presented as something only senior people with deep experience do.

Strategy is simply about choices

Strategy is not the business's long-term revenue and profit targets – though this is an important part of framing a brand or business's ambition. Strategy is a plan to create value. Strategy articulates the choices a business or brand will make to achieve its goals. Given the challenges we face in businesses being overly busy, and often hedging their bets, good strategy often makes clear what the business won't do.

So, strategy is about priorities for growth. A strategic process for the total business will typically start with the company's vision and mission, the long- and short-term goals it wishes to achieve – often financial, but not necessarily so in not-for-profit and other organizational contexts. Then, through a process of analysis and framing the business will select what it will prioritize to achieve those outcomes, and articulate the choices it has made to investors, employees, and other stakeholders.

These choices are typically communicated across the organization to ensure people and resources are focussed on the things that matter the most. Strategic choices affect all elements of an organization – including its design, capabilities, and activities. Finally, strategy is translated into a plan.

Having a clear strategy creates many benefits – having everyone on the same page regarding the organization's vision, mission, and goals, and its prioritization of finite resources in service of them. An effective strategy also ensures a business has plans to mitigate against external threats and create a proactive culture enabling it to effectively respond to opportunities created by the changing environment.

Different types of strategy

This view of strategy – clarity on the choices made to deliver business goals, and to enable the creation of focussed plans – is something that works in other situations where we talk about strategy – especially portfolio and brand.

Portfolio strategy articulates the roles different brands play in delivering company-wide long- and short-term business goals. It helps us understand which are more or less important, and proportion resources appropriately.

Brand and innovation strategy follow the same pattern as the process for delivering a total business strategy, but at the level of brand, either within a geography, or across its different geographies considering its stage of development. Brand strategy shares those common characteristics – long-term ambition comprised of vision, mission, and goals, the choices to deliver and measure them, and the ability to translate that into plans.

With clear strategy, brands can balance long-term aims with short-term performance, make sense of which external events may be important to respond to, and achieve more with the people and funds they have. In contrast, brands without these foundations tend to react to what's going on, burn resources on the short term, and never somehow find the time to undertake those tasks which create long-term value. They may hit their short-term performance goals, but over time such brands open themselves up to becoming less relevant to their target consumers, being overtaken by competition, becoming commoditized, and ultimately less interesting to their customers as well.

Reflections

Am I and my team comfortable with what strategy is and how it is used?

Do we have a clear brand strategy and is it clearly linked to the organization's strategy?

Am I clear on the role each brand plays in the portfolio, and in turn the organization's strategy?

How does the strategy and planning cycle work with the business cycle?

As should be clear from the above, brand strategy sits within your business's overall view of how it will achieve its goals, and its strategic priorities. As such it's important to lay out the process by which you conduct brand and innovation planning alongside business planning, taking into account dynamics like customer lead times and expectations, and other seasonal factors – the impact of cultural events, sports seasons, holiday seasons, etc.

This may require some trade-off as customer timelines may require work developed ahead of confirming an annual business plan or budget. If you are a business with multiple countries, you may find the customer dimension is even more complex due to the mix of different customers and channels – formal, informal, modern, traditional, independent, or multiple chains.

There is a further tension in ensuring that, while you plan for the long term and create programmes in a timely fashion, you can respond to changes in your environment. In general, the pace of change in consumer habits is such that a 3–5 year horizon for articulating a long-term ambition is suitable, and a 12–18 month horizon for developing activation plans works adequately. Whereas sales teams focus more on the sharp end of delivery, while not losing sight of longer-term customer and category planning, marketers should work more on an average two-year horizon, not losing sight of short-term delivery.

If the time frame is too short, plans are developed which are inevitably more reactive and tactical – driven by short-term needs and customer expectations. A short time frame limits the kinds of activities marketers can create. The opposite can be true if work is developed too far in advance – it can appear dated, especially in certain channels. A good example of this would be brands deploying user-generated content and using influencer partners. Social media fads tend to last about 90 days and therefore require a more agile model if such things are part of your execution.

The answer to this is that marketers need to be comfortable working on different time frames – maybe a 10-year horizon where research and development, technologists, and other experts are working on long-term initiatives to crack some of your biggest questions; a 3–5 year horizon to ensure you have a clear path where growth will come from; a 12–18 month horizon to develop and execute joined up consumer facing plans; and a 1–3 month horizon to monitor and evaluate performance.

To develop a planning calendar, identify:

- key trading periods and customer lead times;
- timings for business cycle horizons – 3–5 year, annual, in-year delivery and forecasting;
- the implications of the type of business you are – short or long purchase cycles, highly seasonal, long lead times of product development or fulfilment.

Brand strategy and annual planning process and output

Define the steps in the process you will use. For the purposes of this book, I suggest seven steps which take you from analysis into strategy and planning over the course of a financial year. The process forms a loop, but it is also iterative – looking backwards and forwards will help you consistently learn and improve what you have done.

There are key tools and tasks within each which are detailed in Figure 8.1.

1 Situation analysis
2 Brand ambition
3 Growth priorities
4 Brand foundations
5 Brand campaigns
6 Integrated planning
7 Annual plan

The first three steps deal with analysis and the identification and prioritization of long-term growth opportunities and are covered in sequence in the

FIGURE 8.1 Brand strategy and planning process

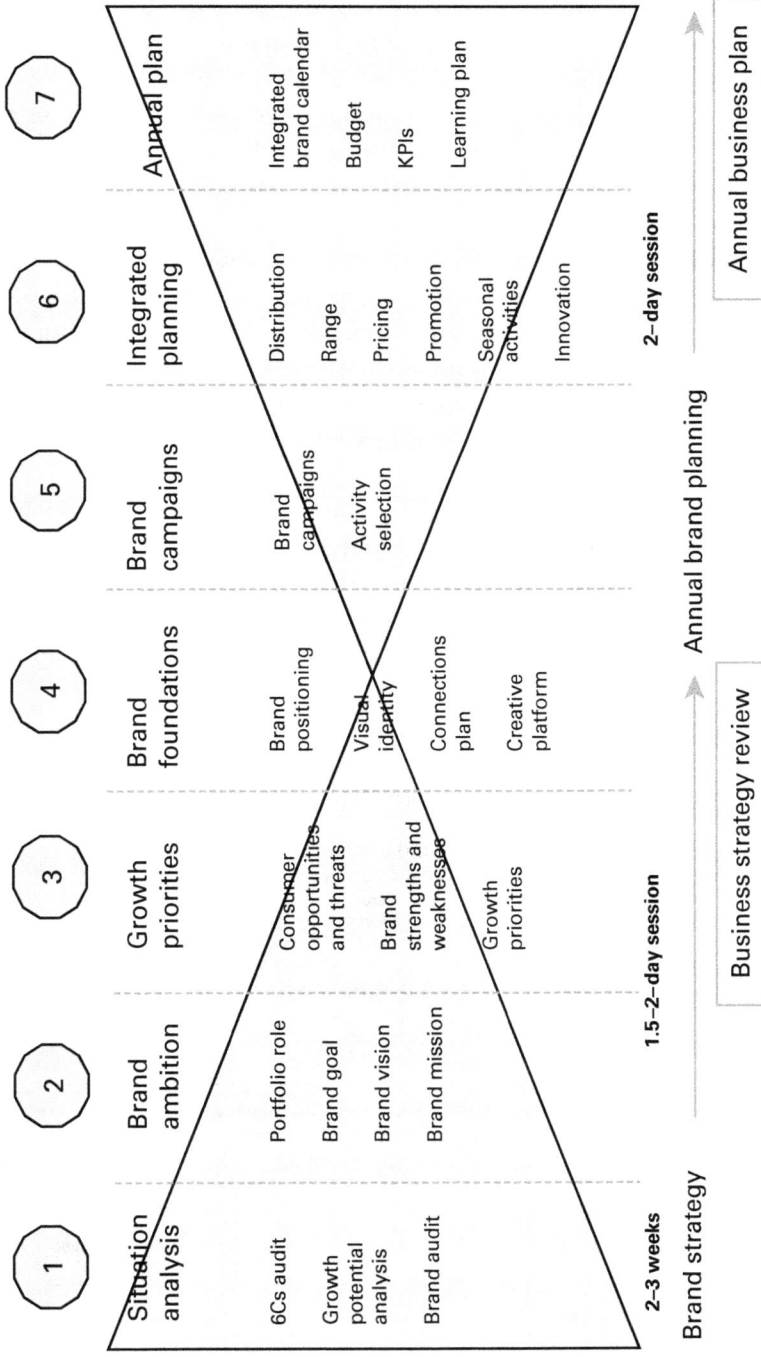

	1 Situation analysis	2 Brand ambition	3 Growth priorities	4 Brand foundations	5 Brand campaigns	6 Integrated planning	7 Annual plan
	6Cs audit	Portfolio role	Consumer opportunities and threats	Brand positioning	Brand campaigns	Distribution	Integrated brand calendar
	Growth potential analysis	Brand goal	Brand strengths and weaknesses	Visual identity	Activity selection	Range	Budget
	Brand audit	Brand vision	Growth priorities	Connections plan		Pricing	KPIs
		Brand mission		Creative platform		Promotion	Learning plan
						Seasonal activities	
						Innovation	

2–3 weeks 1.5–2-day session 2-day session

Brand strategy

Business strategy review

Annual brand planning

Annual business plan

next three chapters. Brand foundations necessary to turn these choices into consistent consumer-facing work are covered in Chapters 12 and 13, with steps five and six covered in Chapter 14, and step seven in Chapter 15, with final thoughts on measurement in Chapter 16.

What we are trying to create as an output is simple – a plan on a page which makes it clear what you are trying to achieve long term, where you are placing your bets against the different opportunities you have to grow, and then how that will show up in consumer-facing work which aligns a broad range of brand activities behind these priorities.

Figure 8.2 illustrates this, assuming as many as three growth priorities, although seeding and scaling brands may have fewer, and a mature brand conceivably may be able to fund more. The model will make more sense as we move through the next chapters, but use it as we go to build and refine the model by which your brand grows effectively. Adapt it to reflect your brand identity.

Culturally, how does your business view planning? What is the balance between a bottom-up view of growth and a top-down expectation? Typically, there is a negotiation between the two, and it is worth considering the range of behaviours and expectations this creates. Think back to Chapter 3 when we considered the impact of things such as reward, information flows, and

FIGURE 8.2 Effective brand house

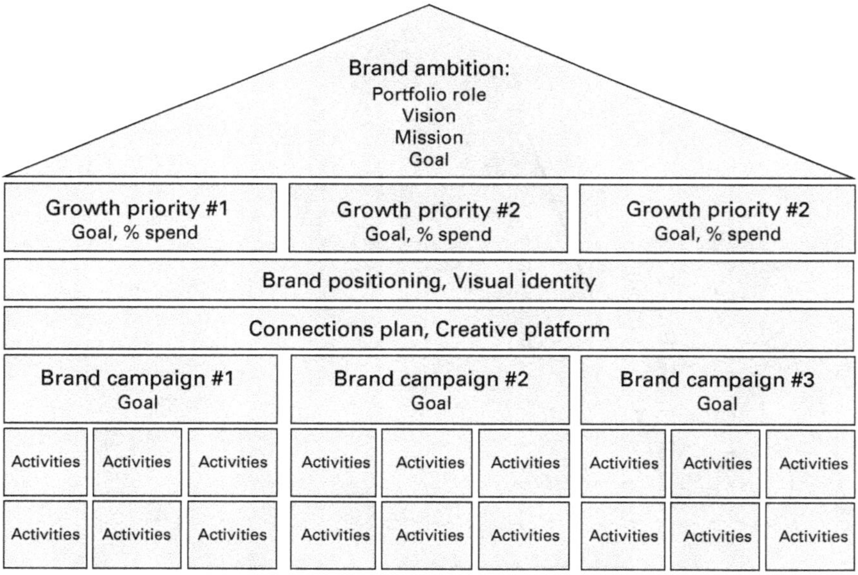

decision-making. Is your business transparent and collaborative? Do factors such as reward impact planning – e.g. a business leader attempting to 'low ball' a plan so they can overdeliver and be rewarded versus creating an ambitious plan which balances long and short term and has robust thinking for mitigating risks?

To place a stake in the ground, let's look at an approach based on a typical financial year. It is neither right nor wrong, but should enable you to iterate a version to suit you. The point is to be deliberate – effective brands focus most of their time on execution, but make time for strategy and planning, and measurement. Without this, especially in the highly volatile times we live in, the planning cycle can feel like a hamster wheel.

A brand-building cycle typically runs 3–5 years. The core of what a brand offers, often captured in brand positioning, should endure way beyond this – 10 plus years, maybe decades. A 3–5 year horizon is often the time frame in which a brand can respond to new challenges, develop and deploy work, learn and make improvements, and further deepen its understanding of how effective it is in achieving its ambition.

This can be tough in a world where financial objectives are shorter term, and people rarely remain in role for more than three years. Organizations without a short- and long-term mindset tend to lack the patience for brand building – they revisit brand strategy too often, they don't allow work to breathe, killing it rather than improving it, and react to the next internal prompt versus holding the tension for the long game and using data and judgement to steer the course.

A stake in the ground:

- Conduct 3–5 year brand and innovation planning at the beginning of the financial year in period or month 1 or 2 – including checking portfolio choices and category priorities. If you do this robustly in year one, for the subsequent years the work is to challenge assumptions and understand what may have changed.

- Conduct 12–18 month brand and innovation planning in period or month 4 or 5, for implementation at the beginning of the financial year. This should be ahead of your annual business planning cycle, so it enables a strong conversation on what growth is achievable and what is required to fund it.

Take some time to understand your business's approach to integrated planning. What are the critical points? When and how are key decisions made? Who owns the process? How should you formally connect your brand planning process? What will you need to communicate, to whom and when?

If you can align brand strategy and planning work to those points and understand the basis for key decisions in language the business understands, you are more likely to build belief in your plans and secure the right resources.

Reflections

Do I have a clear brand strategy and planning process?

Is it aligned to the business planning process, influencing choices and
     investment at the critical long-term, annual, and quarterly time horizons?

Are key people aware of how the brand planning process links to business
     planning and their responsibilities?

How do I embark on the process?

Get out of the weeds

Approaching this work requires a different mindset to everyday working. We get bogged down in the weeds, focussed on micro-level decisions, maintaining momentum, and delivering. Often, the more senior and experienced we get as marketers, paradoxically the more distant we get from adding value and applying our experience to our brands.

Too much of our time can be taken up maintaining a healthy business system in which our brands can thrive, managing vacancies, recruiting, and being involved in other cross-functional committees and projects. Productivity can be an issue as organizations are often over-resourced and artificially busy, creating mission creep.

Making time for strategy and planning can seem difficult, but remaining in the day to day encourages incrementalism. Making marginal gains is important and is one of the ways brands focussed on measurement compete effectively. However, this should be balanced with time spent on developing transformational strategies. To do this requires adopting a different mindset and signalling this to your team – looking longer term and being open to seeing and creating possibility.

Think like a disruptor

It's important to approach a strategic planning process with a critical eye, objectivity, and a challenger mindset. This is true for all brands but especially so of big established brands. I've heard more than once in my career someone stand up with a business or brand strategy and remark to an audience that their main competitors will probably have 'the same strategy'. They want to make the case that difference lies in execution. Though there is merit in this, and a relentless focus on execution matters, there is competitive advantage in transformational strategic thinking. Stand in the shoes of your competition and if the basis for how you will add value to your consumers is the same it is unlikely you will do it in a way which is remarkable.

Take the example of Yorkshire Tea in the UK, the no. 1 tea brand in 2024. It climbed from being fourth in the category to the top not by having a differentiated product from Tetley, PG Tips, and those other household names, but by a relentless focus on making the brand famous. Since 2016, Yorkshire Tea has used a creative platform 'Where everything's done proper', recognizing that while people might not care about tea, humorously using perceptions of what Yorkshire people are like might land the idea that every- thing the brand does is 'done proper'. The company is based in Yorkshire – the tea no doubt comes from India or China.

Challenger mindset is not about size. Consider brands such as Apple and Red Bull. When Steve Jobs returned to Apple as CEO, he was dissatisfied with big box computer retail and believed the shopping experience was crit- ical to the brand's success. At the time this was met with scepticism but today there are over 500 Apple stores in 26 countries. There are many other examples from Apple of having a challenger mindset. By doing things differ- ently to the big soft drinks brands, Red Bull is a $10 billion brand, selling at a premium price per millilitre of over 30% to Coke, depending on the vari- ant. Red Bull does not just partner and sponsor extreme sports but owns the teams, demonstrating long-term commitment to 'giving wiiings to people and ideas'.

Being a disruptor is about having the courage to see and upend the status quo. Often, they are smaller or niche brands able to see the world differently. Think Allbirds, Wealthsimple, Waku, Noted Aromas, Cook, Swytch, Sostrene Grene, Dice, Milliways, 7879, Mejuri, Postmates, Hulu, Knix, Peloton, Fair, Zwift, Spotify, Everlane, Casper, Zappos, Robin Hood, Jiffy, Warby Parker, Beyond Meat, Slack, Soylent, Away … You get the point! Look up some of the brands you have not come across. They cover many consumer segments – from traditional products and services into tech and beyond.

There are some disruptive established brands which have reinvented themselves in entirely different product or services. Think Nintendo, Fuji, IBM, Disney, Western Union, and Netflix. Over a couple of decades Netflix transformed from a postal DVD rental service challenging Blockbuster to a streaming service, and then again to be a remarkable content creator. Unfortunately, this is not always the norm for the establishment.

Too often, success breeds complacency. Scale, and the short tenure of people in role, means brands opt to avoid the big questions and ignore creeping change around them. It is not always true, but established brands can become risk averse, defensive, overly process driven, and analytical. The need for certainty can become bureaucratic. A strategic planning process should be designed to create possibility, challenge thinking, and not simply prevent mistakes. How you approach it will determine the outcome.

Often new ideas are counter-cultural and those people who think differently are rejected by the DNA of an organization. It is a fine balance with a mature brand or business to decide whether to keep going and refine, or to disrupt. Successful established brands find ways to incorporate challenger thinking and experiment without destabilizing their scale business – testing, learning, and experimenting.

As you enter this process, signal permission to think differently, bring to life relevant examples of challenger brands close by, and bring urgency to the question of where future growth will come from as culture slowly undermines your business.

Gather diverse thinking

Engage diverse thinking in your team – this means ensuring you embrace diversity in all its forms. People with different life experiences will see things differently and enrich your conversations.

Bring in people from other functions to key strategic sharing meetings, especially sales, IT, commercial finance, and research and development – they bring understanding of the customer, technology, economics, and so on. If your brand is present in multiple markets, how will you represent that? Include agency partners, especially strategists who will bring perspectives from other brands, categories, and culture.

Keep in mind that all of you are experts in your field, and although you will have perspectives on your consumers you are not them. Remember to bring the consumer into the conversation.

Remember also that this process is not democratic. While being open to transformational thinking, it's important to signal how decisions will ultimately be made and by whom.

Engage stakeholders

Done well, people will shift from being uncertain about this process to excited about it. Even in organizations more comfortable with action, people will become curious and want to become part of shaping the future, becoming stakeholders themselves in the brand and not just participants. Make it simple and bring people along, and the resistance you may find even in businesses with high control and low appetite for risk will wane.

Beyond your team and the concentric circles of participants around you, it is important to think about engaging stakeholders in this process. This is to build awareness, to create understanding and permission, and to empower them to be able to meaningfully add value to the process at key junctions. Especially in a business where a way of working like this is unfamiliar, it is key to demystify what you are doing, and link it to the outcomes and the things different stakeholders care about.

Have a plan to actively communicate with key stakeholders so they support the process and commit the time required to do it. Be mindful of taking them on the journey and letting them see the tangible plans and actions which come from the work. Make it real and commercially focussed. For each key group, capture what they think or feel today, how you want that to change, and reveal a relevant and motivating way to achieve that. Planning actions around this approach is the basis of winning hearts and minds.

Use signalling behaviours with stakeholders – make it clear when you are informing, seeking input, or asking for a decision.

Create the right environment

It's important to make this strategy work feel different. This means thinking about where and when you do it – off site and face to face if possible. Think about the environment you create and how you make it special. Be aware of working and thinking styles – not everyone is at their best thinking live in a workshop, and for some, having pre-work allows them to prepare their thoughts independently first. Think about what work you will do as a smaller group, and what's best done with a broader cast.

Workshops fulfil a dual role – in generating new thinking, but also in deepening connection and alignment. Often it makes sense to include people who may be the least well disposed to this way of approaching things – it will flush out issues in the moment if it is facilitated well, which will help you in the long term.

If you have a portfolio business, you can approach this work with more than one brand. In fact, there is benefit in having brands which play in different segments within the same category doing this work at the same time as there will be common inputs, and you can also ensure you pull them apart. Contrasting brands going through the process together can foster good challenges and fresh perspectives.

Reflections

How do you make time for strategy and planning? What are the barriers and enablers?

What is the mindset towards strategy in your brand and organization? Are you able to challenge and disrupt constructively?

How do you bring diverse perspectives to build your thinking?

How do you bring the consumer into the conversation?

Who are the key stakeholders you need to engage to ensure this process is effective?

What have their past experiences been, and what might you need to consider?

Who might support you in championing this process?

How can you connect this work to what your stakeholders care about, and explain it and the outputs within that framework?

How can your choice of timing and environment support brilliant thinking, deep alignment, and decisive actions?

References

Apple store list, www.apple.com/retail/storelist/ (archived at https://perma.cc/P3NG-K6JX)

BBC Radio Four (2023) The bottom line: Does funny sell? (Yorkshire Tea), 27 July, https://www.bbc.co.uk/sounds/play/m001p246 (archived at https://perma.cc/79FM-EX7M)

9

What is the situation
my brand faces?

What is an effective brand-building audit?

This chapter is about understanding the situation your brand faces, conducting a brand audit, and setting you up to make choices about how to grow.

Why conduct an effective brand-building audit? A brand-building audit:

- aligns your brand to the ever-changing external environment;
- connects people to a common narrative about what your brand needs to confront to achieve its ambition;
- ensures your work is focussed on the biggest opportunities to grow, especially increasing penetration.

At its very simplest, an audit serves to answer these five questions:

- Is the brand winning in the market?
- Does the brand have a winning consumer proposition?
- Is the brand winning the hearts and minds of consumers?
- Is the brand winning at the point of purchase?
- Is the brand driving profitable growth for the organization and its partners?

Though you as a marketing team will champion this, remember that everyone in your organization is in the business of building brands – this work will enable everyone to grasp what needs to be done and why.

A brand-building audit combines data gathering, analysis, inspiration, decision-making, and storytelling. Though there is a sequence, the process is iterative, and is as much about rigour as it is belief.

Robust inputs

You know the phrase 'rubbish in, rubbish out'. Marketers typically feel as though they have insufficient information. How much is enough? The quality of outputs is only ever going to be as good as the inputs, so it is worth ensuring you have a good foundation but recognize that having 70–80% of what you would like is probably sufficient.

This phase naturally feels messy – information inevitably comes from disparate sources which may been compiled with different objectives in mind, and it takes patience to piece together a picture of what's going on seen from different angles, different start points, and levels of detail.

Plan time to do this phase adequately. Breaking the task up helps, so engage your marketing team, insights, and category or sales teams in helping collate the information you need.

The point of this data gathering is not to boil the ocean but:

- to see things dispassionately and with objectivity;
- to base decisions on the best available information;
- to inspire your team to think boldly and with imagination.

A good audit will typically contain distinct parts:

- 6Cs audit
- growth potential analysis
- effective brand audit

This is all about starting with the external environment, understanding the potential for growth among your consumer base, before understanding the latent strengths and weaknesses of your brand, and making choices about the biggest opportunities for growth.

How do I conduct a 6Cs audit?

This is a framework to help you synthesize the relevant information about the external environment and your consumers and enable you to identify all the possible consumer and market opportunities for growth, especially penetration growth. There are alternative models such as Porter's 5 Forces which you could use.

What are the 6Cs?

Context

Category

Competition

Consumer

Customer/Channel

Commercial/Company

CONTEXT

What do we mean by context? This considers the shifting macro context – including socio-cultural, technological, economic, environmental, political, legal, ethical, and demographic, sometimes called STEEPLED. What are the key trends, what may happen in the future, and what are the things which will have the most significant impact on consumer behaviour and the category?

What kind of data should you consider? There are rich and freely available data sources at country level which allow comparison across markets. For an in-market brand with domestic ambitions locally sourced data is likely to be more granular and independent, such as the Office of National Statistics in the UK or the US Census Bureau. As a place to start, data sources with broader international coverage include the World Bank, the Economist, IFS, UN Data, Eurostat, CIA World Factbook, and suchlike.

CATEGORY

What do we mean by category? Consider the category not just through the lens of the trade, but how consumers might define it. For example, a clothing brand would look broadly across fashion, an airline would look beyond air travel to include rail, road, and sea. A chocolate brand would look beyond chocolate into sweet and savoury snacking, and broader food trends.

Once defined, seek to understand how the different categories have performed and are likely to perform in the future. What are the dynamics and drivers of growth, which segments are gaining or losing share, what is the impact of contextual factors on the shape of the category?

What kind of data should you consider? The main sources of data for this will be retail audits and consumer panel data for your core categories, supplemented by syndicated data and snapshots of the broader category context. Many industries will have bespoke datasets and there are also neutral third-party providers such as Global Data, Euromonitor, Mintel, Economist Intelligence Unit etc.

Even if you are working on a brand present in one market you should consider looking at category dynamics in other markets – especially where the category may be more mature or is being disrupted.

Ensure your sales colleagues bring perspectives from customers and retailers about the category and cross-category dynamics for what can be learned.

COMPETITION

What do we mean by competition? When looking at competitors you should look at your current competitive set as well as smaller and emergent competitors. Look at their performance – who is outperforming the market and gaining share, who is declining? Consider what the strategic choices of each may be and what activities they are deploying and how effective they seem to be. Consider any innovation which has been launched in the last few years – how well is it doing, what is sticking, why is it working?

Consult interesting case studies, covering scale and insurgent brands which may still be in niche distribution and perhaps only available online.

What kind of data should you consider? Use the data you gather to look at category trends, but augment this with brand strength data, consumer panel data covering buyer profiles and purchasing dynamics, retail audit data to look at distribution, pricing, promotion, rate of sale etc., and media data to understand relative marketing investment overall and by channel. Also, look at any ad-hoc qualitative and quantitative data you may have conducted which may contain perspectives and references to competitors.

CONSUMER

What do we mean by consumer? Who is your target audience – considering both existing and potential buyers. How many of them are there? What are their lives like? How do they behave? What else do they buy? What are the triggers and barriers which influence their choices? How can you segment them based on attitude or behaviour, their motivations, or usage occasions?

What kind of data should you consider?   Remember that a penetration growth strategy requires maximizing reach, which in turn requires defining a sufficiently broad target of potential buyers to deliver new growth.

Use many of the same data sources you use to understand competitors, especially any consumer purchasing or usage panel data you may have. Look at brand strength data, any usage and attitude, demand space, or consumer segmentation data you may have.

Also look at syndicated data, data from your agencies on media buying habits, trends in consumer behaviour and attitude etc.

Having a view of your market through the lens of how many people participate and their characteristics complements a category view. It will help you determine growth potential and link changes in consumer behaviour to performance in category and business outcomes.

CUSTOMER/CHANNEL

What do we mean by customer/channel?   How is the route to consumer changing? Which channels – including on- and offline channels, direct to consumer, subscriptions etc. are growing and which are declining? What are the forces shaping these changes? Who are the key brands, platforms, and retailers, their strategic choices, and what are they focussing on for their shoppers? How might this evolve over time?

What kind of data should you consider?   This is an area where you need to tap into your sales and category teams. Additionally, there is publicly available information on retailer strategies and campaigns, syndicated reports, and trends on the future of retail, shopping, and so forth.

Agencies supplying retail audits, category strategy projects etc. will also be good sources of thought leadership in this space.

COMMERCIAL/COMPANY

What do we mean by commercial/company?   This comes down to understanding your own organization's growth expectations in the next three to five years and the choices it has made. Where your organization is made of specific business units, consider the role and desired outcomes for each, and any tramlines such as expected profit margins, manufacturing thresholds, and other information.

The outcomes your business seeks to deliver in the next three to five years, especially revenue, volume, and profit are the critical context for this work – broken down by brand within your portfolio they provide a guide to the level of growth your brand needs to deliver. The work you do on your brand should also inform and iterate that total organizational expectation – is the ambition under- or over-stretching based on the market and consumer opportunity? What investment is required to deliver it, and what should you focus on to achieve it?

What kind of data should you consider?   Look at your total business strategy, each business unit's share of delivering that strategy, and how the business has translated overall strategic choices into a roadmap. Be clear on short- and long-term commercial goals, and the commercial, supply, HR, and other work which will work with your brand strategy to ensure the organization is fit to deliver the growth.

How to conduct the 6Cs audit

ASSIGN AN OVERALL OWNER
This person's role is to coordinate, set the time frame for the audit, compile and maintain a catalogue of the relevant data sources, and set up the working session from which you will derive key implications.

ASSIGN OWNERS FOR EACH OF THE SECTIONS
It makes sense to divide up the audit, assigning different components to people who may have specialist knowledge or understanding. This enables you to benefit from divergent points of view before you bring it together, avoiding consensus thinking.

The task of each owner is to compile the information, and then to synthesize what they have learned. The inputs should be comprehensive and detailed. This is the one occasion over a year you take time to deeply understand the implications of what is going on out there.

Once you get into the habit of this, each year becomes more of a case of understanding what's changing in your assumptions versus building a comprehensive picture of the external system in which your business operates.

Audit section owners should prepare a synthesis of what's emerging about the situation you face through the lens of that 'C' as pre-read to a working session. Though the inputs may be rigorous, the output should be focussed – it helps to specify a limit of two pages of a Word document or two to three slides.

As part of the brief, you may ask section owners to highlight what's consistent, what's increasing in importance or is new, and what's decreasing in importance or no longer relevant. This creates an evidence-based narrative, highlighting headwinds and tailwinds.

The overall owner might specify a format and approach so that the different sections can be brought together coherently as a pre-read.

RUN A WORKING SESSION

Consider who should be present. A working session is a significant investment of time, so think carefully about the right mix of people. You certainly want good cross-functional representation – marketing, sales, research and development, and finance, but consider the cast carefully to include those people who you think will make the most significant contribution, bring challenge, and fresh perspectives.

There is a balance. With a broader group of people, you may be able to get more buy-in to the overall narrative regarding the most significant forces shaping your brand, but it may also slow down the process as you will have more input to manage, not all of it incremental.

My recommendation for this work is to keep the group relatively tight, but that does not mean a senior group only. Select a broader mix based on capability and recognize there are other ways to involve and manage senior and junior colleagues. Strike the balance between this being an important event and creating the fear of missing out.

The objectives of the working session are to debrief the key findings from each area and group themes. It can be done over a morning or afternoon, ideally linked to a working session on brand ambition, and a day on translating your findings into opportunities for growth which we will consider in Chapters 10 and 11. It makes sense to integrate the brand performance review covered later in this chapter into this working session and provide the effective brand audit output as part of the pre-read.

Proposed flow for brand audit session:

- Set up and introduction (30 mins)
- 6Cs debrief part one (60 mins)
- Break (15 mins)

- 6Cs debrief part two (60mins)

- Long break (60 mins)

- Brand performance review (30 mins)

- Clustering themes (30 mins)

- Initial prioritizations (30 mins)

- Break (15 mins)

- Sharing in plenary, reflections, and close (45 mins)

All participants should have digested pre-read in advance, and completed a pre-task to capture their top five opportunities and threats.

In the 6Cs debrief, each section owner takes 10 minutes to highlight key opportunities and threats, followed by a moderated discussion to capture any areas which attendees wish to build on and believe are important but not included. With Post-it notes and flip charts, an understanding of each 'C' can be created with input from everyone.

The order in which the 'Cs' should be covered is up to you, but there is a logic to how they have been presented here. It makes sense to start with 'Context' as it is the broadest, and end with 'Company' as although it is critical to link the outside world to the business's aims, leading with that tends to constrain thinking to the status quo.

Once each area has been considered, take time first to cluster themes within each 'C' to see where most energy is. If you are working on a portfolio of brands within a category this is where it makes sense to split into brand groups.

For the second and final exercise, look across 'Cs' for connections and patterns. From this, a smaller group may create a summary of the top two or three threats and two or three opportunities the brand faces. If you are working on more than one brand it makes sense to compare where you get to at this point. Are the lists similar or different? Consider the role they play in your portfolio – the target audience and consumption occasion – and ask whether you need to think in a more nuanced way about the threats and opportunities.

In this session you do not need to consider implications and actions. In fact, it is important to keep people in the mind set which ignores operational implications for the moment.

Reflections

What are the most important data inputs for your brand to understand the situation it faces?

Are these inputs catalogued, accessible, with people clear on their relative strengths and limitations and how to use them?

Are there any big gaps in your data and if so, how do you plan to address them?

What are the biggest opportunities and threats your brand faces on its path to growth?

How do I conduct growth potential analysis?

As you assess the opportunities and threats you have identified you must consider the growth potential of each.

This will enable you to understand the headroom for growth and set a stretching but achievable goal for your brand, which can then be translated into a business goal such as revenue.

As well as enabling you to set a measurable target, this analysis will provoke you to figure out the connections between the opportunities and threats you have uncovered in your 6C audit, and understanding of the different consumer targets and segments where growth might come from – brand buyers, competitor brand buyers, non-category buyers.

Being able to articulate the connection between the forces shaping consumer behaviour, the actions you might need to take to recruit consumers, and the change in revenue which will result is one of the simplest ways to demystify the connection between the effectiveness of your marketing activity and growth.

A note on comparing internal data and external data

Put simply, revenue is a function of the number of people who buy your brand, the frequency with which they buy your brand, and the amount they spend each time.

Sales = Number of people who buy × amount they buy (frequency × amount per occasion) × price paid

The difference between sales to a consumer and revenue earned by your business is accounted for mainly by taxes, and retailer or wholesaler profit margins. Assuming there is no significant change in these things, and you can measure sales to a consumer accurately, the magnitude of growth or decline should be similar. Whilst the absolute numbers might differ between internal and external data, it is the relative movements and trends over time that are of most interest and importance.

The only other key factor worth considering is that of potential lag. If, for example, you are selling directly, or through reseller websites where you fulfil sales, there should be no lag in your datasets. There is likely to be a lag where you are selling physical products through retailers – especially where there is a wholesaler or distributor between you and the retailer, or consumers pay an initial deposit, as they may for a service such as a vacation.

This lag should be predictable where stock held in trade is managed in line with demand, and it is easy to see this pattern if you reconcile datasets – meaning an unexpected drop off in your sales out can be a precursor to seeing a change in consumer demand, and a sudden upturn in consumer demand can predict an upturn in your sales. This pattern is less visible in instances where stock levels held in trade fluctuate perhaps because a business uses that to manage its own sales targets within acceptable accounting practices.

How do I assess growth potential?

Growth potential analysis asks the fundamental question; where will future growth come from?

We know from significant cross category analysis that growth in penetration correlates most with sustained revenue growth, not an increase in the frequency of purchase. As we discussed earlier in the book, most people have a natural ceiling for their purchase requirements in a given category.

So, will growth come from recruiting people not currently buying the category? Will it come from people who are already buying the category but not your brand? Perhaps for a market leader growth may come from getting existing buyers to fulfil more of their requirements using your brand? Perhaps it is about getting new buyers by entering adjacent categories or even markets.

We can sum these approaches to penetration growth as:

New faces – growth from new category or existing category buyers who come in or back into your brand.

New spaces – growth from having your brand present in new or adjacent categories and/or occasions that get your buyers to buy your brand for some of their other needs.

New places – growth which comes from entering new channels, or new markets making your product available to new consumers or consumers on different shopping missions.

An alternative way to look at this is using an Ansoff matrix which considers new and existing markets, and new and existing products or services as sources of growth.

To do this well you need good estimates about the size of these different sources of growth, an understanding of who the consumers or occasions are, and how you might target them.

Use segmentation data, secondary syndicated data, or population data to get the best assumptions you can.

For example, to understand the potential for 'new faces', you need to understand:

How many buyers are there in the category over a given period?

How many buyers buy your brand? Who are they, what are their motivations?

How many buyers buy the category but not your brand? Who are they, what do they buy, and why? What are their motivations?

How many people do not buy the category?

How is this likely to change, if at all, in the next few years?

For this last question it's worth trying to break it down to understand the potential. For example, are there people who do not buy the category because they simply do not experience the relevant motivation? Or are there barriers which you will not be able to overcome (consider trying to convert a vegan to meat, or a non-car owner to buy car insurance)? Converting buyers into a category is hard so consider the barriers – price, relevance, life stage etc. Are there people who may be more predisposed who are lower hanging fruit?

You can plot each potential group on an x–y chart as illustrated in Figure 9.1, with x a hard measure of the number of available buyers in each group, and on the y axis a more qualitative view on how accessible they are from hard at the bottom to easy at the top.

FIGURE 9.1 Size of prize versus accessibility

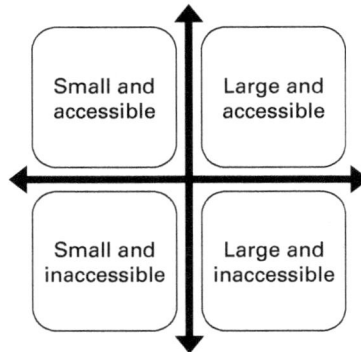

For example, in emerging markets you may find that there are large numbers of non-category buyers in lots of common consumer goods categories. An examination of these groups may lead to you conclude that, for most, affordability is a critical issue, and in the most part they are content with the alternative they use – for example, they may use an all-purpose soap in place of laundry detergents or household cleaning products. There may, however, be a mirror image of your current category users with a similar demographic profile who may represent a sizeable and accessible group who you may be able to recruit. What might the trigger be to recruit them?

Similarly, among category buyers who do not buy your brand, you may hypothesize discrete groups based on your data suggesting why they may not buy you – they are not aware of you, they may not have strong perceptions of your brand. Remember the meaningful, different, and salient framework from Chapter 6! For brands which are seeding and scaling, unaware consumers are likely to be the biggest source of growth.

For mature brands where penetration is strong, you may be reaching saturation, and this is where you should consider the opportunity for new spaces or new places. Use data to quantify the size of these adjacent subcategories, channels, or markets and consider what a share goal might be for your brand, and how accessible they are.

With this approach, the x axis gives you a measure of size, but the y axis acts as a proxy for complexity and therefore relative weight of investment you may need to unlock that growth. Defending your existing buyers and recruiting select groups with more of a propensity towards your brand is likely to be the most reliable way of growing, but it may not meet your growth ambition, meaning you may consider a third group.

This growth potential analysis gives you the basis on which you should conduct target audience understanding. Who are they? What are their lives like? What are their motivations? What is their category behaviour? What is their relationship to your brand? What are the triggers and barriers? What kind of messages do they respond to? What influences their choices? What is their media behaviour?

The point of this is make the connections between the potential for growth your brand has within its market, and the opportunities and threats you have uncovered in your 6Cs audit.

This analysis will also enable you to construct a consumer goal to quantify how to deliver your business goal. If for example, you are targeting 10% value growth net of inflation, and you assume the average amount bought by your consumers will be stable, what is the change in buyer numbers that will deliver this growth? What share of this change in absolute buyers needs to come from each of the segments you have identified?

This will create a measurable, numerical goal linked to your business growth which will help guide investment choices.

Reflections

What are the different consumer groups or occasions you might target to achieve your growth ambitions?

How sizeable and how accessible are each of these groups?

How many of these groups might you need to target to grow?

What might be the barriers you may need to overcome and the triggers you may need to deploy?

What are the connections you see between the opportunities and threats you have uncovered and the measurable size and nature of different growth opportunities?

How strong is my brand?

Understanding the strengths and weaknesses of your brand allows you to understand your readiness to tackle the potential opportunities and threats you have uncovered in your 6Cs audit. There are two key elements – a brand performance review and a brand audit.

A brand performance review covers the effectiveness of brand campaigns, including both mental and physical availability over a 12–18 month period. As well as understanding what to stop, start, and continue, it can flush out quick wins such as distribution opportunities.

A brand audit conducts a full safety inspection on the brand against the critical dimensions of a brand building model. Not to be confused with brand positioning tools, brand building models come in many forms like wheels, triangles, and squares and capture the outputs of good brand building practices against a range of measurable criteria, or check lists. We will consider a model below, Figure 9.2.

Brand performance review

As with the 6Cs audit, the inputs to this may be rich, but the aim is to get to a succinct story. Set a limit of no more than three pages of text or six slides. This creates focus on the most important things.

A good performance review should reveal what we know about the drivers of brand performance – from the nuts and bolts of distribution, changes in promotional spend, the intensity of competitive activity, pricing, and innovation, and the relative share and effectiveness of communications, through to the effectiveness of brand campaigns and activities, and understanding changing consumer attitudes to the brand and the impact of culture and the environment.

Datasets are similar to the 6Cs and it helps to bring perspectives from sales and category management colleagues to ensure the review is robust and holistic.

Consider things such as:

- Brand performance by season and period, by core product or service lines and innovation
- Current pricing performance – are you achieving the pricing index versus the category or key competitors you have established?
- How has your promotional intensity changed? Is it where you expected it to be? Are you promoting as frequently and at the depth you had planned and are your promotions profitable? Are they getting your brand the digital or physical displays which get you noticed and get incremental sales versus subsidizing sales of people who were going to buy your brand anyway from your main fixture?

- Do you have the right products in distribution and the optimum range available by store type and channel?
- What are the results and returns from your other physical availability work – seasonal campaigns, shopper programmes etc.?
- What have you learned about the return on investment of your brand campaigns and activities?

Brand audit

Many businesses, especially multi-brand, multi-market ones have a brand model, focussed on the criteria they believe are critical for success in their industry.

Brand models can be practical in that you can evaluate on a single page how strong the building blocks of your brand are, and pinpoint where action is required to strengthen a particular foundation. It gets everyone on the same page across the organization, and as it covers off all four of the classic Ps of marketing – Product, Place, Price, Promotion, plus mental and physical availability – it brings marketing and sales activities together. Organizations 'traffic light' these factors using a combination of data, consumer research evidence, and judgement.

In the context of the marketing audit, brand models serve to identify strengths and weaknesses which we can combine with the opportunities and threats to growing penetration derived from the 6Cs framework.

Below is a suggested effective brand building model – to ensure your brand is as distinctive as possible and more likely to be chosen over alternatives. It works conceptually across different types of brands – be it a physical product, a digitally delivered service or app with a free to use version, an ad-free version, and a premium version with extra features, a sports team delivering content across different channels or platforms, a travel or insurance company with different product or service bundles to meet the needs of different households or travellers, and so forth.

However, it should be adapted to reflect the specific nature of your category and brand. Make it specific to what matters to you, adapt the language, and ideally design it in line with your brand to make it proprietary. Consider how you will evaluate each element to be consistent and avoid bias.

FIGURE 9.2 Effective brand building model

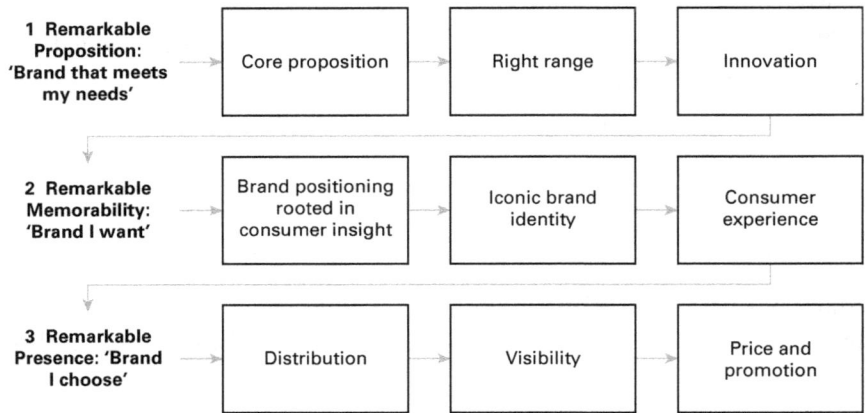

Let's define what these elements are succinctly:

1 REMARKABLE PROPOSITION: 'BRAND THAT MEETS MY NEEDS'
Core proposition: a competitive product or service that meets or exceeds consumer expectations.

- Consistent with the brand
- Delivers profit margin in line with business expectations
- Consistently equals or exceeds competition on desired characteristics of the consumption moment (e.g. sensory testing or user experience testing)

Right range: the right pricing, format, offering by channel, or consumer type to increase penetration and profitable revenue growth.

- Range architecture model including hero variants against which execution can be measured for key consumer types, consumption moments, and channels
- Based on clear channel segmentation and shopper understanding
- Enables brand to access different price tiers

Innovation: innovation that increases penetration by recruiting new consumers or accessing new spaces.

- Pipeline of innovation being developed and commercialized for test and launch

- Based on prioritization of consumer opportunities the brand can credibly access using new product, service, technology, etc.
- Meets or exceeds criteria for consumer, size of prize, and profitability

2 REMARKABLE MEMORABILITY: 'BRAND I WANT'

Brand positioning rooted in consumer insight: single-minded expression of what the brand should stand for in the mind of target consumers.

- Relevant to target consumers and their consumption moments
- Credible from the brand
- Distinctive from competitors
- Inspiring creative springboard

Iconic brand identity: remarkable visual brand codes that ensure the brand is instantly recognizable.

- Logo, colours, wordmark, communication style, tone of voice
- Distinct from the competition
- Owned by and associated with your brand exclusively (not the category)
- Suitable for and used in every touchpoint
- Inspiring creative springboard

Consumer experience: remarkable, relevant, engaging brand communication, content, and experiences in all touchpoints.

- Creative platform which brings brand positioning to life and integrates brand identity
- Inspires creative ideas which unlock defined opportunities to grow penetration across a range of consumer-facing touchpoints including communications, content, experiences, partnerships, product, and service design
- Based on understanding where, when, and how to connect effectively and efficiently with target audiences

3 REMARKABLE PRESENCE: 'BRAND I CHOOSE'

Distribution: available and in the widest possible distribution.

- Based on channel segmentation
- Right range in distribution and available to buy or experience
- Includes optimizing search on search engines and on retail websites or apps

Visibility: stands out in every buying situation.

- Permanent and secondary visibility materials to increase penetration
- Temporary visibility materials to maximize cultural moments and seasonal periods

Price and promotion: least amount of the most effective promotions to increase penetration and maximize profitable revenue

- Strategic pricing guidelines versus category or key competitor including headline pricing and target average selling price consistently executed and updated as the environment changes
- Right depth and frequency of promotions to increase penetration, integrated with brand activity
- Meets targets for efficiency (cost to implement) and effectiveness (in line with incremental profit and revenue expectations)

Many brands traffic light each element of the model

- Is the element in place, up to date, and validated?
- Is it executed in relevant touchpoints consistently?
- Is it keeping pace with the market and competitive environment?

Reflections

What has been working well on my brand to increase brand penetration?

What has been less effective on my brand in increasing brand penetration?

What are the strengths of my brand?

What are the weaknesses of my brand?

10

What is my brand's ambition?

Let's recap. Right now we are clear on:

- the most significant opportunities and threats the brand faces to grow penetration from the 6Cs work;
- where growth might come from based on analysis of potential consumer targets;
- the strengths and weaknesses of the brand based on recent performance and an audit of the foundations of an effective brand.

In the next two chapters we will describe how to bring this together to create an effective brand strategy. For brands in multi-brand businesses, the first step of this is to establish the role the brand plays in the portfolio – its role in delivering the total business goals.

Brand ambition is comprised of three elements – clarity on the role the brand plays in your portfolio; an external or market and consumer view of the brand's potential for growth and appropriate investment; and the brand ambition itself – its vision, mission, and goal. If you refer to Figure 8.2, we are placing the roof on the brand strategy house.

Let's take these elements in turn.

How should I organize my portfolio?

In multi-brand businesses being clear on the role that different brands play is essential to ensure each gets the right level of focus and resource and plays its part in delivering the total business ambition. Often this is not the case – people running global brands find it is the smallest markets paradoxically hungry for resource while the biggest growth opportunities may not want their assistance. Within a market or single market multi-brand business resource is often split more evenly than it might be given the relative growth potential of different brands.

A model to frame portfolio choices

Introduced in the 1970s and still a strong reference point today, the Boston Consulting Group (BCG) growth share matrix is a great way to start the conversation on portfolio choices. It has two key dimensions – relative market share and growth rate. Relative market share is expressed as a brand's market share relative to the market leader.

This model has four quadrants:

High share, high growth. These are scale brands with strong future potential, called 'stars' in the model and ripe for investment. They are typically in the scaling stage of growth.

High share, low growth. These are maturing brands, often in mature categories with less headroom for growth. With less potential the priority is to milk them for profit to invest in the stars. As well as considering appropriate investment rates these are brands where maximizing profit by looking at cost of goods, having efficient formats etc. can make a massive difference.

Low share, high growth. The model calls these 'question marks' and the logic is either to invest or divest. Often businesses do neither with real intent. Given that these are the future stars and are brands in the seeding stage, it is essential to be deliberate – decide which are those on which you place your bets and invest accordingly. Sometimes organizations hope these brands will grow on their own, or chop and change investment from one to another too soon. You can't lose patience with a seeding brand – you must stick with it and be clear on the point at which you would stop investing.

Low share, low growth. Often called 'pets', these are brands which have neither scale nor growth potential. They eat up resource and should be sold or discontinued. This may not happen in a business with a short-term horizon or trading mindset as they may be worried about short-term revenue losses, not recognizing these brands stifle effective brand building for their 'stars' and future stars.

The model was popular – big brands make better returns, and brands with high growth rates have potential to create attractive future businesses.

Although market share remains an important measure, it is less predictive than it once was. Market share is reflective of how categories are defined in a retail space – they reflect how shoppers behave today. While categories may have been more stable in the past, technology has created much more opportunity for consumers to meet their needs in different ways – think about the transformation of the banking industry, the different ways we have to consume entertainment. This means that portfolio thinking for effective brand building needs some nuance.

It's still important to consider core financial measures – future revenue and profit, investment and return on investment, if you have that information. Alongside that you should consider brand and category stage of development, which roughly reflect the core BCG model criteria.

The key difference is, however, to increase focus on ensuring your portfolio reflects your understanding of evolving consumer trends and behaviour, and how they will impact category and sub-category growth. This means being more deliberate about managing experimentation in your portfolio – it will focus you more deliberately on ensuring you pick fewer 'question marks' to be future stars.

Aligned to this notion of experimentation is being smart about exploiting your scale brands with lower growth potential. Unless you can reinvent your brands into more profitable segments, as brands such as IBM and Nokia did in the past, you should maximize their profitability relentlessly by reducing cost of goods or service provision, having an efficiency mindset, and using their scale to ensure your brand investment is the right size.

Doing this will enable you to accelerate your star brands to reach their potential and give you more of a chance to make future stars.

Being rigorous should prompt more brutal conversations about the 'pets'. Even in the most sophisticated of businesses people struggle to let go of brands which do not play a role in future growth – either because they are declining and out of step with current consumer behaviour, or because they remain emotionally attached to them and the past. Overinvesting in this segment is common and spending resources on 'pets' limits the potential of stars and future stars.

Assigning portfolio roles

Though the BCG growth matrix remains a useful concept, the choices you make need translating into more descriptive names to help people in your organization understand the role and therefore focus on each brand. Here are some examples:

'Core', 'foundation', or 'fortress' might be how you describe the 'cash cows' or brands in the maturing stage of development. With scale, they generate revenue efficiently and therefore typically provide a strong contribution to your cost base and high levels of profitability to invest in the 'stars'.

Depending on the complexity of your portfolio you might want to differentiate within your 'stars' or those brands in the scaling stage of development. Medium-sized brands with faster growth might be 'accelerate' and larger ones 'scale', the difference between these being 'accelerate' brands will typically deliver more profitable revenue growth given their stage of development, and 'scale' brands should deliver increased profitability, approaching that of your core brands. Be careful of anti-competitive language, but if a brand is important in a particular segment to mitigate strong competition it might be termed a 'fighter'.

Finally, 'seed' or 'nurture' better describes those future bets than 'question marks' and captures a sense of their stage of development and how to treat them. You may also call out those brands which you want to remove resource from as 'deprioritize', or 'reignite or kill'.

Other lenses on portfolio

In Chapter 6, we considered how businesses should develop a view of their marketplace based on the drivers of consumer choice, or 'demand spaces'. This creates a complementary view of where your brand portfolio plays versus consumer demand and competitors.

Such a view might split the market according to different motivations and perhaps segment sub-motivations and pricing tiers within these – value, mainstream, premium, and perhaps super-premium, if relevant. Further cuts might be customer segments, product, or service types.

In this fictitious example, table 10.1, a functional or sports beverage market might be made up of segments including 'Hydration', 'Performance', 'Recovery', and 'Natural Energy' displaying the percentage of the total market each segment represents in volume, value, and profit, or what it is predicted to be.

Assuming you further segment each by price point, you can place your brands and those of your competitors in the grid to give you a consumer view of the extent to which you effectively cover consumer needs at different price points, where there may be white space, and where there might be most intense competition.

TABLE 10.1   Example market segmentation

	Hydration 35% volume 10% value	Performance 30% volume 35% value	Recovery 25% volume 35% value	Natural energy 10% volume 20% value
Premium				
Mainstream				
Value				

In this fictitious example the two largest segments by volume are also the cheapest, whereas the two smaller segments achieve higher price points. If the business had a foothold in 'hydration' and 'performance' segments which also happened to be highly competitive and had developed value offerings, it may choose to focus energy on or expand into 'recovery' and 'natural energy'.

This exercise would enable it to call out category priorities such as:

• defend core hydration and performance segments;

• win in performance;

• develop natural energy proposition.

It is not uncommon for brands to conduct this exercise using a more orthodox retail view of the category, especially where this is drawn more along product type lines than it is on usage – think insurance types, financial products, classes of vehicles, personal care. A shopper view is useful if it includes focus on the changing dynamics of those segments.

Bringing it all together, a simple portfolio strategy will capture:

• the overarching trends shaping the category landscape;

• the category and subcategory priorities for growth – typically category segments, but may be consumer segments.

• a clear role and ambition for each brand with desired goals.

Those goals might include revenue and profit growth in absolute or percentage growth terms, and what they represent today as a percentage of your brand's revenue or profit in three to five years' time.

Reflections

Do you have a portfolio strategy aligned to business goals?

Does it make clear choices based on deep understanding of the market, consumer opportunity, and attractiveness of different market segments?

Is each brand owner aware of what this means for their brand and the role it plays?

How should I consider marketing investment choices?

Before we get to the question of brand ambition, it is worth addressing what portfolio thinking means for brand investment choices. We talked above about the benefit of a business and portfolio strategy in ensuring resources were allocated to priority initiatives, and the same principle should be true for deciding how to apportion your finite marketing budgets in service of the most profitable growth.

The conversation on effective brand investment is always a live one within the marketing industry. It has become hotter in the early 2020s given the exceptionally challenging situation we have all been living and working in. These times have been characterized by major disruption in so many industries. Years of shockwaves in supply and logistics impacting cost of goods, inflation, and political and economic uncertainty. While industries have benefitted through the acceleration of underlying consumer trends – brands such as Zoom and Teams – all have had a rollercoaster of fluctuating demand.

Under pressure of cost price inflation and low growth in the last couple of years, we've built stronger net revenue management muscles – beyond the more obvious headline pricing, shrinkflation, and portfolio management, brands work hard behind the scenes to obliterate inflation in their cost of goods by sourcing ingredients, raw materials, and even changes to primary and secondary packaging to save costs while delivering an identical or improved consumer experience without degrading their environmental or social impact.

With the likelihood that the next several years will be equally as disrupted, we need courage to make bold and responsible investment decisions on our brands to stimulate demand, take market share, and ensure pricing remains resilient.

The uncertainty of the external environment has also created performance anxiety for many brands – what if latent category demand is less than expected? What if there are unforeseen increases in the cost base? Brand investment remains vulnerable, and that's why we have seen brands be cautious at best for the last couple of years.

Let's assume for a moment, though, that the confidence is there, and your business wants to seize the moment to get ahead. What should you be thinking about? For businesses managing portfolios of brands, this is where the conversation should start. It must come before consideration of investment in individual brands.

So how much marketing spend should go across each of the brands in your portfolio? Start with your portfolio thinking– clear as you are on the different roles for your brands and the different levels of revenue and profit you want them to contribute. Even with this in place many businesses still split their budgets across brands roughly in line with their relative size. The first thing to look at therefore is the split of your brand investment, not in comparison with your revenue today, but against your future portfolio ambition.

Differential levels of investment can come from comparing the relative future profit potential of your brands. You can determine this future profit potential by considering the latent category and segment growth of each brand for the next two to three years, and its track record in growing market share which may increase its share of future category revenue. Also consider the effectiveness of brand investment if you have that data – relatively speaking, which brands return more per dollar or pound spent on marketing? Finally, factor in the different gross margin of different brands to work out the profit from this future growth and arrive at a different view on how attractive investing in each brand may be. In essence, give funding more generously to those brands which will deliver better incremental profit from the future and steal from those which won't.

Strong brands can judiciously take a pause in brand investment, often without experiencing decline in the short term, albeit ensuring the pause doesn't create false confidence and break the good habit of maintaining continuous levels of spend. This may well be true of your 'core' or 'foundation brands' whose scale may mean they inherently display stronger return on investment but given their low growth a dollar or pound spent on them may actually be less effective than spending it on 'accelerate' or 'scale' brands.

Though the industry rule of thumb of investing ahead of a brand's share of voice has strong evidence, because of how significant digital media spend in walled gardens, closed platforms such as Google and Meta, has become it is tricky to measure. The approach also overlooks the portfolio choices and finite total budget businesses have – you can't typically overinvest in excess share of voice across all your brands, so picking winners is important.

As well as the prompts above, you can challenge your thinking further by looking at brand strength relative to competition and its relative market share – that is your market share relative to the strongest competitor. Businesses often overspend on their biggest brands which can be the most efficient and miss opportunities for brands which are of similar size to competitors but may have stronger equity – really investing hard behind those can cause the biggest swing within your consumers' brand repertoires in your favour. This is how to win when your brand is head-to-head with others in repertoires of acceptable brands.

Though having things like marketing mix modelling can strengthen some of this thinking, most of the inputs here – likely category and segment growth, relative market share, brand strength, and profitability are foundational pieces of data for marketers.

In a world where businesses can be hesitant to invest and where there are finite resources, these approaches can help you place your bets, demonstrate the likely incremental profit between different approaches, and ultimately invest behind the most profitable growth. As you succeed in delivering what you laid out to your partners, you will start to build the case for investment across all brands, ideally getting to the point where it is finance and general management asking how much more you can spend.

Reflections

How is brand investment decided today in your organization?

Does it consider the future profit opportunity?

Are you polarizing your allocation of marketing spend across brands in line with growth potential, or are you spending in line with brand size or an expected reinvestment rate?

How might you think more selectively about how you deploy available budget?

What is my brand ambition?

Great brand strategy and planning begins with the end in mind. Understanding what you want to achieve on the brand over a longer-term horizon is essential to ensure your effort, resource, and activities go towards a single-minded and shared view about what success looks like – for you, your team and employees, your consumers and customers, investors, and other stakeholders including society and the environment.

In Chapter 5 we called out the importance of a brand having a clear mission, based around what the business sees as its role or purpose in the world. Brand ambition builds on this by articulating the brand's role in the portfolio, its vision, and mission, and a stretching goal or target.

Stretching goal

Having a stretching goal is about quantifying what the brand aims to deliver in a given time frame, be it three or five years. A time frame is important as it gives you a destination from which to work back, but within a horizon which you can predict with some degree of certainty. Thinking too long term is meaningless – no one can credibly predict what will happen, and as a result it becomes difficult for people to relate to, especially as most of them realistically won't be involved in the brand in that time and therefore may have no commitment or 'skin in the game'.

A three- to five-year horizon is meaningful as you can translate the ambition into building blocks for growth based on your understanding of the current situation your brand faces and foresight into what's to come. Typically, most brands will work on a three-year horizon which correlates with the life span of your team, and a typical brand building cycle, often extrapolating the further out years.

Good data is the foundation for a stretching goal, and this is something you should revisit based on a bottom-up view of the work we looked at in Chapter 9. The process is iterative.

Think about:
  Category dynamics

- Your brand's track record of growth
- Your prediction for likely category growth in the next three to five years
- Your brand's track record in gaining share

Consumer dynamics

- The universe of potential consumers in your brand's segments and categories
- Your brand's current penetration and the headroom to grow
- The likelihood and cost of acquiring new consumers

Use the growth potential analysis to determine from which consumer targets growth will come. How many new buyers will come from 'new faces' and, if relevant, 'new spaces' and 'new places'? This will give you a specific and measurable goal regarding the change in penetration which will support the overall revenue goal you set for your ambition.

The work you have done should help you interrogate these numbers and ask 'what if …' based on the potential impact and likelihood of the things you have identified.

From these inputs create a low, medium, and high scenario. 'Low' might be simply continuing to deliver growth which is consistent with what you have been delivering recognizing any fluctuations in the category growth rate or limitations in the available consumer base. 'Medium' would push this further, perhaps considering more aggressive investment, growth in adjacent spaces. 'High' would reflect your highest level of ambition – pushing more aggressively core growth, adjacent spaces, and perhaps opportunities for growth such as new market entries.

Typically, the numerical element of a brand ambition includes core financial measures, penetration, and perhaps market share numbers. In a not-for-profit context, financial measures may be replaced by fundraising income, scale of impact, or other critical measures of success.

In each instance capture the goal, and the assumptions about the market, consumers, activities, and investment levels which will generate the outcome.

In *Stretchonomics*, Pye and Wright (2018) talk about stretch ambition versus stretch commitment. They encourage teams to take a stand and create a target which feels just out of reach. Their model helps navigate between data and belief – if you set too stretching a goal without your or the organization's commitment you are dreaming and will create unmet expectations with consequences. If, however, you have high commitment to a target which reflects a lack of ambition you are missing opportunities and opening the door to competitors. The provocation in the model is to find the stretch zone – beyond what makes you comfortable, but which balances ambition and commitment from your team and the organization.

This is a helpful model as setting a brand ambition is a combination of maths and psychology. You need the right numbers and the right assumptions, but use the process to make a collective leap of faith and be able to inspire your organization.

Vision and mission

Brands sometimes talk about having a North Star. This may be broken down into vision and mission, sometimes one or the other or both. Vision describes the end point – 'being #1', 'being an icon of …' – whereas mission describes what you are going to do to achieve it in a more action-oriented way – 'champion …', 'enable …', 'create …'.

As we saw from the examples of mission in Chapter 5, including Nike, Lush, and Airbnb, this is about creating an inspiring statement which defines how, why, and for whom we will create value, expressed in a way which will motivate the team to deliver it.

Think:

Nike Brand Ambition

Vision: To be the most authentic, connected, and distinctive brand.

Mission: To bring inspiration and innovation to every athlete in the world.

Goal: Insert revenue, profit, penetration, market share, image statements etc. as relevant.

If we achieve our vision:

- How will we have positively impacted our consumers?
- How will we have performed versus our competitors?
- What will we be known and celebrated for?

Crystallize this into a vision statement which describes the outcome – for us, our consumers, and our business. Also craft a mission statement which will focus everyone on what you will need to do to achieve it.

It takes time to develop something legendary like Nike's mission to bring inspiration and innovation to every athlete in the world. A powerful statement such as this motivates your team and employees and acts as a short cut – are we spending our time on mission-critical things over *the short and long term?* Contrast this with how Nike sees its vision; *'the most authentic, connected, and distinctive brand'* – an inspiring and measurable outcome, not an action.

Brands typically connect the stretching goal to their ambition. In so doing the brand is clear on the value it seeks to create and is single-minded about how it will do it. As we discussed in Chapter 5, this is powerful when it is meaningful to different stakeholder groups, and less so when it is written in bland corporate language. Ask yourself:

- Could this ambition be true of any other brand or business?
- Is it grounded in something of value to consumers and customers?
- Will it motivate my team and organization?
- Will it inspire and guide action?

With the help of their creative agencies, brands sometimes translate their ambition into an inspiring manifesto, bringing to life the kinds of actions the brand will and will not do as a result to deliver it, what it will feel like, and so on.

Developing a brand ambition can be completed in a morning, following on from a working session understanding the external environment, determining growth potential, and reviewing the strengths and weaknesses of your brand.

In groups, spend about 90 minutes on the overall goal or stretch target, and 90 minutes on expressing the vision and mission. Remember to do this in the context of the role the brand plays in the portfolio and organization's total ambition. Iterate your work to create razor-sharp and motivating statements.

Reflections

What is your brand's ambition?

Does it make clear the role the brand plays in the total organization's goals, the brand's goals, its vision and its mission?

Are the elements well connected and logical?

Is it stretching?

Are people familiar with it across the organization?

How might you further develop your brand ambition to bring people together against a common but stretching goal?

References

BCG growth share matrix, www.bcg.com/about/overview/our-history/growth-share-matrix (archived at https://perma.cc/L4QG-49TE)

Pye, N and Wright, J (2015) *Stretchonomics*, Silvertail Books, Kidderminster, UK

11

How do I prioritize opportunities for growth?

How do I make sense of my marketing audit?

This chapter will help you break down your brand ambition further by identifying the two or three long-term priorities for growth, the next level of our brand strategy house (see Figure 8.2). This is about determining the red thread which connects understanding of the external environment and your ambition for growth to the activities you execute in market.

There is a logical sequence to this combining rigour and creativity. Doing this well will enable you to move effectively between the micro and the macro elements of your brand plan – micro being the activities which help you win in market, and macro being the long-term future you seek to create for your brand and business – your ambition.

Let's walk through this step by step, defining terms as we go. In so doing you are starting to translate long-term opportunities for growth into investment choices and ultimately each individual execution the consumer will see, moving them towards choosing your brand over the competition.

As with Chapters 9 and 10, this can be workshopped with your team, which will build belief and alignment as well as capability muscles.

SWOT analysis

The first phase of this work is to compile a SWOT analysis. This is a simple model, enduringly popular since the 1960s. It's not the only suitable tool but is useful for sifting through the audit you have completed and shifting from understanding to prioritization. It's unlikely you would present or share a SWOT analysis more broadly than within your team – see it as the workings out which help you frame the choices you make.

SWOT is composed of four boxes – strengths, weaknesses, opportunities, and threats. Strengths and weaknesses are focussed internally on your brand and organization, while opportunities and threats are from the external environment, in this instance specifically related to penetration growth.

This distinction is useful as you may find that, in the brand strategy and planning process, colleagues are drawn back into the internal world of the organization, even occasionally mistaking an action the brand might take as an opportunity. Putting this model together will ensure your focus remains first and foremost on generating opportunities to grow penetration before defining solutions.

Use the outputs of your 6Cs and brand audit workshop to synthesize the situation your brand faces. You should aim for a maximum of five opportunities and five threats and attempt to rank them.

For strengths and weaknesses, take the salient points from the brand performance review and 'effective brand' audit. You may already have summarized these if you completed the reflections exercise at the end of Chapter 9. This encapsulates learning from recent brand activity, especially brand campaigns and activities which have been effective in growing penetration, and areas which have been less effective. In addition, using the traffic lights from the brand audit, categorize key strengths (green elements) and weaknesses (red elements).

You do not need to catalogue everything. You should identify the most salient points of the analysis. It is typical at this stage to have too much information. You should limit yourself to listing no more than five strengths and weaknesses. Ask yourself how significant a contributor to growth each of the strengths are, and how significant a barrier to growth each weakness is. This will enable you to focus on fewer things with greater impact.

The conversations to get to this synthesis are important. You are not leaving behind the great work you have done to get thus far, but making choices. Debate them in your group. Be conscious of the biases present in the working environment – such as the impact of seniority, groupthink, and status quo bias. To foster rigour in the conversation it is useful to lean into differences of opinion. If someone wants to champion a specific strength or weakness, ask them to prepare a defence. Ask them to consider why they are passionate about the area and provide evidence to support it.

To do this well, appoint a decision-maker and a separate challenger as 'devil's advocate'. In a workshop environment the pace is such that people may not listen deeply but be waiting to make their point. This technique can be effective in ensuring you focus on the right things, move on with a sense of alignment, and practice deep listening. Where you have differing opinions, appoint roles, give a short period for reflection and preparation, allow three minutes for defending the proposition, three for devil's advocate, succinctly collect any points not covered, decide, and move on.

Opportunities and threats

A well-constructed opportunity or threat will typically contain a quantified observation about something happening in the market (consumer, category, segment, channel, occasions etc.) and why (trend, driver) which the brand can capitalize on for growth, or needs to overcome to avoid decline. During this exercise people may reflect on activities being carried out by their brand but these are not opportunities or threats – they are brand activities, not consumer opportunities.

As a checklist, ask:

- Is this opportunity or threat an evidence-based view of what might positively or negatively affect penetration?
- Does it explain why this is the case?
- Is it specific about the consumer group, channel, customer, occasion, trend, market gap, or motivation?
- Is it something my brand can credibly access or address?

Each opportunity or threat should quantify the change not just present it as a general observation. Remember that brand actions such as 'Launch ...', 'Increase distribution ...' etc. are not opportunities.

Think carefully about whether each opportunity or threat is relevant to your brand. They may be more suitable for other brands in your portfolio. For example, purchasing directly through social media channels such as TikTok may be growing rapidly amongst young adults. This may be an opportunity, but only if your target audience is present on the channel and buying other brands in that way.

Rank your final selection according to their biggest potential impact on your growth using available data.

At this point in the thinking, we are focussed on opportunities and threats – strengths and weaknesses will play a role in helping us work out which we can best access.

Reflections

What is the impact of your brand's strengths on the opportunities and threats to growth?

What is the impact of your brand's weaknesses on the opportunities and threats to growth?

How do I turn opportunities into growth priorities?

The next step is to align on the most attractive consumer opportunities your brand can credibly access. It's tempting to hedge your bets and go after several opportunities, but it is rare to be able to fund each opportunity to a level sufficient to have real impact.

At this point, it can help to reframe threats as opportunities. For example, if you were a snack food manufacturer and saw a trend for health and well-being eroding your core business, you might reframe that as a growing need for healthy convenient snacking. You may decide you can access that with your core brand, with innovation on your brand, or another brand from your portfolio.

Two key dimensions help us evaluate the opportunities – size of prize, and ease of access. You can map these using a similar grid to the one we used in chapter 9, Figure 9.1.

For size of prize, consider how big the opportunity is today, how it will evolve in the next three to five years, and whether your brand can potentially access all of it or just a proportion.

For ease of access, you should consider internal and external factors:

Internal – is it consistent with business strategy, do you have the right assets and capabilities to access it (including things such as supply and manufacturing, technology), and will it get the level of focus it would require?

External – how competitive is the opportunity, does it involve changing existing consumer behaviour, and are there existing customer or channel barriers or even positive tailwinds?

Ensure you use the best data available to estimate size of prize and bring a cross-functional lens to plotting ease of access.

This exercise should yield two to three priority growth opportunities. Realistically, only mature, well-resourced brands can resource more than two opportunities, and it is fine, especially for seeding brands, to have only one.

Now articulate the change in consumer behaviour or attitude required for your brand to access this consumer opportunity. This takes you from the broad set of opportunities you considered in the 6Cs audit into something sharper and which will help create consumer-facing creative ideas, brand campaigns, and executions.

This is called different things in different organizations using similar approaches, and here we will call it the 'consumer challenge'.

Here are the ingredients you need to crystallize it into a clear statement:

- Who: your target audience
- What: we need them to think or do
- When and where: on which occasions/in which channels
- Instead of: what they do today

Later, we will also introduce the added notion of 'by' – to address the trigger or barrier your brand needs to leverage or overcome.

For example:

Let's assume New Insurance Co has seen new growth in the premium segment of car insurance after years of downward pressure on pricing and understands that this premium growth is driven by a wealthier segment of consumers concerned about the impact discounting may have on the quality of service in the event of a breakdown or accident. Old Insurance Co seems to be winning in this segment of the market. New Insurance Co might start to express its core consumer challenge as:

> How do I get affluent car owners to choose New Insurance Co instead of Old Insurance Co for their car insurance?

Other examples might be:

> How do I get cross-country cyclists to choose Brand X puncture-free tyres over Brand Y standard tyres on their weekend rides?

> How do I get busy families to choose McDonald's on their weekend home delivery takeaway occasions instead of KFC?

To unlock this challenge requires a powerful consumer insight, often based on leveraging triggers to purchase or overcoming barriers. Use the approach described in Chapter 7 on generating and applying insights. In the insight generation process, the salient points of the consumer opportunity you observed will be critical in helping you identify what will unlock the change in consumer behaviour you desire.

Do you remember our cycling example? *How do I get cross-country cyclists to choose Brand X puncture-free tyres over Brand Y standard tyres on their weekend rides?*

In that instance the brand had understood that cyclists worried about getting a puncture and found carrying a puncture kit to be a nuisance. The insight was '*getting a puncture can ruin a cyclist's day, cyclists want the freedom of cycling without worry*'.

What insight might help New Insurance Co? Beyond a competitive product it might be something to do with reassurance over service levels, transparency, or flexibility should personal circumstances change. Its affluent target might be unwilling to compromise on a cheaper product if they perceive the risk of inconvenience in the case of an accident or breakdown. Remember to consider what the consumer is seeking, what is credible from the brand, and what will unlock the change in attitude or behaviour.

What about McDonald's, who we saw in Chapter 7 had an opportunity for growth from home delivery? Might a relevant insight be something to do with having something for everyone on its menu, perceptions of food quality, experience, its perceived reliability versus competitors, or the role the brand is known for playing in UK life?

Now, it is becoming clearer what each brand might do to access the opportunity it has uncovered. Before thinking more about this, we should take a final step to quantify the growth potential of this and link it to our brand ambition.

Growth priorities

In this phase of brand strategy, we are constantly iterating and refining – seeking inspiration from what's shaping our consumer, but also checking that the choices we make will deliver the desired growth.

Just as with our brand ambition we combined a motivating statement of what we wanted to achieve with numerical goals; each growth priority needs to be measurable. This allows us to check if it holds sufficient potential to deliver the growth we need and see later if we are on track.

Using the growth potential analysis from Chapter 9 is a good way to check if your choices are sufficient, and to be clear on how you might measure them. If you remember, we simplified this to new faces, new spaces, new places.

From Chapter 2 we know brands are constantly churning buyers, so as well as recruiting new buyers, brands must also focus on ensuring existing buyers come back on their next occasion, ideally increasing their share of requirements. Filling the leaky bucket, by retaining as many of your existing buyers as you can, is essential to maintaining your existing business, never mind driving growth.

Does the challenge you have identified relate to new faces, spaces, or places?

- Existing faces – ensure existing buyers return and/or increase frequency, share of requirements, or how much they value your brand.
- New faces – get non-brand buyers to buy your brand.
- New spaces – get brand buyers and non-brand buyers to buy new offerings beyond your core offering.
- New places – access new buyers in new markets.

Don't forget premiumization! It's worth pulling out the ability to charge more explicitly as our focus on recruitment sometimes misses what is arguably your brand's most valuable growth driver – being able to hold or grow a premium position.

What is the annualized percentage growth rate required to deliver your brand's ambition? Based on what you learned from the growth potential analysis, is this feasible?

- What growth can your brand achieve from existing users, followed by new users?
- How much beyond that will have to come from innovation, and trickiest of all, launching in new markets?

Capture these answers as specifically as possible.

For example, if you need to grow revenue 10% each year to achieve your brand ambition, what is the change in penetration which will deliver this?

Let's illustrate this with an example. Assume for a moment we are New Insurance Co and the relevant insurance market has 10 million buyers a year, static over time. Let's say our brand has 2,500,000 buyers a year today, who each spend an average of £250 once a year.

If inflation is running at 5%, and prices to customers grow in line with this, it will deliver half our growth with a new average spend of £263. To achieve 10% growth means increasing the buyer base in year 1 by 120,000 people, totalling 2,620,000. In the base year brand penetration is 25%, and in year 2, 26%. What assumptions might we make to extrapolate this forward? In this instance, if we assume inflation drops to 3% in year three, the recruitment goal remains about the same to deliver the growth.

In this example, we would capture our growth priority as 'increase % market penetration by 1% each year by adding 120,000 new buyers to New Insurance Co's Car Insurance'.

New Insurance Co believes this level of recruitment to be achievable and sustainable. Let's say, however, this was not sufficient to deliver the desired level of growth; it might look at the other consumer opportunities it had identified and select the next one based on size of prize and ease of attainment.

Equally, New Insurance Co may believe it has capacity to do more and may decide to revisit and stretch its brand ambition.

So, for New Insurance Co, it has:

- a business goal of +10% revenue growth per annum;
- A growth priority increasing its penetration by 1% each year, recruiting 120,000 new buyers into car insurance from Old Insurance Co.

Let's link this back to the consumer challenge we articulated above.

How we get after this growth will depend on our insight. Let's assume for a moment New Insurance Co understands that perceptions of the speed and efficacy of response during and in the aftermath of a breakdown or accident are what its target consumers most value in the event of an accident or breakdown. New Insurance Co also understands that people perceive that Old Insurance Co does better than it on this critical dimension, even though it knows its own response times are better in reality.

With a clear insight you can translate a consumer challenge into a **brand growth priority:**

To access the opportunity to …

We must …

By …

For New Insurance Co this might be:

> *Brand growth priority statement*
>
> *To access the growing opportunity* in the premium car insurance market
>
> *We must* recruit affluent car owners concerned about the service they would receive in the event of an accident or breakdown
>
> *By* making New Insurance Co famous for having the fastest response times in the market

From the growth potential analysis New Insurance knows what is achievable and the scale of change required to deliver its business goal. This would be articulated as the following consumer goal:

> Increase %penetration in the next three years from 25% to 30% by adding 120,000 new buyers a year

For many brands, especially scaling and maturing brands, it is likely that there would be a second or perhaps third growth priority, which together would deliver the long-term brand ambition.

The definitions of these growth priorities, derived from a clear understanding of what growth is possible and from where (growth potential analysis) and how to unlock it (consumer opportunities), are the key pillars of a brand strategy.

For our cycle tyre brand our growth priority could be expressed as:

> *Brand growth priority statement*
>
> *To access the growing opportunity* for premium cycling accessories
>
> *We must* get cross-country cyclists to choose Brand X puncture-free tyres
>
> *By* dramatizing the freedom they get from using them
>
> Goal: Increase %penetration in the next three years from x% to y% by adding z thousand new buyers a year.

Where a brand has more than one area of focus, you need a growth priority statement for each. For example, if New Insurance Co determined that recruiting that number of buyers consistently each year was overly ambitious, it may work up its second consumer opportunity.

Once your brand can articulate this, you have made the leap from spotting a consumer opportunity to defining what you need to do to access it and being clear it has enough scale to deliver your brand ambition, and by extension that of your organization across the portfolio. You are also clear on how you will measure it as a financial (revenue) and consumer (penetration) goal.

Find a pithy way to express each growth priority to populate the effective brand house (Figure 8.2). Think about what you must do to access the growth for your brand, such as 'build trust', 'demonstrate quality', 'win occasion x' which will act as powerful shortcuts for everyone working on the brand.

Different organizations have different terminologies here. Some of your colleagues may be familiar with the 'OGSM' (Objectives, Goals, Strategies, Measurement) framework of which 'growth priorities' are broadly 'S' or 'Strategies'. You may hear the phrase 'jobs to be done' to describe broadly what is discussed here. Derived from a framework for innovation (Ulwick, 2016) it describes the consumer's situation, pain point, and desired outcome and therefore what the brand needs to say or do to help them. As such it is useful for brands beyond innovation (Ramli, 2023). The only caution in substituting 'jobs to be done' for 'growth priorities' is that the phrase has become overused, sometimes describing the action the brand is taking, its goal or objective, rather than capturing what it must do to meet its prospective consumer's need, or 'job to be done'.

Workshopping this phase

The work to identify the most powerful consumer growth opportunities and translate them into clear and measurable brand growth priorities follows on naturally from the marketing and brand audit, and the work to define your brand ambition.

It makes sense to have similar attendees and utilize the rich inputs into your audit work and the synthesized outputs.

With good preparation you can workshop this phase in a day, ideally following on soon after.

Inputs: Brand ambition, 6Cs audit, brand performance review, effective brand audit, growth potential analysis, and a completed SWOT analysis as pre-read

Tools and Templates: Brand ambition, SWOT analysis, consumer opportunities, consumer challenge, insight development, brand growth priority

If you work straight from a workshop on the audits the previous day, you can add in an hour to create the SWOT analysis, with one group taking 'strengths and weaknesses', and another 'opportunities and threats', and take a further 30 mins to debrief and finalize.

Growth priorities working session

- Set up and introduction (30 mins)
- SWOT analysis (90 mins)
- Break (15 mins)
- Crafting consumer challenge statements for top two or three opportunities, including insight generation (60 mins)
- Long break (1 hour)
- Crafting brand growth priority statements (90 mins)
  - Consumer opportunity
  - Goal
- Break (15 mins)
- Bringing it all together and sharing back (60 mins)

You can workshop different brands together and create time to challenge and build each other's outputs, or within one brand split the team so you can contrast and refine the best outputs.

Reflections

Are you clear on the two or three consumer opportunities which represent the biggest and most accessible options for growth for your brand in the next three to five years?

For each one are you clear on the consumer challenge, or the change in behaviour or attitude you need to tackle to access the consumer opportunity?

Are you clear on your brand growth priorities, or what your brand needs to do to access them?

Are you clear on the scale of change required to deliver your business goal in terms of new faces, new spaces, and new places and is this credible?

References

Ramli, J (2023) The JTBD formula for content marketing, news.marketingpowerups.com/p/the-jtbd-formula-for-content-marketing (archived at https://perma.cc/2FHJ-2MCP)

Ulwick, A (2016) *Jobs to Be Done: Theory to practice*, Idea Bite Press, Beaverton

12

What are the fundamentals of an effective brand strategy?

What is consumer-centric brand positioning?

Positioning is a critical element of effective brand building. It's worth starting with an obvious point which gets lost in many organizations, especially internally focussed ones; day to day, 'brand' is used to mean the products and services, or lines of products and services under a common name, that an organization sells. You may hear statements such as 'our brands are our most important assets' but realize people are referring to product or service lines.

A brand is intangible. For better or worse, a brand exists in the mind of your target audience. Your consumers hold your brand, their perceptions of your product or service based on prior usage, what they can recall from what they may have heard about it, or what communications they may have seen. As previously discussed, a brand with strong associations is more likely to come to mind in a buying situation and this will help you win against the competition.

Brand positioning describes where a brand sits in your target audience's mind relative to their motivations and to competitors. It is composed of all those things mentioned above – what a consumer thinks and feels about the brand, including what they understand the brand can do for them – ideally something salient, credible, remarkable, and compelling.

In our busy lives as marketers, brand positioning has often become relegated to a tool and a template, secondary to short-term sales and organizational targets. Brand positioning does use tools, but it is at heart the art and science of managing those seemingly intangible perceptions to the benefit of your organization long and short term. If you don't get this right, so much of the work which flows may not be effective.

How do we use brand positioning?

Proactively defining your desired brand positioning, based on realistic understanding of where your brand sits today, is a central facet of effective brand building. It acts like a beacon at all stages, ensuring that consumer-facing work continuously builds positive associations in line with changing culture, and that what the brand offers is grounded credibly in the product or service and how the consumer experiences them. By being present at relevant moments, your brand can achieve what great brands do – fulfil human motivations better than the competition.

Codifying brand positioning, based on real understanding of how the consumer sees your brand today versus the competition enables you to:

- make clear and credible choices about where and how to grow – it informs the process from defining brand ambition to brand growth priorities;

- manage your brand consistently across touchpoints, including when a brand stretches into adjacent categories or markets;

- build shared understanding across the whole business about what the brand is about;

- inspire creative people working on your brand to create remarkable work which will engage your target audience.

Context and inputs

There are lots of brand positioning tools and models out there – pyramids, wheels, keys, diamonds. They all have similar characteristics – making the linkages between what's at the heart of the brand, its product and service features, what it's known for, how consumers describe what it is and what it does for them, and how it makes them look or feel.

These can be overly complex models in which the consumer's motivations and perceptions get a bit lost, and there can be lots of repetition and jargon. The characteristics of remarkable brand positioning are simple:

- relevant and motivating to consumers and their needs;
- distinct from competitors;
- inspiring springboard for creative people.

Effective positioning work removes subjectivity about what is 'on' or 'off' brand from your conversation.

You need a model, but the most important thing is to be consistent in using this model over time, and across the different brands you have. What will make the difference is building this model from the consumer back, not from the brand out.

Great inputs start with deep understanding of the situation your brand faces, and what it wants to achieve. Great news is, if you have been developing this, you will have this information to hand. Unless you are starting a brand from scratch, this will be a process of iteration. Unlike much of your brand work, brand positioning should endure for five years as a minimum, requiring you to keep the learning and expression fresh and relevant, not changing it as a reaction to market conditions. Remember, a brand exists in consumers' minds – this is about building and maintaining competitive and relevant associations.

Inputs to brand positioning

1 Who is the target consumer?

Brand positioning starts with the target audience, derived from understanding of market segmentation. Build a vivid portrait of who they are. Though growth will come by recruiting from all category buyers, it's useful to have a specific view of your bull's-eye consumer. You should have this information from your 6Cs audit:

- Who are they? – demographics, age, gender, social-class, psychographics
- What are their attitudes? – socio-cultural, political, ethical
- What is their lifestyle? – work, family, friends, leisure
- What are their values and motivations? What's important to them, what do they aspire to, what do they want to feel, how do they want to be seen?

- What is their consumption and shopping behaviour? Where? When? What? Why? With whom? Capture the key consumption moments for your category, pain points, and shopping channels linked to different needs

- What else do they consume? What other brands appeal to them and why?

- How can we connect with them? What media do they consume? What and who influences them? What are their interests and passions?

2 What is the context around the brand?

As per Chapter 6, what is the category? How do consumers define the category? What are consumer motivations and the characteristics that satisfy them? What is the competitive set?

What are the forces shaping the category, brand, and consumer behaviour that you learned from the 6Cs audit?

What are the most recent brand and category dynamics? Taken from your brand performance review in Chapter 9, ensuring you look at brand guidance data we discussed in Chapter 6.

What do consumers call the brand? What would they say about the role it plays for them? How does it make them look and feel? What would they say about the brand, both positive and negative? What about key competitors? Use all the available consumer research you have, including sensory information and customer satisfaction information.

Get immersed in brand touchpoints – look at current and previous communications, packaging, and all other visual materials. Do the same for key competitors. Consumers never see your brand positioning and strategy documents, just the materials you put out in the world, so look back through their eyes.

3 What is the brand trying to achieve?

What is the brand ambition? As per Chapter 10, what is the brand trying to achieve in the longer term for the organization and its target consumers? What is the change in behaviour over the long term that will help it achieve its goal? What is the brand's vision and mission?

What are the brand's growth priorities? From Chapter 11, these capture the consumer opportunities you have prioritized, how you will access them, and how you will measure success. Growth priorities ladder up to deliver the brand ambition.

The core of brand positioning

Having worked with many models over time, I want to recommend one which is straightforward, Figure 12.1. The model is simple, but doing it precisely takes time and effort.

At the heart of any brand positioning model is a promise – the most credible, single-minded, motivating expression of what the brand can do for its target consumer. It's a statement of why the brand exists, the role it plays in the world, and what it stands for in the mind of the consumer. There are other names given for this – including brand benefit or brand purpose. Until the 2000s, many businesses used 'benefit' language, sometimes using it to reframe the most salient functional attribute of the brand in a way which was relevant to the consumer. Benefit was overtaken by 'purpose' as a deliberate attempt to elevate brands from functional into emotional territories, recognizing how difficult it was in many categories to compete on performance. Despite the intent outlined in the book *Grow* (Stengel, 2011), this attempt has backfired and 'purpose' became synonymous with brands aligning themselves to more societal and environmental outcomes, sometimes losing sight of what the consumer wants, or what the product or service can credibly deliver. As such, 'promise' is good neutral ground.

Great brands manage to make this core of their brand succinct. In Chapter 5 we referred to the core of Oreo's positioning as 'playfulness'. It comes from something remarkable about the product, relates to a consumer need against which there are fertile cultural tensions to inspire creativity. Being so simple acts as a powerful filter for judging any consumer-facing work. Cadbury's positioning around 'generosity' would be another single-minded example (King et al, 2022).

All brand positioning models are an attempt to find and express the connections between intrinsic elements of a brand and what the consumer wants – the things that make it remarkable and competitive. We have discussed in depth, especially in Chapter 7 on insights, that culture has a profound effect on consumer motivations and how they are satisfied and therefore how brands need to show up over time.

The following approach to brand positioning is popular with creative agencies, brand and research consultancies, and many brand organizations. The fact it thrives in all those contexts is another big clue as to its efficacy, given the importance of brand positioning in working successfully with agencies.

FIGURE 12.1 Core brand positioning model

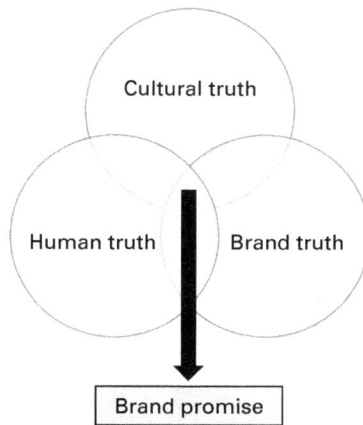

It's an insight-driven model based on the intersection of consumer, culture, and brand:

Cultural truth – the heart of what's going on in culture

Human truth – the heart of what's going on with consumers

Brand truth – the heart of what's going on with the brand

Finding the sweet spot between all three truths enables you to articulate what the brand can credibly offer to the consumer in a way which resonates with culture. Think of it as three intersecting circles.

Let's bring it to life with Childs Farm – a brand of sensitive, sustainable skincare for kids and babies which challenged conventions in its category (Figure 12.2). Three-quarters of parents in the UK say their children have sensitive skin, and the only options available to them are medicinal. Brands designed to facilitate fun and connection between parent and child are seen as unsuitable.

The cleverly worded brand promise, 'funbelievably kind', demonstrates that the brand reconciles the issue parents with kids with sensitive skin face and enables them to enjoy what they and their children are looking for despite their sensitive skin.

Brand positioning should be shown in the context of the brand ambition, its vision and mission, and may also include additional areas so the brand is brought to life consistently. To be effective keep positioning succinct – it should be a page, not a lengthy deck of slides.

FIGURE 12.2 Childs Farm brand positioning

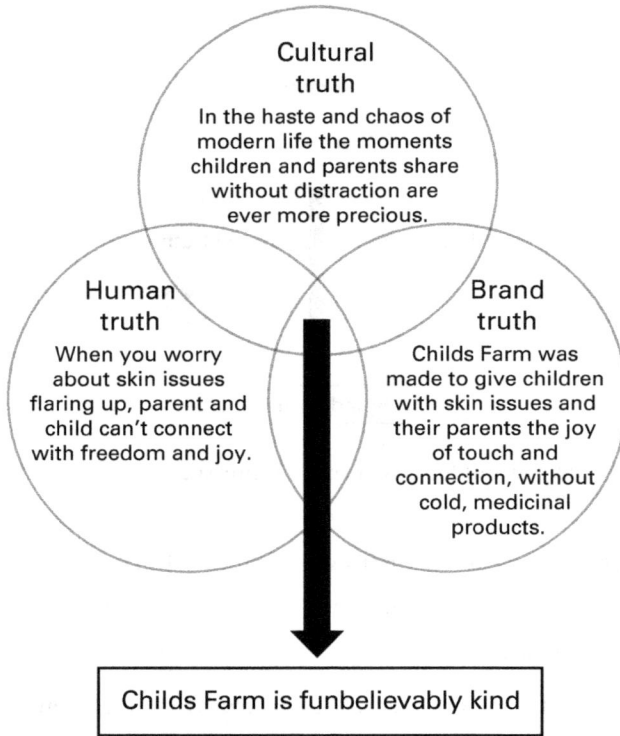

Cultural truth

In the haste and chaos of modern life the moments children and parents share without distraction are ever more precious.

Human truth

When you worry about skin issues flaring up, parent and child can't connect with freedom and joy.

Brand truth

Childs Farm was made to give children with skin issues and their parents the joy of touch and connection, without cold, medicinal products.

Childs Farm is funbelievably kind

Consumer insight: What insight lies at the heart of the brand proposition? In this instance it was the realization which drove the founder to create the brand, 'When children have skin issues, the space for joy and imagination shrinks and their world becomes smaller'.

Product or service proposition: More functional description of the product/service and core attributes. For example, Childs Farm is a range of natural, sensitive, sustainable skincare for babies and kids covering needs for washing and bathing, moisturizing, and protection.

Joanna Jensen had suffered from sensitive skin as a child and so did her daughters. With many children's toiletries unsuitable for sufferers of atopic eczema, the brand set out to give parents and their kids access to the emotional bonding of bath time. As three-quarters of parents believe their children have sensitive skin Joanna had uncovered a consumer opportunity with scale.

There are some final elements to brand positioning which help ensure the brand shows up with the right tone and depth. The first of these is values and beliefs:

Values and beliefs: Care without fun takes the joy out of childhood.

The final element is character. This helps a brand find a distinctive tone of voice. Just as interesting people have different and often contrasting elements to them, so too do engaging brands. Brands often use Jungian archetypes to develop their character and typically these archetypal attributes will mirror the characteristics which drive the consumer's needs.

Character: Mary Poppins. Real and magical. Joyful and practical.

The words chosen here relate to two contrasting archetypes – caregiver and jester. A caregiver brings order to the world, whereas a jester brings enjoyment and enables connection. It is no coincidence that the brand personality is consistent with what the consumer seeks – the structure that comes from personal hygiene with the fun of connecting with their kids at bathtime.

Workshopping brand positioning

BEFORE THE SESSION
Find a cross functional team of 6–10 people, including your agencies. Attendees should be passionate about your brand, consumers, and growth agenda.

Provide key inputs ahead of time as described above.

Get people to spend time with your target audience and answer the questions outlined above so they arrive at the session with a strong affinity for your consumer.

Create an environment for the workshop which brings to life brand and competitor communications.

IN THE SESSION
After introductions, practice the three circles model – take a famous and enduring brand and a brand from your own category and work up the three truths (cultural, human, and brand) and the brand promise.

Review the brands' current positioning – what's working well, what needs attention.

Review key competitors – a great way to do this is to review brand communications.

Map your brand versus key competitors. You may have a market map with key dimensions you can use to do this or decide amongst you the dimensions which most distinguish brands in your category.

Present and discuss your learnings about the target consumer.

Generate the three truths.

What does this mean for the brand promise?

Screen potential brand promise statements:

- Is your statement credible, single-minded, and motivating?
- Does it capture what the brand can do for the target audience?
- Is it distinctive from the competition?
- Is it easy to explain?
- Will it be an enduring springboard for creativity, suitable for unlocking the brand ambition and growth priorities?

Reflections

Do you have a common approach to brand positioning for your brands?

Are you clear on your brand promise?

Does your brand promise reflect what the consumer desires, and what your brand can credibly deliver in a way which is consistent with culture, and competitive?

Will your brand positioning enable your brand to access the growth priorities you have decided on?

What is iconic visual identity?

Brands exist within culture, and can also reflect an organization's internal culture. Consumers shape and are influenced by culture, and so are brands. One way of thinking about culture is as a complex system of signs, including linguistic and visual ones, which convey meaning relative to each other and over time. It's critical for brands to be attuned to this shifting landscape, understanding how the meaning they convey exists in relation to the system in which they operate.

More simply put, consumers understand things about brands intuitively as much by non-verbal cues as they do by verbal ones. It has always been this way, and yet it is probably only in the last decade that brand tools have recognized the importance of visual codes as much as verbal ones.

This is the product of a few things – the understanding that most brand decisions are made using more instinctive system 1 thinking, and the role that distinctive brand assets (Sharp, 2010) play in getting a brand noticed. It has also been influenced by a shift to short form content online and in social media, which puts consumers more in control of what they interact with or pass by, and how long they dwell.

It is useful to think about media types from this perspective – length of attention versus extent of control. For example, in the cinema you have a captive audience with no real choice other than to watch your content with the best possible media experience, right through to an advert in a social media feed which may get no more than a passing glance before it gets swiped.

A cinema advert gives a brand the opportunity to tell its story well, whereas an advertisement on the side of a passing bus or online must work harder to make any impression at all.

The point of this is that there is more to the codes a brand uses than simply standing out. It's great if you have golden arches or a swoosh as a recognizable and unique device – it means your brand is so big it's likely to be part of your consumer's vocabulary already and you can deploy it in all touchpoints, being inventive in how you do so without sacrificing recognition.

For most of us, the brand work we need to do is to develop our distinctive brand assets and visual identity in a way which will enable our brands to be recognizable, while building relevance and meaning pertinent to what the consumer seeks.

To address this, it's important to develop a brand's visual identity alongside brand positioning. Visual identity is a key part of being deliberate in developing the world your brand will convey, consistent with its positioning and what the consumer seeks, while establishing distinctive brand assets suitable for placement across all touchpoints.

Distinctive brand assets

Distinctive brand assets, also referred to as brand codes, are the unique visual, auditory, and verbal elements which target consumers attribute to a brand, often in combination – think logo, including brand marque or icon, colour palette, typography, sonic branding. It can also include things such as a strapline, tone of voice, imagery, advertising style. For packaged goods, the primary elements are often derived from packaging as the key touchpoint.

Distinctive brand assets act as a trigger at the point of purchase for the associations the buyer may have about the brand and help it stand out. The need to stand out is critical – remember, people buy from a repertoire and you need to be present and visible. Secondary elements such as the style of communications can help consumers recognize materials from your brand and increase your likelihood of being noticed and creating an impression.

In their busy lives, consumers struggle to recall brands from communications, so stacking the cards in your favour matters – it is possible to be creatively engaging and brand-centred without inelegantly slapping a giant logo on everything.

CASE STUDY

Tropicana is a much-told case study on the perils of ignoring established distinctive brand assets (Andrivet, 2023). In 2009 work was undertaken on Tropicana's pack and brand identity in North America to evolve and modernize it. The work saw the brand lose the unique orange with a straw which communicated taste and convenience on pack. The new design updated the logo, changing the shade of green, and presented it sideways instead of as an eyebrow shape. The pack included new imagery, a new lid, and a new slogan '100% squeezed' which linked to the relaunch advertising campaign.

The brand announced it was returning to the old packaging the following month after a backlash and significant fall in sales. Changing so many elements at once caused consumers to question or perhaps not even recognize what they were buying. Whereas with communications marketers have more licence to experiment, packaging needs to be recognizable and consistent with shopper expectations, as it is the final trigger, or in this case barrier, to purchase. Packaging can reinforce consumer expectations and provide information to reassure, or it can cause doubt – even as to whether it is the same product inside, or that it may be counterfeit.

It's not just about products with physical packs. Think about finding an app on your phone. What do you look for? You don't look for a brand name but a colour and an icon. When this is not distinctive it's easy to waste time finding the right app, and if it changes significantly, you need to spend time learning a new reflexive habit.

To make it easy for consumers to find and choose your brand, you must codify distinctive brand assets, then define a consistent approach to deploying them, and take care when refreshing them.

In general, the assets you choose should be elements that are both unique versus the competition and attributed by consumers to your brand. For new brands, brands in the seeding phase, or brands without recognizable assets you may need to create them, thinking about how they will work on and off pack.

Beyond those codes which are unique and memorable, be aware of the other brand assets your brand has. If you have codes which are unique but not memorable you may need to take time investing in them to make them memorable. Memorable but not unique codes are likely to be category-wide codes which play a role for shoppers, and those which are neither unique nor memorable are likely to be design detail which may still play a role overall in conveying quality, craft, provenance, or heritage. Consumer research can help – either in a small-scale consumer test where you might ask people to draw your pack from memory, or in a more robust quant study.

Once you are clear on your distinctive brand assets, develop simple guidelines to prescribe how to deploy them in all touchpoints. Should they be presented in combination or alone? What size should they be? How will they work consistently in different media – be it a pack, a piece of large format outdoor communications, or a more constrained format? If it is important to you, think about how they would be recognizable in user-generated content while being suitable for that less produced environment.

Once guidelines are defined ensure all parties creating work adhere to them. It is good practice to create a brand room with your agencies and work through creative output quarterly or bi-annually to see what opportunities you have to improve and ensure your work is consistent yet fresh.

As mentioned, seeding brands need to define their assets, while scale brands are investing to ensure they are unique and recognizable. Maturing brands may have more licence to be creative. Think about brands such as McDonald's, Cadbury, Coke, or Louis Vuitton which have been established over decades. Johnnie Walker Scotch whisky has been doing it for over two centuries! Most of the brands we work on do not have that licence and are more likely to confuse rather than entertain potential buyers.

There is no hard and fast rule as to how often core packaging and brand codes should be updated, but many consumer goods brands refresh them subtly every two or three years so they remain in keeping with how design language evolves around them. If you look online for the evolution of packaging and logos of brands such as Lay's or Walkers, Kit Kat, Cadbury, and Budweiser you will find good examples of managing this. Contrast Pepsi with Coke and you will see less coherence in the former.

Brand world

As well as defining distinctive brand assets, being deliberate about the visual look and feel of your brand enables you to create work which is consistent with your brand positioning – true of the brand, relevant to the consumer, and in step with culture. Think about it as the visual equivalent to your brand's tone of voice.

A brand world is a vivid expression of what you wish to convey to consumers, makes your brand recognizable, and reflects the desired emotional state your consumer seeks. Think about the example we used in Chapter 6 about McDonald's where the 'slice of UK life' remained consistent and recognizable over many years despite the brand tackling different business threats.

A brand world is developed by a design agency in collaboration with an advertising agency as it is deployed in all brand touchpoints. Typically, it provides a visual reference of the idealized world the brand seeks to convey. It's not a mood board but will project how the brand might show up in different environments.

Combined with distinctive brand assets and guidelines for their deployment, the brand world contributes to defining a brand's visual identity.

The combination of your brand strategy from ambition to growth priorities, brand positioning, and visual identity completes the core elements of a brand strategy toolkit, though other elements such as brand architecture, price and promotion guardrails, and other executional guidance may be included.

With a brand strategy toolkit in place, everyone is clear where growth will come from, and you have the foundations to inspire and enable your team and your partners to consistently create consumer-facing work on your brand to access growth effectively.

Reflections

Has your brand codified its distinctive brand assets?

Are you clear how to use them in different contexts?

Are you consistently executing against the standards you have defined?

Do you have a brand world which enables consumer facing work to be recognizable, consistent, and fresh?

Are you able to bring together your brand's visual identity, brand positioning, and brand strategy to provide a common framework to ensure your team and partners are working towards the same long-term ambition together?

References

Andrivet, M (2023) What to learn from Tropicana's packaging redesign failure, *The Branding Journal*, 30 November, www.thebrandingjournal.com/2015/05/what-to-learn-from-tropicanas-packaging-redesign-failure/ (archived at https://perma.cc/VXV9-9BMD)

Childs Farm www.childsfarm.com (archived at https://perma.cc/7GJ9-5Y6B)

King, A et al (2022) Cadbury 'There's a glass & a half in everyone': How intrinsic purpose can transform a brand's fortunes, in Adv*ertising Works 26, Proving the payback on marketing investment*, ed. H Singh, pp 41–75, IPA Effectiveness Awards 2022, IPA, London

Sharp, B (2010) *How Brands Grow*, Oxford University Press, South Melbourne

Stengel, J (2011) *Grow*, Crown Business, New York

PART THREE

How to win and keep winning

13

What are the fundamentals of creative ideas and media connections?

With a clear strategy in mind, you can now think about how to win. Unlike the principles behind strategy and insights which are more universal, the model for execution is more dependent on industry – the frequency with which the category is purchased, the price point, type of consumer, channels, the nature of the consumer experience, and so forth.

In this final section of the book, we'll spend less time on specific tactics and actions to deliver your growth, and more on the practical steps you as a marketing leader need to take to develop a plan your organization is ready to execute. Up until this point the work has been mostly internal, but this is a significant pivot point at which we start to pass the baton to our agencies. Think about how close you are to the choices you have made and the rationale behind them, and therefore what you need to do to get people up to speed. Your role changes at this point, and therefore what different people may need of you to collaborate effectively.

As a case in point, developing a connections plan and nurturing an effective creative platform are things typically delivered with agency partners. Your role is to:

- have a clear strategy and know what you want;
- inspire and excite people about the work;
- be able to brief consistently – setting the task and providing context;

- ensure everyone understands the consumer, including their path to purchase;
- understand how ideas work and what your creative ambition is;
- build great relationships – partnerships which enable brilliant, appropriately rewarded, work;
- manage your internal stakeholders and organizational dynamics;
- hold your nerve – everyone wants you to chase the next big thing.

There are three elements to consider in this chapter – how to think about connecting with your target audience, how to brief, and how to develop an idea which will unlock your brand's growth priorities. What will make the difference is your ability to create an effective extended team and align your team and business behind acting on and investing in the work you create together with your agencies.

How should I think about connecting effectively with consumers?

What are the fundamentals?

A connections plan is a holistic view of how to connect with your target audience with the right message, in the right place, and at the right time. It is built on understanding your consumer's journey or path to purchase.

A connections plan is often thought of as an output of a plan when it should be an input. You should be clear from your brand strategy who your target is, and now address how to connect with them meaningfully. This ensures any activities you create are developed to work appropriately in the channels in which they appear – covering practical matters such as format and size, as well as how they are consumed – dwell time, attention, appropriateness of context etc.

To get clear on scope let's make a distinction between consumer experience and connections planning. Consumer experience covers all aspects of a consumer's interaction with your brand – touchpoints include what happens in the period before they decide to buy, the purchase occasion, and things such as customer service and after-sales care, including interactions on- and offline.

Defining and managing consumer experience is critical to delivering consumer satisfaction and re-recruiting, but here we are focussed on connections planning. Strong connections planning is essential to reaching and influencing prospective consumers to choose our brand over the competition and achieve our business goals. Remember the funnel we considered in Chapter 2? Media is a complex and specialist area, and as your brand increases in scale more of this work will be undertaken by in-house specialists and agencies, albeit the fundamental considerations remain.

Connections planning includes all potential touchpoints and channels by which we can reach consumers with brand messages. Most of the heavy lifting will be done by 'paid' media that you buy or rent, but you should also consider 'owned' media such as your website, blogs, social channels, and mailing lists, as well as 'earned' media or publicity generated for your brand in other channels – other people's blogs, newsfeeds etc.

'Owned' and 'earned' play a role, but you need to be realistic about them – will your target audience really come to find your brand, and is it interesting enough for people to write or talk about you, or share your content? It tends to be industry specific, but there are lots of powerful examples of luxury brands or in tourism where consumers sharing content reels of their vacation could hardly be a more credible way to connect with a prospective and relevant audience.

Working with a media agency, you should define priority touchpoints by applying the target consumer understanding you developed in the 6Cs audit and in your brand positioning work to understand:

- What are the key points on a consumer's path to purchase which influence their brand decision?
- Which media channels best enable you to reach your target audience?
- Which media channels have the most relevance to your consumer? This may be relevant to the brand, the motivation, or the consumer's life more broadly.
- Are there differences depending on shopper missions?

For a brand in its seeding phase, this means choosing just one or two channels to achieve some scale, whereas for a scaling brand it may include partnerships and channels that deepen connection, while for a maturing brand investment levels allow presence across a broad range of channels.

Good connections consider relevance and context as critical – talking to the right audience with the right message in the right environment. It's about achieving reach, but in the most engaging and meaningful manner possible.

The final consideration is budget – how can you balance getting the highest level of reach without compromising relevance and context? The highest levels of reach may be achieved affordably, but this may include 'clickbait' websites designed purely to display advertising alongside minimal content.

Prioritizing channels based on your budget, audience, and objectives provides clarity on the nature of the different formats and assets you and your agency will need to create before writing a brief, and your work will make more sense to your audience as a result.

Some brands build a media plan based on logic – prioritizing the first channel and investing until reach is exhausted, and then selectively adding in other channels to access incremental consumers. Others will consider a blend, combining reach with more consideration of the impact of context. There is no one right answer and it will depend on your category, and also on the subtly different roles media channels play individually and when they are combined. A successful multi-channel plan can be more effective than any single channel by playing to different media strengths and working right across the consumer funnel.

Though a connections plan will primarily be concerned with media, it is worth integrating these channels with other investments managed by sales colleagues, such as retail media online or instore point of sale.

What are other considerations?

REACH MAY BE THE PRIMARY CONNECTIONS GOAL BUT WHAT ABOUT FREQUENCY AND IMPACT?

In the last 20 years media plans have shifted focus towards reach as the key metric, reflecting our increased focus on driving penetration. 'Frequency' is the number of times someone in your audience will see your content over a given time frame. It is generally accepted now that the first media impression is the most potent, and most brands ensure they place caps on frequency to avoid wastage, recognizing that perhaps beyond a second impression it might be better to spend money on reaching someone new.

'Impact' is about choosing certain sites or channels where the context may be especially valuable – for example, the use of high-quality print like *GQ* or *Vogue* for luxury brands, iconic locations such as Times Square in New York, the Sphere in Las Vegas, online publications such as *The Wall Street Journal*, or during communal experiences like the Superbowl. 'Impact' often goes hand in hand with high production values, perhaps with celebrities, and maybe longer formats which might not be viewed online without the context creating a sense of fanfare. The reach which TV channels achieve does not qualify them as 'impact' media but choosing them still says something about the status of your brand.

MASS VERSUS TARGETED

This is a consideration especially for seeding and scaling brands. With small budgets, it can be difficult to reach everyone in the category and it may be necessary to narrow down audiences to those who may be most predisposed to trial or purchase. In contrast to this targeted approach, the most extreme version of mass reach might be programmatic advertising where placement is created by automated technology and reach is placed above contextual considerations. Where should your brand sit on this continuum?

No matter where you sit, it's worth addressing how you might tailor your media. Personalization uses individual data to curate a more bespoke media experience – perhaps with tailored content leveraging information about individuals or audience segments to help brands stand out more. An example might be where someone buys direct from a brand, and with data it has harvested it is able to contact them in a time frame which corresponds with a typical replenishment window or recommend something else which might be relevant – think pet food or beauty products. This also reduces the chance of the consumer's next purchase going to another brand in their repertoire.

Overly focussing on personalization may cause you to neglect people who have not interacted with your brand and may represent incremental growth. You may also forego some of the shared experiences that may create word of mouth, although 'Spotify unwrapped' is a good example where personalized content delivered at scale resonates with individuals while being shareable. Focus on how much your brand growth is reliant on recruiting new buyers versus re-recruiting existing buyers.

As you think about the blend of mass versus targeted media types, consider the quality of engagement versus the extent to which the consumer is in control – video formats such as cinema, video on demand, and certain social platforms can be highly engaging, compared to many where the consumer will just drive past or scroll through. Think about the relative cost of different channels – for example, static or digital outdoor might outperform expensive cinema advertising per exposure, which is why cinema seldom features on many mainstream brand plans.

Other channel considerations regarding creative include duration, and ability to effectively brand content either explicitly or through a recognizable style, aspect ratio etc. Like different magazines, social channels have different characters – Instagram feels more like a magazine compared to the raw feel of TikTok – shifting content from there, especially user-generated content, onto a different social feed or even TV can feel out of place. Are you going to grab people's attention, or look out of place?

CHANNEL CONSOLIDATION

Though advertising revenues have consolidated (Statista, 2022) with 60% of global media revenue currently going through Google, Meta, and Amazon, reach is harder to achieve. Almost all media is now digital and targeted, including much TV, but subscription models, skipping, and so forth mean consumers can choose more than ever whether to engage or not.

Consolidation has happened for many reasons – search remains critical for many brands as consumers research how to fulfil their needs, and retail media plays a role as an important conversion driver – consumers tend to go to retail sites not to research but when they have decided to make a category purchase and brand choice can still be influenced.

These platform media channels tend to be sold directly and sit outside the part of your media that would be planned by your agency. Being clear on your consumer target and their journey is critical to ensure you select channels strategically versus in isolation. How much do you wish to invest in building the brand versus converting sales? Building a connections map and thinking about how you move people through it is critical.

HOW TO THINK ABOUT DATA

Data is abundant in media – enabling targeting and measuring what is placed and what response it elicits. If you have a clear strategy – a clear consumer target, priorities for growth, and insight into what you need to say or do to win consumers over, you have a framework for using data to make channel choices. It can help you at a macro level, and at a micro level – for example, if most people do their main shop towards the end of the week, advertising Thursday–Saturday afternoons might prove most effective and efficient, and early evening for takeaway deliveries.

Without this, you risk becoming overwhelmed with data – much of it provided by specific platforms for whom data and analytics are integrated into their approach to sales, or by AI or biddable media – both of which have their role especially when aligned to clear objectives. The way to avoid being overwhelmed is to ask what data would help you reach and understand your audience better.

The industry's response to the removal of cookies to track consumers online has been to push brands to collect more personal data. There may be a role for this especially in high-end categories where consumers are more prepared to give you data. It may not be so true in categories such as soft drinks and snacks where the effort required to collect the data might be less powerful than other more readily accessible data types. In any case, you must be aware of and adhere to regulations regarding data privacy in every territory in which you operate.

FINAL CONSIDERATIONS

We'll address things such as the balance of short- and long-term media and measurement further on in the book, but final considerations might be:

- Responsible placement. The media choices you make have an ethical dimension to them. What are the media types and publications you want to support and align with your brand values?

- Inclusion. How do you actively avoid toxic media types which do not align with how your brand sees the world, and actively engage and include minority audiences so often overlooked by brands' obsession with a mainstream 18–35 audience?

Reflections

Do you have a clear connections plan built on understanding your consumer path to purchase, mapped to media and other touchpoints?

Do you have clear targets for things such as reach which correlate with your penetration goals?

Do you have the right media principles for your brand? Think reach, frequency caps, how continuously you aspire to be present throughout the year?

Are you clear on how to use context to make media choices resonate more with your target audience and your brand values?

Are you using the right formats on the right platforms?

Have you considered the ethical dimensions of media placement?

Are you outspending the competition?

Are you maximizing your deployment budget by minimizing development costs?

Do you have a plan to measure how effective your media is in achieving your brand goals?

How should I think about creative ideas?

There is a strong interplay between connections planning and creative ideas. Brand owners need to know what kind of creative work they aspire to, while being conscious of balancing long-term vision with unlocking the opportunities and threats to growing penetration today. What do we need to be aware of?

Creative platform

For long-term success, effective brands try to develop a creative platform. Sometimes called a 'big idea', this is typically the creative means by which a brand consistently brings its brand promise to life in all its brand campaigns and activities. To build the kind of consistency and impact you need over time, it helps to make the distinction between a creative platform and individual creative or execution ideas. Think about the creative platform as a description for internal use of the rules or formula you follow across different brand campaigns and activities, and executional ideas as individual expressions of the creative platform which consumers will see or experience.

A creative platform is not born overnight. It takes time to develop and recognize the blend of strategic and executional elements of which it is composed. Some famous examples of creative platforms from the last couple of decades include Snickers 'You're not you when you're hungry', Foster's 'Good Call', Progressive Insurance 'Flo', Dove 'Campaign for real beauty', M&Ms, Guinness 'Made of more', Allstate 'Mayhem', Patek Philippe 'Generations', and Mastercard 'Priceless'.

Having a creative platform makes your brand memorable over time. It may also be flexible enough to address the different growth priorities you have identified. Take one of the examples above that you are familiar with and look at some of the creative work. What do you notice? There is no hard-and-fast rule but creative platforms that last many years often have recurring characters, a common narrative framework, they may use personification, metaphor, hyperbole, humour, as well as common stylistic attributes – music, pacing, direction etc.

Most are built on an ingenious consumer insight, reframing the challenge they sought to overcome in an imaginative and attention-grabbing manner, repeating the same core message. Creative platforms have a framework, but they don't all follow the same formula. The formula may be buttoned down and tight, sometimes looser, and it will typically develop over time but still within a framework. Creative platforms help brands stand out, be instantly recognizable, consistent yet fresh.

If you take the Snickers creative work, it uses diva celebrities in everyday situations to dramatize the social risk you face when being hungry makes you behave out of character. In the adverts, Snickers is the solution to this problem. The story is generally the same, but with different celebrities and different situations. There are other common elements such as the end line, pacing etc. Are all executions the same? The IPA winning multi-market execution featuring Mr Bean differs in that, although well known, Mr Bean is a character not a celebrity and the advert does not feature the transformation from celebrity back to normal person on eating a Snickers (Fenlon, 2016). In this instance, using a character who was well known enough to allow the creative work to travel caused the brand to tweak the formula. It seems there is an art in defining the guardrails of an idea – too narrow and perhaps it will become exhausted, too broad and it lacks cohesive power.

It is a choice. You cannot request a versatile platform off the shelf, but you can work with your agency consciously to achieve it – taking time to work out whether there is something in a specific execution or campaign which can inspire other executions, work in different channels, and so on. You also must focus on cracking the code, identifying what elements are core, and what can be refreshed over time without losing consistency and brand recognition.

For example, Apple's advertising approach has evolved over time, recognizing different product lines need to land different messages. There are, however, common elements – the product as hero, demonstrating the benefit not the features, and a simplicity in design and execution which makes Apple's creative work easy to recognize.

Dove also uses more than one idea – its work has remained fresh by tackling different cultural tensions regarding the portrayal of women and girls in media, with more product-focussed work. With common branding elements, Dove's work happily co-exists to promote its point of view on culture and its products. It uses different, but related, ideas for Dove Kids and Dove Men+Care.

Nike's work has two veins to 'inspire the athlete' in each of us – some work celebrates the best of American athletes, while some work heroes the everyday American. The McDonald's UK work we discussed in the chapter on insights works similarly – common elements, but more creative freedom given the very different issues it needed to address.

You should also think about the different growth priorities you may have. Some creative platforms are so versatile they can stretch across different market segments. For example, All State insurance uses the same 'Mayhem' character to personify humorously reckless behaviours that can lead to insurance claims in different sectors. Mastercard uses its priceless platform to cover everything from core products, to innovation, and its loyalty scheme. A creative platform which can stretch so broadly is hard to create but hugely valuable – priceless has been used since 1997 and is part of culture, entering the vernacular.

A single creative platform over time is the gold standard. What are your organization's beliefs around creative brand ideas? What can you find in the brand's history which may give you clues for creating work which will resonate today? Even if you don't go after developing a creative platform, what elements will you keep consistently over time?

The Effectiveness Code (Hurman and Field, 2020) proposes a categorization of ideas at different levels. All levels describe effective marketing, but the higher the level the greater the impact and effort required to deliver it. It can be a useful way to think about your current work and frame your creative ambition:

1 Enduring icon – create long-term brand and sales growth

2 Commercial triumph – create sustained sales success

3 Brand builder – improve brand health

4 Sales spike – create short-term, temporary sales growth

5 Behaviour breakthrough – change consumer behaviour

6 Influential idea – overachieve campaign metrics

Most of the well-established examples cited above as creative platforms would achieve the sixth rung of the ladder. Regardless of whether you aspire to a long-term creative platform or are using different ideas to address different brand growth priorities when the creative platform will not stretch, all creative work must integrate your brand's distinctive assets to ensure it is properly attributed to the brand.

In this book I use the term 'brand campaign' to describe a bundle of individual activities designed to address a brand growth priority. Terminology differs between agencies and organizations, but most recognize these three levels – creative platform, brand campaign, execution or activity. Be fluent in your ability to describe the difference, have common terms, and be clear with your agency about the kind of work and approach appropriate for your brand in its stage of development.

A connections plan sets up the mix of channels in which a creative platform will need to work. Media and ideas are intimately connected – just as we considered the importance of context on media channel selection, so will it have an impact on the type of idea and what may constrain or enable it when it appears in the world.

It is the combination of these things – clarity on your strategic intent, the integration of your distinctive brand assets, visual identity, media choices, and your approach to idea development which combine to make your brand memorable.

Why do we need a creative platform?

CREATIVITY IS GOOD FOR BUSINESS

Creativity has been shown to increase effectiveness and efficiency. An Effies study (Whiteside, 2020) demonstrated that it was the main driver of effectiveness after brand size, and in *The Link between Creativity and Effectiveness* (Field, 2011), Peter Field found that creatively awarded campaigns were more efficient than non-awarded ones in the market share growth they drove relative to their investment in excess share of voice, and in their pricing power.

Having a creative platform on your brand accelerates effectiveness because it engages your audience emotionally and creates a foundation on which you can balance being consistent over time and fresh. It saves you money in the long term in time, agency fees, and production costs, so it is efficient too. Quoted in the Gift report (Brand Finance, 2016), Janet Hill OBE, former director of marketing strategy at the IPA, claimed creativity 'is the cornerstone for sound business management'.

This evidence connects to what we've learned about consumer behaviour and the need to be remarkable. In essence, a creative platform is a device which gets your message across and creates an emotional response from your audience. Creativity plays to the instinctive system 1 brain, in contrast to a rational message which seeks to persuade the rational system 2 brain. The buzz consumers get from creativity makes your brand more memorable and can be applied to the different growth priorities your brand needs to address.

It doesn't matter what category you are in, and perhaps it could be argued the lower engagement the category the more need to create memorable work. Think about insurance. Which brands come to mind? It will, of course, depend on where you are in the world, but look at the effort brands such as Progressive, Geico, State Farm, Direct Line, and price comparison sites such as comparethemarket.com and gocompare.com put in so they more readily come to mind. Of course, they must offer the right product, but mainly they dramatize what their brand stands for, often using humour and characters. Think geckos, cavemen, hitmen, meerkats, Transformers, and opera singers. Of course, in the 20 years since insurance has shifted from rational persuasion to entertainment you could argue the whole category has a formula which someone now needs to subvert, but the success of these campaigns has been documented – Progressive's character, Flo, has been in well over 1,000 spots since 2008 and is now part of a cadre of characters who have become a cultural phenomenon in their own right.

It's not an affront to say creativity can have a formula and still be magical. What's the formula for your brand which will enable it to be creative and fresh? Musical genres are like this, even the most revered band like the Beatles were creative within a framework. Think about the best film franchises or TV series – they have an idea and point of view about the world brought to life with a distinctive style which resonates with their audience. This helps them tell different stories. Often when a series goes off the boil, or 'jumps the shark', it is because it loses sight of what it is at its core, introducing incongruent elements. The same is true of brands and brand ideas. Refreshing a successful creative platform becomes difficult over time for different reasons but it is the ultimate goal.

Understanding the potential impact of ideas

Alongside knowing your growth priorities, it's important to know where you are in the creative cycle. This often correlates with the brand's stage of development. In their scant channels, seeding brands are typically trying to build awareness and meaning – helping prospective consumers understand what they offer. As brands build more momentum into the scaling phase, building awareness remains a priority but they may start to focus more on what makes them remarkable – how they challenge the status quo. Maturing brands may have the biggest budgets, but they may also have the most mouths to feed – re-recruiting buyers to hold onto their position, remaining relevant, launching and sustaining innovation. As brands move through these stages, they tend to climb the creative effectiveness ladder – towards a flexible creative platform.

You may remember the adage about poets and farmers, representing creativity and practicality? To be an effective marketing leader you need to be both – or an architect and a builder, if you prefer. With so much pressure to chase the next big thing, and so much sales pressure, it's easy to be swayed. Without a strong brand idea, marketing leaders can end up more like plumbers fixing leaks or allowing their brand to go with the flow.

As well as doing the right thing by your brand, you need to understand your organization. Aside from its ambition, what is its character? Organizations can be humble, altruistic, adventurous, conservative, hyper-rational, reckless. Brands tend to soak up organizational qualities and those characteristics show up in their attitude to creativity. Don't underestimate your business. Essity was part of a Swedish forest products company until it was spun off in 2017 with the recognition it could make more money from paper-based products such as tissues, diapers or nappies, and feminine hygiene products. You might be mistaken for assuming such a business would be quite conservative when it came to creativity, and yet since 2017 its brand Libresse has tackled taboos around women's bodies and menstruation, subverting category conventions and tackling societal stigma and shame. Look at BrewDog – whose forthright creative output reflects the uncompromising challenger attitude of its co-founder James Watt.

Marketers face pressure to be creatively brave from within the broader marketing community, often in a way which is not congruent with what creative is effective or the character of their organization.

Should creativity require bravery? You may need to champion work that excites you and may challenge the organization, but ultimately ideas need to change consumer attitudes and behaviours, not play to industry tastes. Being fluent in the anatomy of an idea, understanding why it has the potential to work, can demystify creativity, and increase your agency as a marketer. Creativity should be conscious – we may need to be bold in overcoming internal opinion, but great work is built off the brand, its growth priorities, and understanding of consumer motivations and culture. Just as brands reflect organizational characteristics, so too will what they seek from creative ideas.

Without destroying its potential, you should be able to explain the creative work you develop, even if consumers experience it in the most visceral of manners. Doing this with respect can enable creative magic, not constrain it.

Creative testing

Learning from consumers in a qualitative and quantitative setting can help. Knowing that advertising is consumed 'system 1' first and most research, even research which tries to recreate that state, will need respondents to engage system 2 thinking does not render it useless.

There is good evidence that pre-testing methods can be predictive of in-market performance, and yet for many marketers it is seen as an affront to their capability. Some organizations won't run advertising unless it passes the test, and others don't care – it's more about attitude to risk, approaches to decision-making, and personal bias than it is whether the research method works or not. You can be both a poet with a vision for the kind of work your brand needs, and a farmer getting the most out of each execution with humility to keep learning about what works.

Research should come down to an appreciation of critical learning questions. A new piece of creative from a long- running campaign producing multiple executions a year may not need pre-testing, but it can certainly help you work out how something new might work, and help you unpick something which isn't quite coming together. We get so close to our work, it can help us see it through new eyes, be an aid to judgement and most importantly enable us to produce the most powerful execution of a powerful idea, image by image. The cost of research is often used as a reason against pre-testing, but it is a small percentage of your investment in media.

Many businesses have mnemonics to help their marketers understand ideas and give constructive feedback. The IPA paper from Diageo, 'Creating a culture of marketing effectiveness' (Geoghegan, 2020), demonstrates the link between creative and improvements in return on investment. When developing work, ask yourself whether the work has these qualities and how you might improve them:

- Is it attention grabbing?
- Will it be remembered for being my brand?
- Will it stand out from the crowd?
- Is it easy to understand?
- Will it generate emotion towards the brand?

The things which most strongly correlate with effectiveness regard standing out or being remarkable (creative distinctiveness 45% and brand distinctiveness 58%) and generating emotion (brand appeal 51%).

Reflections

What legacy does your brand have with creativity?

What type of creative system do you aspire to for your brand?

What brands do you admire which can help you refine your vision for creativity?

What bearing does your organization's character have on its attitude to creativity?

How comfortable are you describing different types of ideas and how they work?

How do you integrate consumer learning with sensitivity into your development process?

Is your organization fluent in the criteria which create the most effective work?

How should I brief brand campaigns?

We'll consider activity selection in the next chapter, but let's turn our attention towards developing a creative platform and a brand campaign to address your growth priorities.

Before you even put pen to paper it's worth reflecting on whether you have the conditions for success. As well as being clear on what you want your agency partner to do, your biggest role is to create an environment in which creativity can flourish with pace.

There are many things which can get in the way: lack of clarity on what you want, lack of organizational alignment, unclear roles, unclear decision-making responsibilities, lack of confidence or belief, feeling intimidated by creativity. It can come down to having the wrong agency for your brand and the work you need to create.

The process of briefing and creating work together should be one which is joyful. It comes easiest if there is truth and candour, care and diligence, respect, and shared goals. You also must have the right commercial relationship – agencies and individuals must feel appropriately rewarded, just as you and your team need to. It should feel like a process of coaching each other. We are feeling our way through to find something exciting and which has potential – ideas need nurturing, but you also need to keep moving forward, taking decisions.

Much of this can be resolved with a good contracting session; a well-facilitated discussion which sets out the soft elements of a creative process – what matters to each of you, how you want to work together, how you will create an environment of trust where everyone knows how to get the best out of each other. Are you all clear on what success looks like? This might require clarity on what work or assets need to be delivered, when and how you will integrate consumer learning into the process, and what KPIs you may have for the work and the impact you expect when it's deployed. There's an intriguing balance here – knowing where you want to go but being open-minded to new possibilities. The process itself may entirely reframe how you think about unlocking the brand challenge you are working on together.

Another aspect of your role as marketing leader is to focus proactively on engaging your own stakeholders. As well as building belief in the work you create and removing potential obstacles later, this is about insulating your agency from the things which can get in the way – those things should be on your shoulders. Your partners should be wondering how to achieve success for the brand, what drives the consumer.

Delivering a brief should feel like an important moment. It is the start of something which should be fun and exciting. It does not have to be elaborate or showy – it's fine to go to the agency's offices or take some time immersing them in a relevant consumer touchpoint – your store, restaurant, hotel etc. A great agency will be curious enough to want to do this for themselves, so if you make too much of an occasion of it you risk detracting from the critical conversation – getting aligned on the core of the brief, how you will work together, and what needs to be delivered. Create an environment which is all about the ideas.

Think deeply about how to engage with your agency as partners and build direct relationships – with your account managers, strategists, creatives, and producers. Balance this with keeping the circle tight – on both sides this should be the people who do the work. You need to be able to interact authentically, and having too many voices, and people uncertain of their role, slows things down and causes confusion. As you contemplate 'team and decision making' it's important to have that conversation on both sides to avoid ambiguity. You may need to formalize this with a 'RASCI' (responsible, accountable, support, consulted, informed) or similar model to ensure there is clarity – especially for senior stakeholders who may inadvertently act as decision-makers despite not being present in the process.

Cracking a brief and getting to ideas can be as simple as ensuring everyone remains focussed on the problem in hand. This is hard when a client gives too much information – it distracts the agency, and often means the client is not sure how to evaluate and feedback on the work provided. How do you know if it is 'on brief' if the brief covers all bases?

Agencies value a brand being clear on the brand's essence, such as the three truths we discussed in Chapter 12 on brand positioning, alongside a tight articulation of the brand promise – what it brings to the world. What do your agency partners value as start points for creativity?

When being briefed and working together, agencies are trying to work out what you want, looking for signals of things you may not be conscious of, assessing the nature of the brand and organization and what kind of creative work it will run.

Creative brief

First determine if you need to create new work at all. You may have existing, effective activities which you can repurpose and reuse. Marketers tire of brand work before it has worn out and reducing spend on production increases available spend for media.

Let's assume, however, you do need to develop new assets. It's useful to have a common approach to briefing to use across brands and over time. It can help to design a short template. Make it tight – constraining the amount of space will pay dividends in encouraging brevity. David Ogilvy's quotation requesting the freedom of a tight brief highlights the importance of providing something succinct which communicates the problem you want your agency partner to solve.

Your job is to tell the agency what you want. Sounds simple, right? However, many briefs are written before the marketer has laser-like clarity on what they need. The great news is that if you've put effort into understanding and prioritizing the opportunities and threats to penetration growth you are almost all the way there. At its core a brief must make clear the scale of the task, the problem you want to solve, and lay out the context and a good start point for solving it – a consumer insight.

The main issue arising with briefs is a lack of decisions in preparing them – marketers are insufficiently clear what they want, overload the brief with too much information, or see it as transactional. To overcome these things, you can collaborate on a brief with your agency to ensure it meets their needs, but in any case, they will typically translate it internally into a format which works for them. As we have discussed at length, so much of how you approach marketing tasks reflects your own organization – how to gain alignment, how decisions are made. This is also true for how agencies work.

What's in a brief?

WHAT ARE YOUR GOALS?

Keep these simple and topline – cascading from business goals (typically revenue growth), marketing goals (the penetration which will deliver the business goal, and perhaps market share), and communications or activity goals (a measure of what will need to change in your audience's attitudes towards the brand which will deliver the change in penetration).

WHAT IS THE OPPORTUNITY OR THREAT YOU NEED TO ADDRESS?

Remember our growth priority statement from Chapter 11?

To access the opportunity to ...

We must ...

By ...

To access the growing opportunity in the premium car insurance market

We must recruit affluent car owners concerned about the service they would receive in the event of an accident or breakdown

By making New Insurance Co famous for having the fastest response times in the market

Be specific about the opportunity, the target audience and the trigger or barrier to penetration, and what you believe the brand needs to do. Consumer insight is critical – especially why it is relevant to the opportunity, credible from the brand, what action it implies the brand should take.

WHAT ELSE SHOULD A BRIEF CONTAIN?

As well as highlighting the opportunity, you need to provide the agency other important information:

- learnings and background;
- specific deliverables, e.g. the priority channels and assets relevant to this brief from your connections plan;
- other mandatories – such as adherence to your brand positioning, distinctive brand assets;
- budget (production and media) and timing;
- team and decision-making.

The approach above is deliberately pitched at the level of developing a creative platform or brand campaign. The approach is relevant for briefing individual activities, and should stretch into developing PR, brand experiences, shopper marketing, and suchlike with due consideration of appropriate objectives for the channel. In an ideal world, and especially as your brand grows in scale, you should brief agencies from different disciplines together if they are contributing to different elements of a brand campaign.

A great brief is a pivot point, not an answer. It makes it clear what the scale of the job to be done is, and is a start point for addressing the challenge, while establishing common ground between client and agency. But it is just a jumping-off point – spend time making it simple, don't overload it, and then focus on creating the culture and environment which will foster great work with your agency and team, and build conviction within your business. Be aware of the nature of your organization, what excites it, and how it makes decisions.

Reflections

Have you got the right agency relationship for the work you need to make?

How strong is your agency relationship?

How does your agency view the relationship with you?

What are the opportunities to improve both hard and soft ways of working?

Do you have a consistent approach to briefing which captures key information about the brand challenge?

Does the brief make clear important considerations such as deliverables, budget, timeliness, decision-making?

How would your agencies rate you on the quality of your briefs and briefing?

References

Brand Finance (2016) Gift 2016, Brand Finance, p 5, brandfinance.com/wp-content/uploads/1/gift_report_2016_for_print.pdf (archived at https://perma.cc/6KUQ-FX8P)

Fenlon, A (2016) Snickers: Thinking like a Hollywood blockbuster, in *Advertising Works 23, Proving the payback on marketing investment,* ed. B Angear, pp 285–301, Case studies from the IPA Effectiveness Awards 2016, WARC, London

Field, P (2011) *The Link between Creativity and Effectiveness,* IPA, London

Geoghegan, A (2020) Diageo portfolio. Marketing catalyst: Creating a culture of marketing effectiveness, in *Advertising Works 25, Proving the payback on marketing investment*, ed. S Unerman, pp 119–145, IPA Effectiveness Awards 2020, Ascential Events (Europe), London.

Hurman, J and Field, P (2020) *The Effectiveness Code*, Cannes Lions and WARC, www.warc.com/content/paywall/article/warc-exclusive/the-effectiveness-code/en-GB/133006? (archived at https://perma.cc/3U2K-W84N)

Statista (2022) Leading media companies worldwide, ranked by advertising revenue, www.statista.com/statistics/261827/leading-media-companies-worldwide/ (archived at https://perma.cc/H93T-7AC5)

Sussman, T (2022) McDonald's. How we got customers lovin' it and kept them lovin' it, no matter what, *Advertising Works 26, Proving the payback on marketing investment*, ed. H Singh, pp 193–245, IPA Effectiveness Awards 2022, IPA, London

Whiteside, S (2020) The top ten drivers of marketing effectiveness from the Effie Awards – and beyond, WARC, www.warc.com/content/paywall/article/event-reports/the-top-ten-drivers-of-marketing-effectiveness-from-the-effie-awards-and-beyond/en-GB/130732? (archived at https://perma.cc/4KFC-YJUW)

14

How do I turn strategy into a plan?

Introduction

We are in the home straight now with everything we need in place to create a holistic plan. This is an active process which will benefit from cross-functional working, as did the development of brand strategy. It makes sense to carve out a couple of days to do this work. Unlike the first working sessions with fewer people, you need a larger cast – salespeople from specific channels or segments and customers, category managers if relevant, and more of your marketing team. This is because the process translates your strategy into consumer- and customer-facing activities – ensuring trading activities are aligned with brand activities. As well as making micro-level choices, it will allow your colleagues to work out as you go what the plan means for the work they need to deliver. Commercial finance partners will work to create a financial model based on the assumptions you make in the sessions.

Planning a workshop

Thinking about the sessions, it makes sense to start with a recap. This could be done online or in person, but should set the scene by ensuring everyone is up to speed on the brand ambition and the chosen growth priorities. It can help people to understand more of the rationale for these choices and to ask any questions.

Draft agenda for annual brand planning workshop

Day 1

- Introduction and expectations (30 mins)
- Reminder on growth priorities (30 mins)
- Breakout groups – mental availability (communications), physical availability (including visibility and seasonal shopper activity but also distribution, pricing, promotion, pack or service offering optimization), innovation (including news/renovation and strategic innovation)
  - o Session one: what are the different activities we might consider for each growth priority? (2 hours plus 15 mins per group sharing back to uncover synergies)
  - o Session two: building a period-by-period activity plan (2 hours, plus 45 mins to review in plenary to drive closer alignment between activities)

Day 2

- Review progress from day 1
  - o Breakout 1 – optimizing the plan (cross-functional groups, 2 hours, plus 30 mins feedback)
    - – Making choices – fewer things with more scale?
    - – How can you improve co-ordination between activities?
    - – Are there any gaps?
  - o Breakout 2 (three groups for 3 hours)
    - – Draft the activity calendar
    - – Investment required and potential growth impact
    - – Crafting the story and sell-in for the plan
- Presenting back – peer review and defining next steps ahead of presenting plan/review (90 mins)

The outcome will be a draft integrated plan, bottom-up assumptions about the growth it will deliver, and a story to bring it to life. Let's explore more of what we will need to consider as we do this work.

What are brand campaigns and activities?

Remember our brand strategy house from Chapter 8, Figure 8.2?

During the strategic process we used various tools to get clear on our brand ambition – its role in the portfolio, vision, mission, and a measurable goal.

We worked out the most critical opportunities and threats we needed to overcome to grow penetration at a level sufficient to deliver the growth we needed.

We converted these opportunities into clear growth priorities, with simply articulated and insightful statements as to what we needed to do – for example, 'Get consumer x to choose our brand instead of y on z occasion by ...'.

We considered some of the fundamental things we need in place to access this growth – strong brand positioning, a connections plan, a creative platform, or at least a point of view on the type of brand we want to be from a creative standpoint.

As you focus on selecting activities for each brand campaign, consider expanding the lens of your connections plan to think about your total consumer experience plan. As discussed in the previous chapter, this covers all brand touchpoints, not just those primarily concerned with building consideration or mental availability and converting that into sales. Consumer experience also includes the brand experience in stores or online, the product or service experience, and anything which occurs afterwards including complaints, returns, disposal of waste etc. When planning brand-building activities, they must be congruent with your total consumer experience.

Remember the McDonald's example in Chapter 7? To rebuild trust and footfall, it would not have been sufficient to remind people what they loved about coming into a restaurant and building perceptions of better food values. This had to be matched with evolving the menu, and ensuring the restaurant environment competed more effectively with the competition. It should be self-evident, but you must think through holistically how your consumer experience will match up with your communications – especially when you are closing a perceived gap such as poor service for an insurance company, a bad reputation for a travel company etc.

Effective brands deploy communications alongside a broad range of levers, including distribution, visibility, pricing, promotion, pack price architecture, and so forth. These elements are integrated into the effective brand model – they ensure you harvest short-term sales as you build your brand for the long term.

At this point we should shift from talking about growth priorities to brand campaigns. A brand campaign describes a bundle of activities designed in combination to deliver growth. The key word here is 'describes' – a brand campaign is not an activity that the consumer sees or experiences but an internal way of describing the totality of activities deployed overtime against a specific growth priority. A brand campaign is not limited to advertising alone and may cover multiple touchpoints. This is an important distinction especially as the word campaign can be used improperly to describe an activity or activities within a single channel, for example, an 'email campaign'. Here our usage of brand campaign is specific and deliberate.

The McDonald's case had four brand campaigns to deliver its overall aim of driving footfall – value, variety, trust, and favourites. Each had a variety of activities. For example, 'value' was a combination of communications, promotions, and value product range, while 'variety' was a combination of communications and exciting product news. We talked previously about some of the activities on 'trust' and 'favourite' – reassuring consumers about McDonald's food and supply chain and reminding people why they love the brand.

Organizing your work around the idea of a brand campaign before thinking about specific activities is important as it will ensure every cent or penny you spend is focussed on the consumer opportunity, for the short and long term. We are rarely looking at a blank piece of paper, so with this framework you can look at the activities you have today – do they combine to tackle something coherent (a brand campaign) which is in service of the growth priorities you established through your understanding of the situation your brand faces? If not, perhaps they can be repurposed, or the money reinvested in something which does drive your growth priorities?

Tesco's turnaround 2015–19, covered in its grand prix-winning IPA paper, is a great example (Gregory and Parnum, 2020). There were three brand campaigns – trust, quality, and value, addressing the three challenges Tesco had identified to increasing footfall. To change the top-line metric against each one there were different activities, for example to shift value perceptions it needed to make its instore and value mechanics simpler for shoppers, to have a trading plan and value products based on shopper needs, and to have innovative products and services which brought value in new ways, such as a Clubcard Plus subscription service which brought Tesco, Tesco Mobile, and Tesco Bank offerings together.

In 2017, Cadbury in the UK faced revenue decline and falling penetration (King et al, 2022). The brand faced several issues following its acquisition in

2010 by Kraft which undermined its status as a prized national institu-
tion – rumours of recipe changes, overseas manufacturing, and an
overreliance on limited editions and new products. To overcome this,
Cadbury's priority was to rebuild penetration by re-establishing the brand
in the fabric of the nation. Though this was one focussed brand campaign to
rebuild love, there were still several activities required – emotionally engaging stories of everyday Britons using Cadbury to demonstrate generosity to
one another, activities to inspire people to show generosity to one another – a
worldwide Easter egg hunt, Secret Santa, also a partnership with 'Age UK'
to tackle loneliness, and initiatives to encourage shoppers to support strug-
gling corner shops.

The implications of these examples are:

- Be clear on the distinction between brand campaigns and activities, and
  indeed the red thread to them from growth priorities which address the
  opportunities and threats to penetration growth.
- Think holistically about your consumer experience – how do you ensure
  communications are congruent with all other brand proof points?
- Consider a full suite of activities. Though this will be truer for scaling and
  maturing brands, all brands will need to consider the interplay of activities
  designed to build mental availability with physical availability, pricing,
  promotion and so forth.

Reflections

Are you clear on the difference between activities and brand campaigns with
your own brand?

Do you understand how different activities work together to affect consumer
perceptions of your brand?

How should I choose activities?

The examples cited above were pivotal moments for those brands – they
recognized they faced challenges and had to make interventions. The cycles
for these interventions were over several years. This means that most of the
time and for most brands we are not creating a plan from scratch, even when

in crisis. Brands in flow typically have a reasonable baseline of activities and good information on which to base decisions.

When we considered investment across the portfolio in Chapter 10, we reflected that investment was typically spread too thinly across brands, especially versus their future profit potential. This is often true within brands, too – they have insufficient investment to cover all the brand campaigns and activities they aspire to do.

It may also be true that the more activities and brand campaigns you have, the more of your budget will go on development costs, leaving less available for deployment. These are just the bare facts of agency and production fees, research costs, and so on.

It's good practice to reuse work. There is great evidence proving that creative wear out is largely in the mind of the marketer (Marketing Week, 2022). I worked on one brand where data demonstrated that a particular suite of assets delivered a better return on investment after five years of being used than during its first year.

The examples above are also brands with scale. It's worth thinking through the lens of seeding, scaling, and maturing brands – the latter, as we saw above, can often be as much about staying on top and avoiding decline. For seed brands we discussed that investment might be best focussed on one or two channels, and probably on one brand campaign – perhaps with only a couple of activities. Scaling brands may be able to stretch their money further, but only maturing brands can fund multiple brand campaigns.

It's good discipline to prioritize. In essence, this means ensuring your first brand campaign is appropriately funded before you place funding on a second brand campaign. Within each brand campaign you also need to ask if you can fund each activity to deliver the appropriate level of reach or impact to drive the attitudinal or behavioural change you seek. This is about recognizing budgets are finite and paying attention to whether you are doing each activity at a level sufficient to generate an impact.

How much is enough?

The conversation about sufficiency is an important one. In essence, how much investment is enough, or if I had another dollar where would I put it? There are lots of different approaches to thinking about sufficiency – be it in media sufficiency or across your whole marketing mix. Think about the three 'E's of activity selection – am I spending *enough*, focussed on the most *efficient* and *effective* activities?

Chapter 10 advocated for spending disproportionately on those brands with the biggest future profit potential and track record of growth delivery. There are many rules of thumb for determining the right amount to spend including reinvestment rate (marketing spend as a percentage of revenue) often favoured by finance and for which there are expected levels for different categories. This approach does not address spend relative to competitors, or brand or category stage of development – smaller brands typically need a higher percentage, and maturing ones a lower percentage.

'Excess share of voice' is another approach – there is strong evidence that brands with a higher share of voice than their share of market will grow (Binet and Field, 2013). Over time ESOV has become impractical for practitioners – it focusses on media rather than total marketing deployment spend and the changing media landscape means it is likely to be based on less than 50% of advertising spend given so much money goes on platforms where competitor spend data is not available. The spend of smaller brands may be ignored entirely, depending on their media and channel choices.

A good starting point, especially for seeding brands, is to look at what you spent last year and see what effect it caused. If you look year on year, you should account for the impact of seasonality, but it is worth considering if there was anything unusual which may have driven your sales rate. Aside from this, consider the underlying effects of any changes in distribution or pricing. In the most basic form, what's left is likely to be the impact of your investment. As it is likely you will have had limited activities on a seeding brand, you can be more certain in attributing any growth to what you have done.

Brands in a scaling phase can eyeball their data to get to a similar starting point, albeit the more activities in play the harder to understand which are working. Within a particular platform, such as Meta, over time the data will begin to point to the right level of spend, and when it becomes unresponsive. Attribution modelling will give you a more precise answer as to how much is enough. At some point as reach increases you start to hit the same people over and over – it becomes wasteful to reach the same people in your audience.

Once your marketing deployment spend reaches or exceeds the equivalent of a million pounds it become sensible to invest a small proportion of that in marketing mix modelling, which we will discuss more in Chapter 16 on measurement. Marketing mix modelling isolates the impact of spend from other variables so you can see what's working individually and in combination.

Using modelling, a scaling or maturing brand will be able to determine more precisely how much to spend and on what, as well as how much profit will be returned. Models generate graphs populated with interesting reach curves which can answer more precisely the question on sufficiency and indicate where there are likely to be diminishing returns.

Optimizing return is an ongoing question brand marketers and media specialists must grapple with – the parameters are constantly shifting based on media prices, competitive investment, and consumer media consumption patterns. From the simplest observation to the most complex approaches to modelling, there are good ways to form a strong point of view. The most evolved businesses have developed tools which can help determine how to spend across a portfolio in a way which is sufficient to deliver against a business objective, or indeed how much to spend on a specific brand and how to spend that money effectively. One such example is Diageo's marketing catalyst programme (Geoghegan, 2020).

A parallel debate to sufficiency is what proportion of spend should be on building brand associations versus converting that to sales. Selling your brand does not inherently damage its perceived strength so we should be careful in our language not to set these types of spend in opposition to one another – it can be divisive, especially in your relationship with sales colleagues. A rule of thumb for consumer goods categories is 60:40 brand building to conversion (Binet and Field, 2013). When you look at your own brand, however, you may find it harder to categorize different activities as purely 'brand building' or 'sales driving', especially in categories with a high percentage of online purchases – so much digital content is shoppable, and media on a digital shelf can serve to build associations for a shopper in a buying situation as well as trigger that purchase. It will be important to seek balance and develop a feeling as to what works for you on your brand, but the 60:40 heuristic is evidence-based and a starting point.

You must understand what your business sees as success in the long and short term, and how you build belief in a model which comprises engaging with your audience on their path to purchase as well as in the moment of choice. In an environment predisposed to short-term sales metrics where performance marketing datasets are well established, how might you make the point for spending further up the funnel? The balance will depend on your brand and its life stage, its category, and route to market. When you recognize that advertising channels such as Google, Microsoft, Amazon, and Facebook spend billions of dollars on advertising to build their own brands it does make you wonder why this is such a thorny issue.

Still, it is good to have a target and work out how to deliver it in practice. If you think about your marketing spend holistically, you may find that it is not all managed by marketers – this may be the case for spend on retail media platforms or CRM platforms which help you identify prospective customers and close sales. Is this sales or marketing?

Beyond sufficiency and balance, the best tool you have for selecting activities is to consider effectiveness versus efficiency. Build a 2 × 2 matrix of high and low efficiency and effectiveness such as Figure 14.1. A simple measure for efficiency would be the cost of reaching a consumer looking at both development and deployment costs, recognizing for activities you are reusing you may choose to exclude development costs ongoing. Given that we are likely to be talking about large scaling brands and maturing brands, marketing mix modelling can help you determine the incremental revenue and profit attributable to each activity. Often these metrics naturally correlate, but it is a framework which will help you determine which activities to stop, which to question and redevelop, and which to continue. Smaller brands may not have all the data, but it is still worth populating it with what you do know. Having all your activities on a page relative to each other will provoke a conversation about which have performed rather than biasing those which your team enjoy implementing.

Judgement plays an important role – let's say you have a bundle of activities designed to overcome value perceptions. Let's imagine it is for a household cleaning brand. You may find that your media is effective and efficient in telling your story, but that an activity providing a brand experience which demonstrates value in real life is effective but less efficient,

FIGURE 14.1 Effectiveness versus efficiency

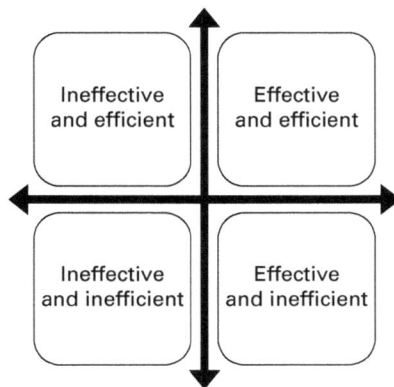

FIGURE 14.2 Brand activity calendar

Brand/Market	Q1			Q2			Q3			Q4		
	1	2	3	4	5	6	7	8	9	10	11	12
Brand campaign #1												
Activity A												
Activity B												
Activity C												
Brand campaign #2												
Activity A												
Activity B												
Activity C												
Core range												
Tactical innovation												
Strategic innovation												
Pricing												
Promotion												
Shopper/Seasonal												
Distribution												

and tricky to deliver at scale. Knowing the importance of the brand demonstrating to consumers its value in an emotional way may lead you to continue or think about how you might redesign the ideas to be scalable. Be bold, however, in ditching the activities which are nice to have and redeploy that money on hard-working activities.

By thinking through the activities required to deliver your brand campaigns, assessing the impact of your existing activities, and identifying critical gaps which may need to be briefed, you are half way to building a draft plan of when and in what combination you will deploy those activities over the next 12–18 months as outlined in Figure 14.2.

In a workshop context, this is achievable using a simple table with quarters or months as columns, with a section for each brand campaign and associated activities as rows.

As you build this with your team it will flush out key questions – what other brand or category activity might be planned at this time? Am I balancing the times when my consumer may be most receptive, with relative peaks and troughs in media and other costs? How will this spend correlate with the business cycle and does that create any risk for available investment should business become pressured?

You are setting the stage for combining media and other consumer activation with the other elements of your plan.

Reflections

How much is enough investment to deliver your goals?

Which are your most efficient activities?

Which are your most effective activities?

How do you select activities to ensure you consider these dimensions and the change in consumer attitude and behaviour required to deliver your plan?

How do I ensure physical availability, shopper marketing, pricing, and other drivers are integrated into the plan?

Integration of media and communications with other critical sales drivers makes for a great plan.

Pricing

From an annual standpoint, the key question you need to address is what pricing actions you need to plan, when, and what impact they may have on your expected performance.

Depending on your organization, your category, channels, and brand, the role of marketing in pricing will differ. Pricing overall is a broad subject – establishing the brand's relative value in consumer's minds, ensuring the consumer's experience is congruent with that expectation, and unlocking long- and short-term brand value through realizing the best price for every sale. Too often, however, pricing is underutilized as an important strategic tool, more focussed on reacting to the competitive environment, and the need to deliver in the short term. Strong brands command higher price points and are inherently more valued by consumers but it is difficult to achieve the balance.

Strategic pricing will be determined by several factors – what the organization needs to charge to make its desired level of revenue and profit over the long and short term, what consumers are prepared to pay, what price communicates to consumers about brand value, and desired pricing relative to competitors in the marketplace.

From a brand standpoint it is good to have determined a stance on strategic price positioning. This is based on consumer perceptions of brand value relative to the competition. Though you need to be cognizant of the cost of providing your product or service, and margin expectations, profitability should not be the start point – instead, consider the benefits you offer and what this means to your target audience. This is typically expressed as an index versus the category average, or in some cases an index versus a specific competitor – it may be versus the market leader, a mainstream brand, or in some instances versus a key competitor in a tightly contested segment. Understanding the impact of market movements on your brand's value index drives the actions you may take.

When we think about brand building, we focus on the long-term incremental revenue and profit generated by building awareness, positive associations, and converting that to sales in the short term. However, the other main outcome is that effective brands are more able to charge and maintain a premium – they are less price sensitive or inelastic, meaning that they can increase price with less impact on sales.

In stable economic times, pricing may be simply a case of keeping pace with inflation – for consumer brands typically measured relative to a consumer price index which reflects the combined impact across many categories of increasing direct and indirect costs in providing a service compared with what consumers are prepared to pay. However, it is an average – as categories mature, they tend to be less valued by consumers and, without innovation, pricing becomes less dynamic compared to newer or more innovative categories – think about how brands such as Nike, North Face, and Patagonia in sportswear were able to keep prices higher compared to price squeezed food and beverages.

Determine pricing recommendations by working out the likely changes in your brand's cost base, your organization's annual goals especially regarding maintaining and growing profitability, and the extent to which you believe you can implement a price change and predict the impact of changes to the price your consumer sees. Few and far between are those brands with the strength to own their own sales channels, and for the rest list prices are a recommendation. In tightly contested segments like grocery retail, for example, intense focus on market share will mean price changes which may negatively influence the cost to consumer of a typical basket will be scrutinized both internally and by retail customers.

In the context of an annual plan, you should be mainly concerned with making pricing changes which balance these considerations:

- What is the business's expectation of revenue and profit from your brand?
- What has changed in the costs associated with delivering your product and service?
- What are the category and competitor pricing trends?
- What may have changed in your consumer attitude to what they are prepared to pay?
- What may have changed in your customers' (resellers/channels) attitudes to price?

When thinking about a price change pay attention to things such as historic precedent, timing, competitor pricing, and other risks. It's tempting to have a trade-focussed view on in-year pricing – it takes belief in the inherent value of your brand to consumers to hold your ground.

It's important to consider the positive and negative consequences of pricing initiatives. For example, what was the average increase or decrease in price in your category over time, looking both at brands and different segments. What patterns can you observe when prices changes are implemented – is there a predictable time each year, a rhythm of one brand, typically the market leader, increasing prices which competitors follow? What is the impact of trade channels on pricing rhythms?

Here we are assuming one pricing initiative a year, but in less stable economies this may be more frequent, sometimes every couple of months or every quarter where inflation is high, and brands must be vigilant managing cash flows and inventory. Having a strong brand can be even more critical in such circumstances – price perceptions are more dynamic and the risk of pricing beyond perceived value for consumers, or under-pricing and risking commoditization, is real. What's fair for your consumers, your customers, and you?

How will you integrate a price increase into your plan? Consider how much and when you will execute. Be clear on any risks there may be in executing a price increase, and what impact it may have, positive or negative, on sales.

Beyond pricing

Pricing does not happen in a vacuum. As you look at the plan, ensure that you have considered how you might mitigate risk from a pricing change through brand architecture, promotion, and innovation, as well as brand communications.

In the section above we reflected on pricing as if it were a single number, relative to an anchor point in the category or in your consumer's mind. As you turn strategy into an action-oriented plan it helps to think about how other dimensions which unlock brand value might work together. You cannot think about price without considering the promotional dynamics and intensity of the channels in which you sell, or indeed the pricing of different formats or tiers of your brand offering and how they may work together to win with different consumers.

This is how you execute pricing, and it means proactively correlating pricing with the different types of benefits consumers are seeking, more than it is about managing changes in your cost base and reacting to competitive pressure. This is the difference between thinking strategically about changes you may wish to make in year, versus thinking tactically or defensively.

The tiers in your product or service offering should be based around the same insight into consumer motivation and behaviour we discussed in Chapter 6. Based on their needs, what are the different benefits consumers are looking for in your category? Some of them will be universal hygiene factors or basics, but others have more value and can be staggered in your offering to create price progression in your range – typically from good, to better, to best. If you are unclear on what your consumer values, you will struggle to use pricing as a clear signal to how to navigate your brand.

CASE STUDY

Let's look at an example to show how an effective brand uses pricing, pack architecture, promotion, and innovation together effectively to build long-term value. Think about the Apple iPhone. Let's make no mistake, despite its high penetration iPhone is a luxury brand commanding significantly higher than average market prices. If you review the 2007 launch communications, one of the first things Apple did was to anchor price in the mind of its target audience as great value – by describing it as 'a revolutionary mobile phone, a widescreen iPod with touch controls, and a breakthrough Internet communications device with desktop-class email, Web browsing, searching and maps — into one small and lightweight handheld device' (Apple, 2007). Immediately our frame of reference is the combined price of these devices, not the mobile phone category.

If we ignore for a moment the value iPhone SE option, iPhone comes in three main tiers – at the time of writing in 2024, iPhone 14, 15, and 16 with an entry price of $599 up to a staggering $1,599. These correlate with an easy-to-navigate classic 'good, better, best' pricing strategy, with a 'better plus' extension of the top two tiers providing the latest tech in a 'Pro' version with a better camera and other features. Pricing is easy to navigate with three variables – age of technology, memory, and screen size, and this hierarchy is reflected in the design of the consumer experience and its coherent inter-tier pricing.

The newest tech is $100 more than last year's, and $300 more than that of the year before. Consumers pay an additional $200 for a larger screen only available in the latest two models, and $100 for each increment of 128 mb of memory, also organized around tiers. Storage particularly represents a great trade-up opportunity – consumers perceive the value of storage in a linear fashion whereas the incremental cost of memory components is much smaller.

In effect, there is an iPhone at each increment of $100, and this clarity makes it easy for consumers to compare the value of these different attributes – for example, an 128 mb iPhone 16 is $799 and a 128 mb iPhone 15 is $699. A similar pattern is seen in other currencies – in the UK pricing for the iPhone 15 starts at £699 and moves up in increments of £100. In almost every currency Apple understands the importance of pricing beneath psychological price thresholds (e.g. £699 not £700) and making it easy to understand value progression.

Promotion and innovation are inherent in this approach. As I mentioned at the beginning, Apple offers older, but acceptable technology, in the form of iPhone SE or 'special edition' – in effect, an everyday low price. Each year, currently in September, Apple uses innovation to upgrade the range – launching a new phone into 'best' with a 'best plus' pro version, and cascading models down a segment, from 'best' to 'good' and retiring the model currently in 'good'. It will probably only break the cycle when there is a step change in technology. Everyday promotion is baked into this approach by discounting older technology. In general, it is only in the short lead up towards the launch of innovation that there will be any other discounting – recognizing the perceived value of existing models may dip just before a technology upgrade.

Of course, Apple benefits from owning its route to the consumer – either through direct sales channels or approved resellers, but this underscores the power of its brand, and its choice to invest ahead in those things, such as retail, as a key part of a remarkable consumer experience.

As well being one of the world's most valuable brands, Apple has an impressive operating margin, despite high investment in research and development. Its approach to building the brand and unlocking value with clear price positioning, pack price architecture, promotion, and innovation is a big driver of this. Though it is an innovation-driven business, it can effectively harvest 'old' technology for several years. Pricing on other ranges follows similar simple core principles.

Alongside advertising, Apple launch events are important brand-building events for the business, enabling it to maintain its edge in the category, and build on its inherent distinctiveness. These events are in fact its annual pricing initiative – timed ahead of the key seasonal trading period and designed to build value in the mind of consumers. The mobile phone market is also driven by penetration – recruiting new consumers and recruiting back into the brand when they upgrade their phone. Apple's pricing ladder, or perhaps more accurately pricing matrix, maps to different segments of the market it sees as penetration targets, right down to the 'SE' model.

What can we learn from Apple about integrating pricing into our plans?

1 Have a clear price positioning versus the market.

2 Map product or service offerings to penetration opportunities.

3 Be clear on the additional benefits consumers care about and charge for them.

4 Use promotion, where possible, to drive incremental penetration and visibility versus subsidizing sales.

5 Integrate innovation, and new or improved benefits, into your thinking and charge for them.

6 Make it easy to shop so consumers can find what meets their needs, easily trading up or down.

When you look closer there are clear patterns in most categories, albeit brands do not always work them through with as much elegance as Apple. If you look at Samsung pricing in comparison to Apple, you can see how the market leader often defines category rules and competitors work within them.

Rules differ by category, and in insurance, breakdown cover, and energy sectors, for example, promoted pricing is used as a recruitment tool, in the hope that consumers will remain after the initial period. The downside of this is that to avoid trading purely on price these brands must also focus on delivering a remarkable consumer experience to avoid consumers going back to the market to seek a discounted price, and in some markets, legislation protects consumers from unfair pricing further down the line.

The Apple example is best in class but look on any grocery shelf and you will see the same principles in action. The global auto-dishwashing detergent brand Finish in the UK has Power, Quantum, Ultimate, and Ultimate Plus following the same tier structure as Apple and with different pack configurations delivering better per-unit price points for higher volume. Ultimate Plus sells at a premium of over 40% to Power, depending on the pack.

Consumer goods brands must typically focus on maintaining a strong average selling price given the intensity of promotions with deep discounts in modern trade across the world as retailers battle for market share. To drive penetration in such markets having a strong brand will enable you to better manage the depth of discount, and critically ensure promotions drive off-shelf display. It's quite simple, on-shelf promotions subsidize purchases that would have happened in any case, and encourage switching, whereas secondary placements will attract new and light buyers who may not have considered buying the category that day. In markets where discount retailers are developed, brands must also contend with everyday low prices and ensuring they have a differentiated proposition to avoid price matching. In such categories shoppers quickly tune in to promotional patterns.

Promotion need also not be price promotion – competitions and prizes are other examples where the aim may be to recruit light buyers but may often end up appealing only to a small core.

As we saw with the Apple example it's important to know how shoppers navigate and judge price. iPhone is anchored in our minds in comparison with multiple devices supported with strong brand perceptions, but ultimately it is absolute price or affordability which matters. It could be price per volume, price per serve, or something else entirely. Shoppers quickly learn pricing and navigate using only system 1 brain power. It's often only during economic shocks and inflation where choices may be actively examined due to price.

In designing pricing architecture across their range of products or services, effective brands consider not only their brand positioning but also the implication of understanding shopper needs and missions, and how shoppers navigate value in the moment of choice. A classic example is Coke, which can sell 500 ml as a convenience format at a higher price to a 2 L bottle which would be part of a routine stock-up shop.

INNOVATION

In your annual plan for innovation or new products, you may need to include something as part of a brand campaign or to excite the trade. Innovation to create news is prevalent in many categories – from partnerships on luxury brands such as Rimowa to fast-food menu items, and flavours or fragrances of ice cream brands or low-cost shower gels. Getting the right cadence of launching innovation may be important to maintain a level of interest for trade and consumer, and it may increase shelf space or visibility for your brand, but it is rarely incremental longer term, and can create undue complexity in your organization.

It's likely, however, that you will include more sustainable and scalable innovation within your plan – innovation designed to recruit new consumers or stretch your brand into adjacent motivations or occasions of existing brand buyers. These are higher risk and higher reward ventures, requiring funding and planning to ensure they work synergistically with your core brand versus diluting spend and potential impact. It can be a challenge to launch innovation at higher price points to your brand's core offering, but it's critical to get this right and avoid giving away new technology or benefits priced in line with your core, ultimately eroding your brand value.

DISTRIBUTION AND VISIBILITY

Annual planning is the perfect opportunity to revisit the other drivers of physical availability – especially distribution and visibility.

On distribution, it may be as simple as understanding the universe of available points of sale for your brand, how present you are in them, with a bias towards those which represent the highest turnover for your category. It is not just about being present, it is important to be clear on the right offer for different channels understanding the shoppers they serve, and ensuring you are always available. You also need to be aware of the cost of distribution – profit margin expectations, trade investment and terms, and so on.

Measuring distribution purely as a percentage can be misleading. Aim to understand not only the presence your brand has, but the quality of that presence, and its suitability for the channel type based on shopper needs. Though this will be ongoing work, building a plan cross-functionally should focus you on how opportunities for distribution can be supported by your broader brand-building initiatives.

Ensuring your brand is visible at the moment of choice is a minimum standard. We discussed distinctive brand assets in Chapter 12 as an important aspect of being recognizable, but visibility goes beyond being present and you will need to make choices about where and how to invest across your distribution base to drive the biggest impact on- and offline.

Focus on these two elements – firstly, ensure your brand is easy to shop all year round in a way that is appropriate for the environment, and secondly, deploy temporary activities which support your brand campaigns. Being easy to shop is highly category and channel specific. Consider categories such as beauty which may have highly branded fixtures within a store, or an online landing page which may both build desire and inform. Effective brands will define and measure the standards they expect to see by channel and understand with real clarity which one or two things have the biggest impact on sales depending on the shopping context. Temporary activities are often known as shopper programmes – as well as being part of a brand campaign these may be seasonal opportunities where consumer and shopper behaviour changes – big public holidays, warmer weather, or pre-planning peaks such as January for summer vacation bookings.

To be successful requires an understanding of what drives the final choice, especially as most consumers tend to have a category purchase, not a brand purchase, in mind before they shop. Focus your visibility items where choice happens – it could be at a shelf, a rack, a table, a bar, a counter, or a page online. How do shoppers choose and how can you influence choice in that moment? Consider things such as advocacy – reviews, salesperson recommendation, as well as product information, and even sensory signals.

Remember how many decisions are made with quick system 1 thinking – visibility is about standing out to shoppers, engaging them if you can, and then sealing the deal. The most important visibility materials will be right where the shopper places the item in a real or virtual basket, but may include proximity media (a shoppable piece of media content, the website landing page, on entering a store) and investing in online and on-platform search. Visibility is, of course, linked strongly to the other considerations discussed in this chapter, especially promotion.

What interventions will you make to increase visibility to support your annual plan? This may include new materials linked to a brand campaign, a piece of innovation, or a seasonal moment. They need to be planned to ensure there is synergy between the things which will continuously drive short-term sales performance, and those which build a remarkable brand in the minds of your consumers.

What all this boils down to is knowing what you are trying to achieve. How do all these things combined enable you to convert all the positive associations you are building in the minds of your consumer into purchase – the right value perception, the right price point to capture different parts of your audience, the right format or service bundle to meet their needs on that occasion, the right promotion to capture lighter and less engaged buyers, innovation to grab an incremental sale, and your brand being available and standing out on a real or digital shelf?

Reflections

What is the strategic price positioning of your brand relative to the market?

What actions will you need to take in the next year to maintain or achieve your desired price positioning?

What actions will you need to take to optimize brand pack and service architecture to support pricing, and unlock profitable growth?

What actions will you take to promote your brand? What guidelines will you follow to ensure promotion has a positive impact on growing penetration, and recognizes different channel environments?

What tactical innovation will you launch next year to provide news and excitement?

Will you launch any strategic innovation and how will you price, promote, and invest in it to ensure success without detracting from your core brand?

What actions will you take regarding distribution opportunities?

What actions will you take to ensure minimum standards of visibility, and where will you invest in visibility materials?

References

Apple (2007) Apple reinvents the phone with iPhone, www.apple.com/uk/ newsroom/2007/01/09Apple-Reinvents-the-Phone-with-iPhone/ (archived at https://perma.cc/A2WZ-QH46)

Binet, L and Field, P (2013) *The Long and the Short of It*, IPA, London

Geoghegan, A (2020) Diageo portfolio. Marketing catalyst: Creating a culture of marketing effectiveness, in *Advertising Works 25, Proving the payback on marketing investment*, ed. S Unerman, pp 119–145, Ascential Events (Europe), London.

Gregory, S and Parnum, J (2020) From running shops to serving customers: The Tesco turnaround story, in *Advertising Works 25, Proving the payback on marketing investment*, ed. S Unerman, pp 47–86, IPA Effectiveness Awards 2020, Ascential Events (Europe), London

King, A et al (2022) Cadbury 'There's a glass & a half in everyone': How intrinsic purpose can transform a brand's fortunes, in *Advertising Works 26, Proving the payback on marketing investment*, ed. H. Singh, pp 41–75, IPA Effectiveness Awards 2022, IPA, London

Marketing Week (2022) Study finds ad effectiveness does not 'wear-out' over time, www.marketingweek.com/study-ad-effectiveness-does-not-decline (archived at https://perma.cc/FR2D-ZH2Z)

15

How do I bring the plan together?

- How do I create a growth plan and a budget? p. 212
- How do I set KPIs and a learning plan? p. 217

How do I create a growth plan and a budget?

Pressure test your plan

The cross-functional working session from Chapter 14 will create a draft plan, integrating and incorporating a full mix of elements. It will require several iterations to button down but will guide action and prepare you for deployment.

As a final exercise, take a step back from your emerging plan. You will have too much material. Some good 'pressure test' questions to ask are:

- If you had to cut 20% of activities or budget, what would you cut?
- If you were given 20% more money, where would you invest?
- Are your activities enough to deliver the outcome you need?
- Are you focussing on the most efficient and effective activities?
- Are you using a blend of existing and new activities?
- For new initiatives, do you have the time and resources to create them?
- Have you captured important actions such as distribution opportunities, price changes, and pack or service optimization?
- Have you balanced activities which will build brand associations with ones which will drive sales?
- Are you placing as much of your available budget on consumer-facing activities, minimizing development spend?

Build a simple financial model

In partnership with finance, this plan on a page can quickly be turned into a high-level model to determine the overall impact on sales in the coming year, and the investment required to achieve the revenue goal. This is a growth plan, a simple version of which can be seen in Figure 15.1. This exercise is valuable as it is another opportunity to link your brand activity to the financial language of the business. For example, as marketers we think about growing penetration where our finance colleagues consider customer acquisition. We may consider the effectiveness and efficiency of our plan, and the budget required to deliver it sufficiently, but finance wants to understand the cost of that growth and risk inherent in it. Taking the time to work with your colleagues to bridge this language divide can pay enormous dividends in building belief in the plan, making it stronger, more focussed, and more likely to be signed off.

The work will help you demonstrate the financial outcome of this plan. Simply put, work out the incremental benefits of all your activities using assumptions based on past work, analytics, and good judgement. Include activities which sit squarely within your growth priorities as well as things such as pricing, changes to your product or service formats and the costs to implement them, promotions, seasonal shopper marketing, and tactical innovation or 'news'. Tailor this list to what is relevant to your brand and category.

This exercise will provoke a conversation on how credible the plan is and where there may be tensions.

Depending on how robust your data is, build up a model at activity level which can be aggregated to brand campaign level to cover the potential incremental revenue, the cost of achieving that revenue, and its effectiveness. Keep it simple – don't get bogged down in thinking about things like staff costs etc. It helps to categorize each element of the plan according to your confidence level in delivering it.

You may, for example, have included some distribution gains – some of them may have been agreed or have high certainty, whereas others may require more work. Use a simple coding system against each activity, for those with a medium or high degree of risk it's good to work out what would need to be true to increase the probability of that part of your plan delivering. Understanding what will need to be created and what actions carried out to deliver a plan where the risks have been mitigated is the basis of the work you need to do to prepare for execution.

FIGURE 15.1 Brand activity cost, return, and risk

Brand campaign	Activity	Role of activity	Investment	Incremental revenue	Risk (H/M/L)

Low		Medium		High	
Investment	Revenue	Investment	Revenue	Investment	Revenue

In parallel consider the cost of delivering each of these activities. Where you have existing work to redeploy, this is about the cost of deployment at the level you are planning for next year, and where you may need to create new activities consider costs which may sit outside of any current agency fees – including cost of production, any usage rights you may need, and so forth. At this stage it's OK to build these costs indicatively using precedent and assumptions. You can refine these later when you optimize the plan.

Use these reference points to compare the cost and benefits of the different elements of your plan. It is not a purely financial exercise but about framing choices at a much lower level of detail. You should still consider activities as a bundle or brand campaign and understand the role of each in achieving the change in behaviour and attitude sought. You may be able to deprioritize an activity which looks ineffective, but not if it's critical for the others to work together – for example, sampling may look costly but if it's a powerful way to drive trial then without it the other activities may lose their effectiveness.

Either for your brand as a whole or for each brand campaign look at the percentage of investment it represents and compare that to the percentage of the overall growth it will give you and its cost. What opportunities are there to take money from those things which may lack scale or appear relatively speaking less effective than other parts of your plan? As a team consider how you might evolve your plan to be more effective – perhaps cutting any low reach activities, focussing spend even more, and looking at how activities are interconnected.

Review your plan to determine whether there are any potential external clashes with other brands or customer activity, including what you may know about likely timing of competitor activity. From an internal perspective consider any pinch points which may be present due to activities from other brands in your portfolio, and whether these may create competing demand for investment which may make funding harder to approve. Are there any other potential issues, and what would it take to resolve them together?

Build a budget

This exercise will also enable you to build a budget of spend requirements for the coming year. It can help to split this into development and deployment costs, sometimes referred to as working and non-working. Using the work you have done to understand the cost and benefit of the different activities you are proposing, build up your budget using Figure 15.2 as a reference.

- Consider development costs – fees for your agencies including creative, PR, design, experiential, and so on, splitting out ongoing costs and variable production fees associated with new activities. Make a provision for consumer research covered in your learning plan.
- Consider deployment costs – separate out different types of spend relevant to your brand, such as media, PR, experiential, sampling, sponsorship, shopper marketing, and so on. You may wish to cut this activation spend by different brand campaigns.

Try to capture the expected return for each line of your deployment costs for the coming year. Remember, we are constantly trying to get the balance right between concentrating spend on the activities which will be the hardest working while ensuring we have the right mix mapped to our understanding of the consumer journey.

Building a budget this way has a couple of benefits. Firstly, it creates a 'zero based' view of the investment required to deliver next year's growth, in contrast to the common practice of taking last year's spend and rolling it forward. Secondly, it enables you to understand the relative mix of spend between development and deployment. It will provoke you to think about whether you are spending enough against the most effective types of activity.

FIGURE 15.2 Brand budget, by brand campaign or total brand

Development	Investment	% Investment	Short-term return	Long-term return
Agency fees				
Production				
Research				
Deployment				
Media				
Experiential				
Sampling				
PR/Events				
Influencer				
Sponsorship				
Shopper/Seasonal				

Effective brands maximize the split of their spend between deployment and development. They are continually seeking efficiencies in their development spend. It is not that this category of spend is not valuable, but it can become unbalanced. For some brands, especially luxury brands, or brands which use costly branded display and merchandising such as beauty brands, there may be a higher percentage against development but for many it may be around 20% of their total annual budget. It is also true that bigger brands and international brands benefit in this regard. If a brand reuses activities, this amount may fluctuate year on year, and it is worth getting into a rhythm for renovation work on things such as pack and comms, so they don't all happen in the same year.

Consider consumer research costs carefully. As we will discuss below, aligning these to a learning plan ensures spend reflects critical learning needs and decisions – valuable investments not costs. You may wish to categorize research costs by those which are continuous, such as consumer behaviour tracking, and brand strength and market share measurement, and those which are more ad hoc – communications, innovation, and pack development, and things such as marketing mix modelling which may not be conducted annually.

As you examine deployment costs, include a view on likely returns as it is another way to provoke a conversation on the mix of spend. Is there enough money against brand-building lines, typically things such as media, balanced against sales driving activities? This 'top down' view might provoke some reprioritization – perhaps you have some elements which are less effective and may not have enough scale. How might you better apportion that money to drive the biggest overall impact?

In a multi-brand business this budget should further provoke discussion about where to invest. Do you remember in the chapter on portfolio we considered investment in terms of the future profit potential of different brands? Constructing your budget with a development/deployment split and a view on likely returns enables a healthy comparison of the cost of growth of different brands – depending on their stage of development and the type of work they require some may be hungrier for funding than others. Transparent budgeting enables you to further polarize spend between brands and within them and create constructive challenge – let every penny count and welcome debate.

Reflections

How could you further optimize your plan?

Could you focus on fewer activities and deliver better results?

What opportunities are there within your budget to focus more spend on deployment and less on development?

Do you have the right balance between brand-building and conversion or sales-driving activities in your deployment spend?

How do I set KPIs and a learning plan?

Setting KPIs

With an integrated activity plan organized around brand campaigns, KPIs, or key performance indicators, can be defined for the coming year. These should be organized around the forthcoming financial year, and where you expect to be at the close of the year. Once you are in a rhythm these will be consistent over time, featuring for example in the brand performance review we discussed in Chapter 9.

KPIs should be aligned to the numerical goals in your three- to five-year brand ambition. If you remember, this included business and brand goals. Business goals included things such as revenue, profit, and volume, whereas brand goals include things such as the change in penetration, market share, brand strength, and net promoter score. Your plan should illustrate the impact of the year ahead in delivering these.

For the year ahead, once you've created a zero-based budget and growth goal, add in the benchmark for each brand campaign. Build a table, such as Figure 15.3, which includes last year, this year (as you expect to finish it), and the following year showing the percentage, percentage point, or actual change as you see it.

What are the key metrics associated with each brand campaign? These will include a subset of consumer metrics such as the change in penetration, but may also include attitudinal or brand associations relevant to the brand campaign. If, for example, you were trying to build trust or quality perceptions you would want to understand the extent to which you were achieving that, probably relative to competition and if possible linked to consumer behaviour. To understand effects, you might capture measures such as awareness (of your brand campaign/activities rather than your brand) and the conversion of that awareness to trial.

In this final section you should include KPIs, setting your desired goal for things such as distribution, quality of distribution, average price, promotional intensity (frequency and depth).

We will consider in Chapter 16 the types of measures and approaches to measurement which should be in your effective brand-building system, but it starts with building a simple balanced scorecard with clear links from activities, to brand campaigns, to overall brand and business goals.

Capture the key shifts – the three or four core metrics which you will focus on. How will you measure them and how often?

Create a learning plan

As you finalize the annual activity plan, growth plan, and budget it's important to reflect on where there are gaps in your understanding about what needs to be true to deliver it.

Reflect on the conclusions about consumers and shoppers on which you have built the plans. What learning do you have that supports these conclusions, and where are there knowledge gaps? It helps to capture these as learning questions, to categorize the level of risk each of them poses and then to work out how you are going to answer them.

You might have learning questions around the potential response to price movements, changes in promotional strategy, or changes to your product offering, or communications. For innovation you might want to understand who's likely to buy, and what they will buy this new product instead of to understand potential incrementality.

FIGURE 15.3 What will be different, year-on-year shifts

	Last year	This year	Next year	%/Chg vs YA	Notes
Business					
Net revenue					
Volume					
(Gross) Profit					
Brand					
Brand strength					
% Penetration					
Frequency					
Value market share					
Distribution					
Promotion weeks					
Promotion depth					
Visibility					
Brand campaign					
Awareness					
Conversion					
Brand image					

You might be able to answer these learning questions through existing research or data you have or by acquiring secondary data or conducting primary consumer research. Alongside capturing critical questions, a learning plan should identify how you will address each question, timing to ensure that learning informs action, and investment to ensure research funding is in place.

A robust learning plan will de-risk your brand plan, enabling you to focus on the least amount of the most powerful data, enrich consumer understanding, and be clear that your plan straightforwardly addresses the opportunities and threats you identified for growth.

Bring it all together as one story

By now you should have confidence in a plan covering the next 12–18 months' brand campaigns and activities, complete with critical supporting actions on pricing, promotion, range, shopper marketing, and innovation. The good news is that by choosing to work cross-functionally you will have built belief in the plan, overcome many internal challenges, be clearer on the risks to delivery, and have a learning plan to support you.

It's worth taking another step back and thinking about how you will create excitement for the plan internally, ensuring it is signed off and supported in implementation. This is another instance where understanding the organization, its mindset, and culture will pay enormous dividends in how you share the plan.

A plan, after all, is a simple story. The payoff for the organization is success in delivering the brand goals which in turn will help the organization succeed in its goals and ambition. The brand is the hero overcoming the challenges it has identified, with the plan explaining how.

Think about the motivations of your stakeholders – telling this story in a way which enables them to see its value, and what you need from them is essential. Beware the traps of overselling or burying the story under too much data.

You have at your disposal key ingredients:

- your brand ambition – the value at stake for the organization;
- the situation the brand faces – the jeopardy or opportunity;
- the choices you've made about the biggest obstacles or opportunities to grow or premium-ize;

- insight into your consumers and shoppers to help you overcome them;
- what you've learnt in the last year which can help you and build belief;
- the actions you plan to take;
- the impact these actions will have on your brand – how they will deliver the goal;
- what needs to be true – investment required, and how you plan to mitigate the things that could go wrong.

Remember to include what you are seeking from stakeholders – belief, commitment to budget, or specific actions to overcome internal barriers or issues.

In bringing plans to life, marketers often spend too much time on the detail of the plan itself and the data behind it when it's better to focus on setting context, sharing what the plan will deliver, its cost, critical risks and assumptions, and building belief that the actions are right for the consumer and the brand/business. Be conscious of the biases and decision-making style and needs of individual stakeholders.

What matters for most stakeholders is the commercial value of the plan you put together, not the minutiae of individual activities or communications messaging. It's useful to illustrate the bridge from your start point today to the end of your financial year, as illustrated in Figure 15.4. Using the work you did on your growth plan, this may be as simple as showing the incremental revenue for each of the different buckets of growth – perhaps one for each brand campaign, with values for range, pricing, promotion, distribution, innovation, shopper marketing, or seasonal shopper activity. This demonstrates visually the balance in your plan, and what proposed investment will deliver. It will also allow comparison in a portfolio business of the relative cost, outcomes, and inherent risk across brands.

The question of what needs to be true to deliver the goal is an important one. Though much of your plan may be based on existing proven brand campaigns, there will still be ambiguity around its achievability. Establish what needs to be true to deliver the plan, what commitments the organization may need to make and by when – this might be in signing off budget or a campaign, or in agreeing a supply solution for a piece of innovation. It is important to articulate risks to delivering the plan and appropriate mitigation – risks may include regulatory approvals, a customer failing to buy into your plan, unexpected changes in the macro-environment. Selling in your plan is your opportunity to flush these out and gain commitment from the organization.

FIGURE 15.4 Projected brand revenue growth

Illustrative revenue in £m

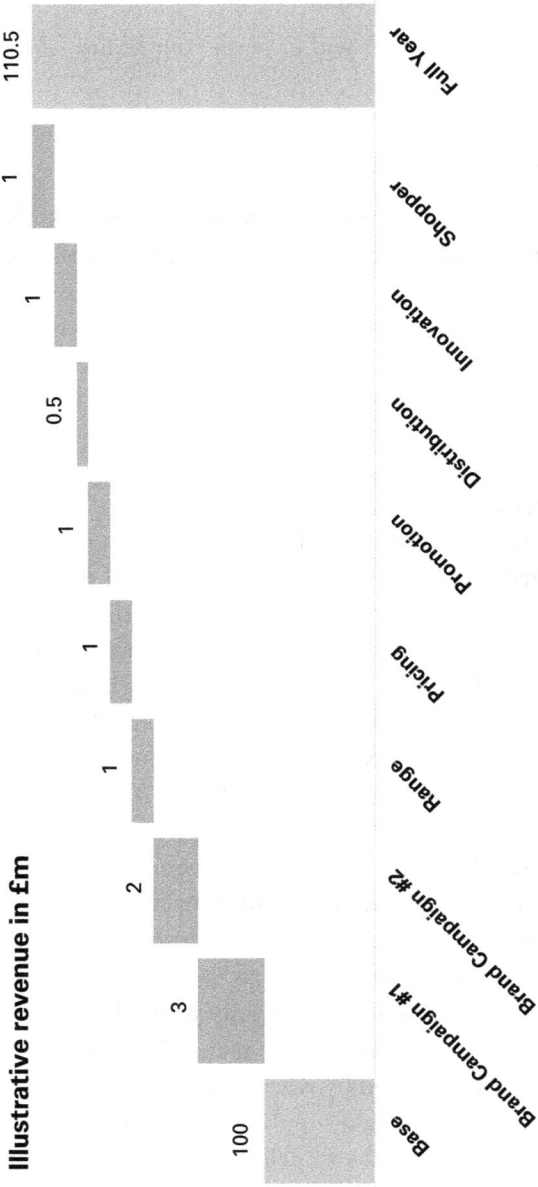

Reflections

What are the KPIs against which you will measure business, brand, and activation outcomes?

What are the key learning questions you must address for your plan to be robust?

How will you tell the story of your plan internally to win hearts and minds?

16

How do I approach measurement?

What is measurement?

Though it may appear we have come to measurement last, we have been discussing the importance of evidence-based judgement at every step. Given the nature of the brand-building cycle, it is logical to think about how we will measure the impact of our work at the end, albeit this sequence often means measurement gets neglected. Developing a bespoke measurement framework for your brand is critical to power the virtuous circle of effective brand building.

What is measurement? Perhaps an odd question in a book advocating marketers to make time for it. It is, however, important as measurement and our attitude towards it is very much cultural. The topic of measurement and marketing effectiveness provokes debate with polarizing views around tools and approaches – these debates are often removed from the context in which brands make decisions and can seem motivated by the marketer's fear that measurement may reveal shortcomings or question individual capability. Measurement is about constant learning and improvement, not about evaluation and judgement.

There has been an explosion of data in the twenty-first century – as consumers we leave a digital trail as we move from one site to another, from one device to another, from online retail into physical stores and brand experiences. This may sound like utopia – the ability to understand consumer responses to marketing at scale. The reality is somewhat different – amazing things are possible, but marketing technology struggles to keep pace, and for most brands data can feel both overwhelming and disjointed.

Marketers are constantly on the receiving end of a hard sell. If your phone rings, typically it is a sales pitch offering some new 'must have' measurement approach. The same is true through LinkedIn.com, and in conversations with the platforms. As marketers we are susceptible to marketing – peer pressure and 'fear of missing out' makes people feel like they must adopt the shiny new, probably AI-driven, measurement tool or data resource.

The conversation on consumer research is similarly baffling. The research industry has undergone a profound digital transformation with self-service tools and data collection methods. There are many benefits – savings in cost and time, and the ability to buy standard or customized research directly, often without human contact. On the one hand, it is easier to see how predictive different research methods are of in-market performance, but on the other it can feel like marketers have lost the expertise they had in understanding the basis for consumer research and benefit less from the social science training which once characterized research practitioners.

We may have better and faster consumer research but not always better and more nuanced answers to our questions. The polarized debate on advertising pre-testing we touched on in Chapter 13 is a case in point. For many marketers it was a badge of honour not to pre-test as it was an affront to their capability, whereas now as pre-testing methods have improved there is a better case. By creating such a polarized discussion, we miss addressing some of the drivers and inhibitors for marketers. Pre-testing can perform a positive role in the optimization of an execution, and in understanding how it works with consumers. It can help in the definition of a creative platform which will save time in the future. It can also reduce creative evaluation to a single score which encourages judgement not learning. An individual piece of advertising content typically sits within a larger brand system and there may be more nuances to take into consideration. Organizations are keen to mitigate risk and avoid poor work but there are stakeholder dimensions which mean it is easy to understand why marketers may be wary of using such tools which can become a stick to beat them.

And we are only just seeing the impact of AI, good and bad. Certainly, there are examples of businesses using AI effectively to collect, process, and analyse research and other data. Equally, there are instances where there may be overclaim, and organizations selling systems which lack understanding of how brands grow and how to influence consumer behaviour. This will be a watching brief as we experiment and learn.

In many organizations measurement has become something of an industry. It can seem as though brands start with measurement in the hope that they learn things which enable them to improve their performance. The aphorism 'what gets measured gets managed', perhaps a paraphrase of Drucker (1954), appears to promote the importance of measurement to improve productivity. A fuller version, perhaps itself a paraphrase of Ridgway (1956) has a different meaning: 'What gets measured gets managed — even when it's pointless to measure and manage it, and even if it harms the purpose of the organization to do so.'

This is a more powerful statement. What this means for brand builders is they must have the confidence to take back power. Measurement must flow from strategic choices. Measurement must be considered carefully against the things which matter to your strategy, ensuring it is effectively delivered. Measurement must be reframed as learning and focussed on making better future decisions versus auditing or policing the past. Prove to improve!

Measurement provides an illusion of objectivity – data is prone to bias stemming from sampling, collection, algorithmic, and cultural factors amongst others. Brand builders must take control of measurement if they are to manage brands effectively to win with consumers and demonstrate value to their organizations. Do not be put off by the nature of bias in data, it is a question of understanding and working with it or creating your own objective dataset.

Data is a profitable industry, and marketers should be as concerned about this as about understanding the implications of changing technology on what's available and its utility. Unlike a balance sheet and income statement, marketing measures are fluid, and are indirect – we are often reliant more on proxies than direct, causal measures. Most data can be critiqued and weaponized. The broad acceptance that acquiring new buyers, or penetration, is key to growth has had a positive effect in linking marketing to sales and revenue, but it's still incumbent on marketers to design a relevant measurement framework for their organization and make it as meaningful and familiar as the monthly financials.

Reflections

How is measurement viewed in your organization?

What are people's beliefs around measurement and its value?

How do I take control of measurement?

Reflect again on the aphorism referenced in the previous section. What does it mean for your brand and organization? Consider the stage of maturity of your brand, whether it is a product or service, the nature of the relationship you have with your consumers be it direct or disintermediated, the data you have, your technical and technological capability to manage data, and internal factors such as the nature of decision-making, stakeholders and so forth.

For a seeding brand selling through its own direct-to-consumer platform and using mainly social media to target and drive traffic, getting to grips with what works and the impact that changes in spend levels, promotion etc. have on traffic flows and purchases can usually be cleanly managed. The same might be true for brands with a similar model at scale – think about online travel bookers and retailers. Often, however, as brands shift into the scaling phase, distribution shifts into multiple channels, and maturing brands may be present internationally further increasing the challenge. It can be tough to wrap your arms around your marketing model and manage measuring it with the grace of an orchestra conductor.

Principles for measurement

1   Keep it objective and impartial

2   Be sceptical

3   It's OK not to measure everything

4   Be holistic

5   Think organizational culture

6   Focus on the future

7   Learn how to influence

Keep it objective and impartial. One example might be how you work with attribution data provided by social media and retail platforms. There is value in these datasets, but it could be argued that most vendors are marking their own homework. It's key to understand the scope of what's measured, for example whether consumers are tracked beyond the platform. Though in-platform data can determine how people react to a certain piece of copy versus another, or report sales impacts due to changes in display, promotion, pricing etc., they cannot determine what else a consumer may have seen along their path to purchase. This may lead to overstating the impact of certain activities, especially as they relate to converting sales, at the expense of those activities which may be more effective in building awareness and understanding which are prerequisites in the longer term for brand choice.

Initially strong returns on incremental investments can become a minimum just to remain present, especially when more than one brand invests and a page in effect becomes monetized. Consider the motivation against which data is provided – is it for objective learning, or perhaps to increase overall investment by brands in sales driving initiatives which align to the growth objectives of a platform?

Be sceptical. As the above demonstrates, it serves you to be inquisitive about data – who collected it, on what basis, and why. As data is prone to bias, including bias you can introduce repurposing it, it helps to know its strengths and limitations and how best to use it. Being sceptical will guide you when buying a slice of data about a market size as much as it will help you remain in control of how much you spend on the platforms. In the instance of the former, for example, ask about the category definition, the universe on which the data was based, the implications of how it was collected – for example, if it was based on collated manufacturer records of sales, retailer data, or consumer data perhaps derived from a sample. All these things will affect how suitable the data is for your needs, and depending on the scale of decision you can choose whether off the shelf data is adequate versus bespoke data.

Ask agencies to open their black boxes so you understand how things work. For new technology-driven approaches it's especially important to validate the underlying model is based on sound understanding of consumers and how they make decisions.

It's OK not to measure everything. Be selective. As we discussed above, marketing relies on proxy measures – things which are indicative of the impact of your work on consumer attitude and behaviour. Recognize that your consumers may be poor witnesses to their own choices and behaviours, that not everything is knowable. What do you need to know to mitigate significant risks, and to measure and learn proportionate to the value at stake?

Be holistic. A great measurement system is integrative. It considers the impact of numerous variables on the overall outcome just as we did in considering our 6Cs audit – context, category, competition, consumer, customer, and commercial. A brand exists in a system with multifaceted and multidirectional causal relationships between these variables. Though this supposes that as brands grow modelling will become important, it is equally important to define a suite of simple measures which act as proxies for demand and may signal changes in the category and for your brand. These might be things such as disposable income, regulatory changes, consumer sentiment or planned future behaviour, certain traffic flows etc.

Think organizational culture. Know your organization's biases, attitude towards risk, and decision-making. Organizational culture is a major driver of the role measurement plays. Strive for a culture which rewards learning, transparency, and continuous improvement. Marketing measurement is imperfect, and it's good to embrace this, focussing more on what you can deduce and act on, versus what is unknowable.

Focus on the future. Another strike against measurement can be that it is a rear-view mirror. Apart from a lack of patience and due diligence, this is often why reviews are not conducted on the outcomes of brand campaigns, innovation launches, or significant pieces of investment including capital expenditure. It can feel like an autopsy, or an opportunity for people to apportion blame or defend actions if things have not gone so well. Think about a post-activity review less as a trial than as a truth commission. If there is a no-fault culture, you can focus on understanding the implications for the future – what activities worked and what didn't, how might you evolve them, and optimize relative levels of spend?

Learn how to influence. Great measurement is about learning and changing future choices. As such it's critical to focus your team on influencing different outcomes. The subject of measurement inherently brings with it a desire for people to show the data and analysis. This is a trap – perhaps it sounds like a paradox but driving impact from measurement is less about showing data, and more about storytelling, and making a confident recommendation with clear actions, backed up with the least amount of the most powerful evidence.

Reflections

What are the positive behaviours around measurement in your organization?

What opportunities are there to improve ways of working around measurement?

How might I organize a measurement framework?

So, how do you go about this in practice? I think the answer is proactively to define a measurement framework, considering what you are trying to achieve and a balanced view of the trade-offs it may entail – including things such as the culture of decision-making, availability of data, and resources to supply it. Figure 16.1 provides an example.

You are not working in a vacuum – this exercise is about taking a step back from what you measure to ensure it is aligned to your long-term ambition, your plan for the next 12–18 months, and what different people in your team and business need to make effective decisions, identify issues, and communicate a balanced view of performance, progress, and risk.

Alongside a measurement framework, you should also develop a toolkit – a common set of approaches answering specific questions you hear consistently over time managed with a learning plan. This will save a huge amount of time and enable comparisons across brands and over time.

So, what should you consider?

Audiences

The first dimension is who your measurement framework is for, and what their needs are. Think about what each audience needs to know to understand performance, how each group influences how brand performance is perceived, and the business and brand decisions they are responsible for or influence.

It is likely that as you define audiences, it will correspond to a pyramid with the most senior folk at the top and junior audiences at the bottom. This correlates with the likely measurement content as well – with top level business and brand metrics at the top, perhaps covering key input and output metrics as well as leading indicators, whereas the bottom level will be more granular and operational in detail.

Depending on how your marketing team is organized, you may have people with sight of quite discrete metrics relating to specific activities or channels, or people with oversight across the whole brand or across the totality of activities within a brand campaign, including things such as pricing, promotional intensity etc.

Consider the ideal frequency of reporting as you sketch out these audiences. Frequency of reporting measures depends on the type of measure and its responsiveness. For example, brand strength measures are outputs of all your marketing efforts and tend to be slow moving. In contrast, activities directly impacting sales are dynamic and data may be updated daily, albeit you may still be trying to discern trends.

Remember the business cycle we aligned brand planning to? A senior audience will want to see performance each period, but perhaps engage less frequently on diagnostic measures, in contrast to the members of your team implementing your plan.

Reporting levels

The next consideration is that of level, which we discussed in the previous chapter. Remember, you are trying to create a holistic measurement framework which ensures you are on track to deliver both your three- to five-year ambition, and the next 12–18 months. Reporting levels should relate to your overall long- and short-term plans.

This structure follows the hierarchy of key performance indicators you will have been creating as you go. At the top level are those metrics which feature in key financial reports – the output measures of revenue, volume, and profit, plus marketing spend. The level below that is likely to be brand measures. As we discussed in the chapter on brand ambition, these should be at an appropriate level of magnitude to deliver the business objectives including metrics such as penetration, market share, brand strength, and other critical measures such as 'net promoter score', a common measure used by many brands.

The level below this starts to get to executional detail – first at the level of brand campaigns. From your plan you should have measures regarding the change in behaviour or attitude the brand campaign was designed to address, with appropriate goals. Each level of measurement framework ladders up to the hard sales delivery, albeit with each step down you make, the link is likely to become less direct and more indicative.

The last level of detail is executional but will also have measures which may be critical indicators for your team both in deploying your activities, and understanding if you are on track to hit your goals. These measures are more likely to be input metrics – useful in ensuring your activities are being deployed with the right pace and scale.

You may have noticed the terms 'input' and 'output' metrics in the text above. It is good discipline to get clear on the difference between them. Output metrics are the results or outcomes of activities, whereas input

FIGURE 16.1 Effective brand measurement framework

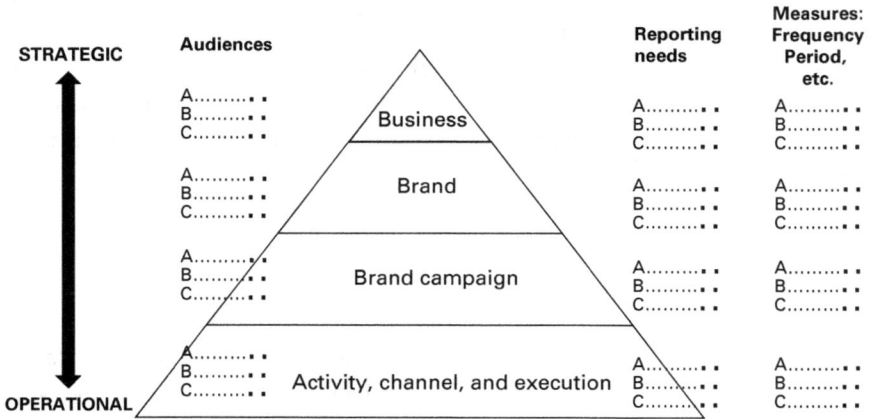

metrics are the actions which will lead to outcomes over time. It is a common – and easily made – error of marketers to present input metrics as if they were results. For example, % increase in media spend versus last year (input) – this doesn't guarantee any output unless your plan reaches more consumers more often than last year (output). There are lots of factors that might stop an input metric becoming an output metric: in this example, higher media costs or an ineffective media plan. In another example, developing new creative material which tests better than its predecessor is an input metric, until you can establish that the new creative has driven better return on investment against a similar media plan and spend – an output metric. You can see how output metrics drive consumer reactions, and influence the next actions you choose to take, whereas input metrics typically just describe aspects of marketing activities.

A slightly different way of thinking about measures is as 'leading' or 'lagging' indicators. Many input metrics are useful leading indicators of sales velocity. In contrast, while brand strength may be highly predictive of future success, it is a lagging indicator as consumer awareness and perceptions build slowly over time. It's great therefore to identify for your brand and category those leading indicators such as a change in rate of sale which can give you a view of fluctuating consumer demand or perhaps changes in your online traffic flows – CTR or 'click through rates' might be a consideration, for example.

Recognizing the uses for input and output measures, lagging and leading indicators helps ensure you are monitoring whether the business is executing things at the scale and cost you believed was sufficient to influence enough prospective consumers to choose your brand, at the desired price, to deliver volume and revenue targets week by week, month by month, quarter by quarter, year on year.

As well as confusing inputs and outputs, it is at this lowest level of detail where the business picture can get distorted if the metrics are not judiciously put together to ladder up to strategic choices. It is easy to look at a tactic which appears to be working and overdo it, and conversely it can be easy to lose patience with more brand-building activities which are consumed passively and may not provide reassuring short-term signals in the way that sales conversion activities can.

At this lowest level of detail, it can help to split metrics according to the funnel and use judgement and experience to determine whether and what signals to use as proxies. For example, further up the funnel you may be content to see if the levels of reach or exposures you are getting are in line with expectation, but you may have clearer expectations further down the funnel as to the amount of traffic you should expect to see to deliver the expected run rate of sales to give you confidence that you are on track.

The precise metrics you define at each level will depend on your business and brand goals, strategic choices, and the laydown of consumer-facing activities. For those wishing to apply Ehrenberg Bass Institute laws of growth theories to brand health measurement and other research, *Better Brand Health* (Romaniuk, 2023) offers advice.

Media measurement example

It's difficult to be specific about metrics – many are generic, and others will be brand- and industry-specific. It might, however, serve to illustrate some of the measures which a brand largely focussed on media might consider.

As we have discussed, there are those which relate to how efficiently media is being bought, how effectively it is being deployed, and whether it is sufficient to drive the scale of impact. These might be things such as the number of impressions (how many times your content has been displayed), viewable impressions (in a way which can be clearly seen by viewers), video plays, attentive seconds (the average attention given before skipping), and associated performance-based measures of cost per thousand (CPM, vCPM, aCPM respectively), and aCPV which perhaps more tellingly captures the attentive cost per view – measuring less the relative cost of the media you have put out, versus that which is seen. You might look at these alongside some of the things we discussed in Chapter 13 on media such as appropriate and safe placement, and a laydown which reflects the other choices you made about when and how best to reach your audience.

As you think about growth through a brand lens, you might want to look at the impact of media beyond reach – the lift it achieved, its incrementality, and associated performance-based metrics such as the iROS (incremental return on investment), or cost per user lifted. These start to paint a picture as to whether specific marketing tactics are having a positive effect, relative to the cost.

At a brand or brand campaign level you would want to look at the total impact of media on business goals – in essence, the leads and sales generated relative to your investment – and therefore at common metrics such as the cost per click (CPC), return on advertising spend (ROAS), return on investment (ROI – typically expressed as profit and includes production and media costs), average order value (AOV).

Organizing measures in a model around key questions helps you shift from knowing if you are getting what you paid for, to knowing if it's having an impact, to being able to work out how much you should spend and how you should spend it to achieve your brand and campaign goals. Aligning measures to questions demystifies measurement – taking it beyond using lots of acronyms impenetrable to the people you need to influence to believe in and invest more in your work, and possibly even to people in your marketing team who may be unclear about what all these terms are, why they matter, and how to use them to drive more efficiency and more effective outcomes from every pound you spend.

Remember the point on audiences – a team member focussed on deploying media across different channels and platforms may need a more granular suite of measures, but a senior marketer may be more interested in understanding the optimum spend for a brand to be on track to achieve its goals. Your CEO or CFO may only care that your marketing is on track to deliver the expected revenue within the planned investment for the quarter, year, or longer term.

As you think about the system around your measurement framework think about how you want data and information to flow between these different audiences. Also check if you can source the data you have included. Is it cost effective to do so? Do you need to measure everything? Have you created an integrated measurement framework which enables you to understand your brand holistically and hypothesize effectively about the drivers of success today and how you might evolve the model for the future?

How will you curate this measurement system? How will you bring the data together? How will you present it? How will you build the capability of different audiences to understand the different measures, their sensitivity, and how to use them? Mature brands are likely to have a marketing data platform and visualization software which can automate reports for audiences, joining the dots. A lo-fi approach in Excel is still worth the effort – the power is in bringing the right things together rather than having them in silos.

At its best, a measurement framework can crack the code for growth for its brand and create real advantage – knowing precisely which levers to pull based on the brand and category stage of development, and how to adapt those assumptions to markets with different trade profiles and so on. Such a model will never be 100% accurate, but it means that the markets of a global brand which are most similar start from the same place in understanding the likely impact of different brand campaigns and are able to start from common assumptions about how much to spend and how to spend it.

Mondelēz, the owner of Oreo and Cadbury, has such a framework built around its understanding of widely accepted principles which drive growth, and which helps it understand the impact of things such as pricing, promotion, media, and other aspects of the marketing mix. As we saw from the Diageo portfolio example in Chapter 13, for organizations seeking to capitalize on the benefits of scale this can be a profitable way to avoid waste and drive profit from brand investment.

Enter awards

It may seem an unusual thing to recommend, but entering awards supports effective brand building. It's not for the glory necessarily, but for the benefit it provides in taking a step back to understand what's going on with your brand. The prospect of winning an award may be the thing which motivates your team to do the work to determine what's happened in the last year, with a view to making better future choices.

It's no surprise that agencies tend to write the best submissions. This is not just because of their storytelling capability, but also because they recognize winning awards helps them win new business.

Writing award submissions develops muscles that help you get the most out of measurement:

- set the scene by dramatically capturing the context and the challenge your brand faced;

- outline the stretching but achievable KPIs you set;
- bring to life the consumer as a key protagonist in your narrative, drama-tizing what you learned about them as you developed the work, and how your brand building influenced them;
- get clear on what it all means – what happened, and what elements contributed positively to the outcomes;
- get clear about what your brand responds to, and what's changing given the evolving nature of channels and consumers.

There is a bigger and perhaps surprising thing to be learned when you put together a case study. Even if you have achieved or exceeded your business goals it's likely you did so in a way which did not entirely follow your strat-egy. It may seem a paradox in a book advocating time spent on consumer-centred strategy to advocate a relaxed attitude to whether it worked precisely or not. Perhaps the real role of brand strategy is to enable focussed and deliberate action which kickstarts a virtuous circle of learning. Consumer behaviour is unpredictable, so gaining understanding of what happened and why will be invaluable. If you have humility, the most important discoveries may happen by chance, leading to the profoundest impacts on your brand.

Reflections

How does information flow around your organization?

Is there a measurement framework in place providing relevant timely information to different audiences?

Are people knowledgeable about how and when to use different measures and how they are interrelated?

What opportunities are there to improve measurement in your organization, including how it is accessed and used to make decisions?

What should be in a measurement toolkit?

Finally, it's worth codifying a set of common approaches to consumer learning. This will include evaluation tools but should also include tools to understand consumer motivations, behaviour, and preferences, and to understand how consumers may react to communications, packaging, product and service innovation, and so on.

The benefits of a learning toolkit are significant in all organizations – be it a start-up or a multinational. Common tools save people time working out how to answer common questions. Common tools allow comparison between markets and over time as you build benchmarks. As familiarity builds, people develop common language to describe things, and know whether and how to use consumer research.

This last point is as valid in a start-up to a multinational. In the former, a founder may have such a clear vision and understanding of their target audience and the opportunity they see in the market that they may only need to research selectively, perhaps around new products or new markets. It can be tempting in a well-resourced business to research far more than is necessary – including when there is existing data, or existing technology or products are being deployed, or the activity is relatively low risk.

Choosing tools requires you to think about the questions you want to answer using consumer research and measurement and determine the level of robustness with which to address them. There is no right or wrong answer and much of this will be determined by what the organization needs to know to feel comfortable in how it markets to consumers.

A toolkit can be organized in different manners, but one approach might be to follow the structure of this book in considering where to win, how to win, and how to keep winning.

For example, in a 'where to win' toolkit, you might select an approach to understanding how to segment demand, how to define and monitor the forces shaping your business and consumer, to understand consumer journeys, connections, and shopper missions.

In 'how to win', you might consider a common approach to evaluating communications, often referred to as pre-testing, to packaging development including online and on-shelf, as well as understanding the impact of shopper programmes and visibility materials. It's useful to have common approaches to pricing, including assessing price elasticity, and consumer promotions.

Finally, in 'how to keep winning' consider how you will measure brand strength, as well as any other continuous studies you may need to track consumer behaviour and measure market share. Additionally, define core evaluation tools. There are products which will enable you to learn about consumer responses to your marketing materials as you deploy them, understanding their impact and how they work in combination.

Seeding brands may not need complex analytics to understand the impact of their work. As previously discussed, it may be sufficient to look at year-on-year sales comparisons to see the impact of marketing, considering any other changes such as price and distribution. As your brand scales you may consider things such as attribution modelling which provides tactical information about the impact of specific channels and activities. This is likely to be sufficient given your activities are still likely to be concentrated.

Finally, as brands grow it is worth considering marketing mix modelling. As a rule of thumb this becomes a smart choice as a brand's budget tips over £1m or equivalent. Marketing mix modelling (MMM) is more data intensive but works by breaking sales down according to different drivers – put simply it can identify the impact of things such as weather, competitor activity, pricing, promotion – and finally decompose media deployment and other activities. MMM is a strategic tool for future planning, only needing refreshing every couple of years or when there is significant change in a category. There is a debate about the validity of return on investment (ROI) as a key measure. Though ROI is a useful way of benchmarking the effectiveness of your activity versus industry norms it is perhaps less useful to your business than expressing the incremental profit attributable to marketing which aligns it to a core business metric.

As well as giving a robust answer to questions on the value of marketing investment, the power of marketing mix modelling lies in its potential for future planning. MMM can help you understand the optimum amount you should spend, as well as identifying the point at which your marketing will become saturated – often this correlates with a point where it becomes harder to reach new people without exposing the same audience over and over. As well as determining the right amount and predicting with a good degree of certainty the incremental profit and payback, it can help you decide how to spend that money – optimizing the mix and weight of different activities based on consumer response and the variable costs of media and other activities. Though MMM is not essential to demonstrate the effectiveness of your marketing, it remains the gold standard in providing a holistic, objective, evidence-based view on your brand's growth model and its future potential – typically paying back the investment in measurement with the gains you will make through its application.

To round off your roster of measurment partners, consider building relationships with qualitative researchers who can be valuable at many stages, uncovering insights and developing brand campaigns against them. Semioticians or cultural insight experts are worth their weight in gold in understanding how culture shapes consumer preferences and brands in ways which people can struggle to do for themselves and providing guidance about how to encode desirable cultural tropes into your full marketing mix.

As with all these tools, your needs will change based on the brand's stage of development. Decide when or whether to commission research by:

- identifying learning priorities;
- identifying existing sources of information;
- considering the level of risk involved in making the decision if no data are available.

If the learning need and level of risk outweigh the value of research, then proceed.

By identifying learning priorities as you complete the planning cycle you will be able to create a costed learning plan.

This may feel like the end, but it's really just the beginning of the next cycle of your work!

Reflections

Do you have a measurement toolkit?

Do you have principles by which people know when and how to use different research and measurement tools?

References

Drucker, P F (1954) *The Practice of Management*, Harper & Brothers, New York

Ridgway, V F (1956) Dysfunctional consequences of performance measurements, *Administrative Science Quarterly*, 1(2), 240–47

Romaniuk, J (2023) *Better Brand Health. Measures and metrics for a* How Brands Grow *world*, Oxford University Press, Victoria

INDEX

NB: page numbers in *italic* indicate figures or tables

Looking for another book?

Explore our award-winning
books from global business
experts in Marketing and Sales

Scan the code to browse

www.koganpage.com/marketing

From 4 December 2025 the EU Responsible Person (GPSR) is:
eucomply oÜ, Pärnu mnt. 139b – 14, 11317 Tallinn, Estonia
www.eucompliancepartner.com

www.ingramcontent.com/pod-product-compliance
Lightning Source LLC
Chambersburg PA
CBHW071550210326
41597CB00019B/3188